PILLARS OF CLOUD AND FIRE

RELIGION AND SOCIAL TRANSFORMATION
General Editors: Anthony B. Pinn and Stacey M. Floyd-Thomas

Pillars of Cloud and Fire

The Politics of Exodus in African American Biblical Interpretation

Herbert Robinson Marbury

NEW YORK UNIVERSITY PRESS

New York and London

NEW YORK UNIVERSITY PRESS
New York and London
www.nyupress.org

References to Internet websites (URLs) were accurate at the time of writing. Neither the author nor New York University Press is responsible for URLs that may have expired or changed since the manuscript was prepared.

Library of Congress Cataloging-in-Publication Data
Marbury, Herbert Robinson.
Pillars of cloud and fire : the politics of exodus in African American
biblical interpretation / Herbert Robinson Marbury.
pages cm   Includes bibliographical references and index.
ISBN 978-1-4798-3596-6 (cloth : alk. paper) — ISBN 978-1-4798-1250-9 (paper   )
1. Black theology. 2. Bible—Black interpretations. 3. Exodus, The—Typology. I. Title.
BT82.7.M356   2015
230.089'96073—dc23   2015010013

New York University Press books

Manufactured in the United States of America

10 9 8 7 6 5 4 3 2 1

Also available as an ebook

Dedicated to my parents,
Chaplain (LTC) Herbert Lawrence Marbury and Annette Robinson
Marbury, who taught me to remember the struggle and to join it.

It is evident that the opening lines of "Go Down, Moses,"

> Go down, Moses,
> 'Way down in Egypt land;'
> Tell old Pharaoh,
> Let my people go.

have a significance beyond the bondage of Israel in Egypt.

– James Weldon Johnson, *The Book of American Negro Poetry*, 1922

CONTENTS

PREFACE: LOCATING THE PROJECT

African American biblical interpretation has taken a decisive turn toward cultural studies.[1] In its nascent stages, the project was burdened by the constraints of the historical-critical paradigm. Its methodological concerns focused black biblical interpretation on excavating a past that preceded the production of the biblical text, whether in ancient Israel or in the Greco-Roman world. Many scholars now find such demands unwieldy as these scholars pursue newer questions that explore the Bible's relationship to contemporary worlds. Even black scholars who were once deeply wedded to historical-critical results now find themselves thinking about the Bible in relation to contemporary cultural questions. Nonetheless, their historical-critical sensibilities remain useful even if they have redirected the orientation of their study.[2]

The inclusion of cultural studies in biblical scholarship has been three decades in the making.[3] During that time, African American biblical interpretation matured into a venerable mode of study within biblical studies that both critically informs and has been informed by its larger field. Even before cultural studies proper found its way into the stock of methodologies of biblical scholars, early studies in the 1980s and 1990s pioneered the new territory. Renita Weems's *Just a Sister Away: A Womanist Vision of Women's Relationships in the Bible* seamlessly blended scholarly rigor and eloquent poetics to interpret the Bible through the experiences of African American women.[4] In 1989, Cain Hope Felder inaugurated the current academic conversation with the first major exploration, *Troubling Biblical Waters: Race, Class and Family*.[5] In 1991, *Stony the Road We Trod: African American Biblical Interpretation* gathered the most prominent African American biblical hermeneuts to demonstrate the broad spectrum of black academic interpretive modes and to explore its most pressing questions.[6]

In the following decade, African American biblical scholars built upon much of this early work and intentionally explored the goods of culture studies for their work. During that time, five major volumes in African American biblical interpretation appeared. Each displayed the broad range of African American interpretive work. In 2003, *African Americans and the Bible: Sacred Texts and Social Textures*, edited by Vincent L. Wimbush, self-consciously incorporated methods of investigation that were not native to biblical studies. The study, written primarily by non-biblical scholars, took as their methodological point of departure the modes by which the biblical text has functioned in African American culture.[7] The second volume, *Yet with a Steady Beat: Contemporary U.S. Afrocentric Biblical Interpretation*, edited by Randall C. Bailey, followed the trajectory of *Stony the Road We Trod*, but featured a second generation of African American biblical scholarship.[8] Bailey's study highlighted examples of African American scholars engaging in interpretative activity with a keen self-awareness of particularity and a commitment to liberation. The same year marked a more than doubling of the number of African American biblical scholars to almost fifty.[9] By 2004, African American Biblical Interpretation had developed sufficiently to warrant a survey text, which appeared as Michael Joseph Brown's *Blackening of the Bible: The Aims of African-American Biblical Scholarship*.[10] Brown offered both a survey and a critical but judicious interrogation. In 2007, Brian K. Blount produced *True to Our Native Land: An African American New Testament Commentary*, the first one-volume commentary that intentionally read the Bible through the lens of black culture.[11] Finally, Hugh R. Page et al.'s *The Africana Bible*, which appeared in 2010, was the first commentary to gather voices from the Continent and the Diaspora into a single volume covering the entire Hebrew Bible, along with certain pseudepigraphic and apocryphal works that many Africana communities hold as sacred.[12]

On one hand, the studies by Cain Hope Felder, Randall C. Bailey, and Michael J. Brown have come to shape black biblical scholarship. Each is interested in chronicling and displaying ways that African American scholars interpret texts and the worlds from which those texts emerge. These studies offer important critiques of the history of scholarship, while presenting new interpretations with keen attention to the marginalizing work of the politics of gender, class, and racialization.[13] Much of the important work in black biblical scholarship, such as the studies by Stephanie Buckhanon Crowder,[14] Gay L. Byron,[15] Cheryl Anderson,[16]

Brian K. Blount,[17] Rodney L. Sadler,[18] Mignon Jacobs,[19] Wilda Gafney,[20] and Love L. Sechrest,[21] has followed this paradigm. To varying degrees, each study takes up biblical interpretation as specialized academic activity largely disconnected from the ordinary cultural forms by which black people apprehend the Bible.[22] Wimbush's work, on the other hand, has focused on black people's discovery and encounter with the Bible as a phenomenon of black culture. In successive works, he advances the project of theorizing this dimension of the larger enterprise.[23] Recently, works by Allen D. Callahan and Margaret Aymer have followed this second paradigm.[24]

Pioneers in both approaches have raised important challenges for the direction of future work. First, Wimbush challenges the scholars to leave "no practice or practitioner in the whole phenomenon without critical attention" and to pursue "not so much [. . .] what 'scriptures' mean (in terms of content), but how scriptures mean in terms of psycho-social-cultural performances and their politics)."[25] Second, Bailey argues for interrogating the political locations of writers and interpreters along with a rigorous analysis of the text itself.[26] Third, Brown's study calls upon scholars to focus on liberating the marginalized even within our marginalized discourse to create for them "the possibility of authentic human existence."[27] Fourth, Hugh R. Page, Jr., calls for African American interpretation to be "both a reflection of *Africana* life and the role that the First Testament has played in it."[28] These four challenges press African American biblical interpretation to rethink itself and its place in the field of biblical studies. Together, they expand the work of African American biblical interpretation and call it to think of itself beyond its current methodological and theoretical boundaries.

This book positions itself between these two types of studies and responds to these four challenges by focusing on textuality, that is, how texts come to mean within cultural fields of significance. It does this in two ways. First, it retrieves a tradition of non-specialist interpretation that preceded and deeply influenced African American academic interpretation. Second, it critically appraises the politics of interpretations as much as the interpretations themselves. In this second endeavor, the book takes seriously the notion of culture as all-encompassing. It understands scholarly activity as deeply embedded in wider "webs of significance" with no radical disjuncture between the academy and the world and traces strands of the larger history of black people's encounter with the biblical text from the antebellum period to the late twentieth century. In this way the book is both informed by and informative of the unfolding black culture to which it is committed. Ultimately, this book contributes to the long tradition of investigating black people's continuing encounter with the Bible by clearing one more mile on the path toward freedom.

ACKNOWLEDGMENTS

Although this project bears my name, it belongs to a rich and broad village. It could not have been completed without those who blessed my journey with their love, support, intellectual insight, and prayers. I thank God for all of them. Long ago, classes and formative conversations with professors and mentors such as Delores P. Alderidge, Gloria Wade-Gayles, Nagueyalti Warren, Rosetta Gooden, Ojeda Penn, Vera Dixon Rorie, Sylvester Hopewell, and Tariq Shakoor, at Emory University, awakened my voice and honed it for writing. I continue to benefit from the work, witness, and friendship of Randall C. Bailey, who was my first "Old Testament" professor. He introduced me to the academic study of religion and launched me on my journey in biblical studies. Renita J. Weems, my adviser, instilled in me a love for the Hebrew Bible that moved beyond simple, mechanical criticism to rich and appreciative critique. Randy and Renita modeled the importance of asking the questions that matter to those communities of mothers and fathers that had formed me and who sent me to academe. I hope that I have done so here. Bishop James S. Thomas and Bishop L. Scott Allen offered advice and encouragement at critical times. Both reminded me of my responsibility to the United Methodist Church. I am especially grateful and indebted to Charles B. Copher, a beacon of biblical scholarship and a devoted United Methodist clergyperson. He believed deeply enough in the task of encouraging young African American Hebrew Bible scholars to give generously of precious time during his final months of life.

Upon reading my first draft, Victor Anderson advised me to forget most of what I had learned about writing for my colleagues in academe, and to reclaim the voice I had honed as an undergraduate literature major. Our conversations sharpened my analysis. Victor listened patiently as I read chapters and, with each reading, I revived a voice that I thought was long lost.

Lewis V. Baldwin remains, for me, one of the finest examples of excellence as a historian. He graciously read and discussed the chapter on the Civil Rights Movement. In our conversations, he generously gave me the benefit of a lifetime of study devoted to the life and intellectual work of Martin Luther King, Jr. Moreover, he and Jackie Baldwin freely offered mentoring and moral support along the way.

Stacey Michelle Floyd-Thomas and Juan Marcial Floyd-Thomas invited me to join them in forming a weekly writing group, "BMW." Together, we read each other's work, offered each other rigorous critiques, and held ourselves to the discipline that routinizes scholarly production. We were only three "Black Minds Writing" for one summer, but the synergy that emerged during our time together generated enough intellectual energy to carry us forward through many projects to come. Their incisive critique helped to clarify my thinking, and pressed me to "produce faster" and to write with more intentionality.

Several biblical scholars and colleagues outside of the field read drafts and offered valuable suggestions: Michael Joseph Brown, Alice Wells Hunt, Jon Berquist, Dexter Callender, Monya Stubbs, Hugh R. Page, Jr., Frank Yamada, Chris Dorsey, Sandra Barnes, Hashim Pipkin, Dwight Hopkins, Anthea Butler, Walter Fluker, Marla Frederick, and Peter Paris. Jon Berquist took the risk to publish my first book and continued to encourage me throughout this project. I particularly thank two doctoral students, Bridgett Green and Kim Russaw, and the students in my African American Biblical Hermeneutics courses, whose insightful questions helped me to write the book that was missing for our work.

My conversations with Dale Andrews, Forrest Harris, Dennis J. Dickerson, and Brad R. Braxton pressed me to make connections with conversations in Practical Theology, Black Church Studies, History, and New Testament. Fernando Segovia's model and encouragement from the "other" canon was invaluable.

My close colleagues in Hebrew Bible at Vanderbilt Divinity School have become friends and trusted interlocutors. Douglas A. Knight, Jack M. Sasson, and Annalisa Azzoni supported my work even as it theorized a reception history of the Hebrew Bible in unfamiliar ways.

I began this work with a leave granted by Jim Hudnut-Beumler, who was then Dean of Vanderbilt Divinity School, in concert with a grant awarded by the Wabash Center. At critical times over the years, Sharon

Watson Fluker and Matthew Williams at the Fund for Theological Education (now the Forum for Theological Exploration) gave me invaluable funding and moral support. I would not have finished this leg of the race without them. I am also grateful to the Louisville Institute, which awarded the project its First Book Fellowship. My year as a Faculty Fellow of the Robert Penn Warren Center at Vanderbilt University afforded me an abundance of interdisciplinary conversations with Emily August, Caree Banton, Richard Blackett, Celso Castilho, Nihad Farook, Mona Fredericks, Teresa Goddu, Jane Landers, Daniel Sharfstein, and the ever-intrepid organizer, Allison J. Thompson.

Well along in the journey, I was blessed to have emilie m. townes take the helm at Vanderbilt Divinity School. She is a Dean par excellence, who understands how to mentor junior faculty while building a scholarly collegium.

I benefited immensely from my time at Clark Atlanta University and conversations with the Rev. Paul Easley, Karen Cole, Joyce Worrell, L. Henry Whelchel, who was my teacher as well as my colleague, Walter D. Broadnax, Joel Harrel, Isabella Jenkins, Newburn Reynolds, Marilynn Lineberger, Rosemary Allwood, Thomas Scott, Devin White, Rick Robinson, Harris Tay, Brad McWhorter, Phillip Golden, and David Claxton.

My friends and colleagues from Southwest Dekalb, Emory University, the Interdenominational Theological Center, Kelley's Chapel and Old National United Methodist Churches, Vanderbilt University, the King's Row Community in Decatur, Georgia, and beyond have remained steadfast even though I have not always been able to reciprocate. The relationships with Mr. and Mrs. Gatewood, Trey and Joy Gatewood, Mr. and Mrs. Hubbard, Thomas and Holly Hubbard, Mr. and Mrs. Kirby, Collis and Torrey Kirby, William "Buck" Godfrey, Dianne Spencer, Gwen Smith, Jeannette and Willie Greene, Kathleen Gray, Jill U. Edmonson, Jennifaye V. Brown, Nakata Smith Fitch, Nikki N. Hildebrand, Darlene R. Herbert, Rita M. Treadwell, Marvin J. Coleman, Eric Croone, Jeff D. Milner, Roderick B. Wilkerson, Sheldon R. Johnson, Nate Mitchell, Kevin Wesley, Phillis Sheppard, Bridgette D. Young, Victor-Cyrus Franklin, Kelly Grimes, Alanis B. C. Dorsey, Sha'Tika Brown, Adrienne Alderman White, Jacque Barber, Brian Perry, Charles L. White, Jr., Aurelio D. G. Little, Paul C. H. Lim, Monica A. Coleman, Marie McEntire,

Amy Steele, Angela Dillon, Victor Judge, Amy Norfleet, and Graham Reside have sustained me along the way.

I am thankful to my Martha's Vineyard "Inkwell" family—Darryl Ballard, Stephanie Bradley, Don Brewington, Roderick Brown, Michael Buggs, Shawn Cook, Africa Hands, Babatu Hansen, Myron Lawrence, Debra Mumford, Joseph Perry, and Monya Stubbs—for allowing me to write when we were supposed to be on vacation.

Hobson United Methodist Church has been my spiritual community since I arrived in Nashville. My colleague, friend, and pastor, the Rev. V. H. "Sonnye" Dixon, Jr., along with Sonja Dixon Beasley, Garlinda Burton, Trey Dixon, Fred Allen, Bill Barnes, Champ, Sheila Jones, Ramona Day, Johnny and Melanie Brewster, Lawanna Coleman, Vida Finley, Crystal Doss, James Milliken, Brad Wright, Pam Crosby, Keisha Williams, Ca'Rissa Day, Alyssa Ross, Dan Joranko, and Chris Davis, among others, continue to bless my soul and nurture my faith in God.

I owe much to my series editors, Anthony B. Pinn and Stacey M. Floyd-Thomas. They early on saw value in this work and believed it worthy to be a part of the Religion and Social Transformation series. Both graciously shepherded it through a process that was for me both strange and, at times, daunting. I could not have asked for more generous and professional editors than Jennifer Hammer, Constance Grady, and Alexia Traganas at New York University Press. From proposal to submission, they have given far more than a due portion of patience, encouragement, and support throughout the process. Many thanks also to Victor Simmons, curator of Fisk University's Aaron Douglas Gallery, and Tammi Lawson at the Schomburg Center for Research in Black Culture, Art and Artifacts Division of the New York Public Library for their assistance with the cover art.

I am most grateful to my family: my aunts and uncles, Bob, Tom, Joyce, and Karla Robinson, Amy Baker, and John and Dorothy Traylor, as well as my cousins Avery, Amya, Eric, LaKeidra, John, Michelle, Latitia, Bo, Melinda, Pete, Jodi, Anwar, Yasmin, Ruby, and Jaida, and my godmother, J. René Carter. I am particularly grateful to my cousin, Alvin Williams, who researched materials on the Reverend John Jasper at Sixth Mount Zion Baptist Church in Richmond, Virginia. Gay-linn Elizabeth Gatewood-Jasho has been my "Rafiki." My brother, Lawrence Andrew, exhorted me over the rough places. My sisters-in-law, Sheryl L.

Marbury and Sheila Jones, and their parents, Rosalyn and J. W. Jones, cheered my work every time I came home to Atlanta. My nephews, Lawrence Johnathan and Jaylan Carter, ensured that I put my pen down to take them to the movies and to do those things that reminded me that I was their uncle long before I became a scholar. My niece, Chloe AnnaRose, brought me smiles. My youngest nephew, Charles Andrew, arrived after the manuscript was completed. It was the hope of his birth and the promise of his generation that kept me pressing on. I hope he will one day see himself in this story. Antonio Q. Meeks continues to bless my life with his unwavering support. His constant demand, "Show me some work!" kept me on schedule. Penny, our four-legged family member, was a constant and faithful companion as I wrote the early chapters. My grandmother, Ernestine Williams Robinson, equipped me with diligence for the journey. She left us just before this book went to press. But from that great Cloud of Witnesses, she, my grandfather, the Rev. J.W. Robinson, my paternal grandparents, the Rev. L.C. and Essie Mae Marbury, my uncles, Alfred and Hosea Marbury, James, Thaddeus, and Frank L. Williams, and my father, lifted me along every mile of the way. Last, I am grateful to my parents, Herbert L. and Annette R. Marbury. They raised me to press my way no matter the obstacles, and their love taught me to pursue my questions no matter where they lead me, because the quest will only bring me closer to truth.

Introduction

He used to read prayers in public to the ship's crew every Sabbath day; and when first I saw him read, I was never so surprised in my whole life as when I saw the book talk to my master; for I thought it did, as I observed him to look upon it, and move his lips.—I wished it would do so to me.—As soon as my master had done reading I follow'd him to the place where he put the book, being mightily delighted with it, and when nobody saw me, I open'd it and put my ear down close upon it, in great hope that it wou'd say something to me; but was very sorry and greatly disappointed when I found it would not speak, this thought immediately presented itself to me, that every body and every thing despis'd me because I was black.
—*A Narrative of the Most Remarkable Particular in the Life of James Albert Ukawsaw Gronniosaw, an African Prince, As Related by Himself*[1]

Contact and Conquest, Orality and Textuality

Ukawsaw Gronniosaw listened, but the book gave him nothing. What went wrong? Gronniosaw was sure he saw the book speak to the captain. Earlier that day, he and the Dutch captain stood on the same deck, but their horizons were worlds apart.[2] In the captain's Western cultural tradition, books—religious or otherwise—do not talk, but in traditional African religions, talismans, amulets, drums, and so forth sometimes speak to believers. Gronniosaw had no reference for reading as a mode to apprehend a book, and the Dutch captain had no reference for listening as a mode to apprehend a religious item. Thus, when the captain read the public prayer, Gronniosaw saw him talking to the book. Then something remarkable happened. Perhaps, in the natural pauses of the captain's cadence, Gronniosaw saw the book respond. For Gronniosaw, conversation was so taken for granted, and reading aloud was so strange, that he

1

saw the book talk. Since the book had spoken to the captain, then why not him? As soon as he was alone, he approached the volume, lifted it to his ear, and listened, but the book gave him no response. Finally, Gronniosaw read the disappointing silence and spoke *for* the book: he knew that it, like everything else in the new world, despised him: because he was black.

Almost fifty years later, upon recollection, Gronniosaw transcribed his story and qualified his experience by adding the words, "for I thought it did."[3] But Gronniosaw retained the trope because it mediated the oral West African culture of his birth and the literate culture of his captivity. For African American biblical scholars, the talking book signified black people's aspiration to hear the Bible speak the Word of God.[4] As Allen D. Callahan contends, black folk en masse, old and young alike, learned to read as soon as it was legal. African Americans knew the book was more than a symbol of the conqueror's religion and power. Because they believed it was a symbol of justice that held moral authority over even their captors, they wanted the Bible to speak this Word of God to them before they died.[5]

However, the deep desire to hear the book *talk* seduces us away from a frightening possibility, and a less explored image in Gronniosaw's experience, namely, the *silent* book. It, too, is signified by Gronniosaw's narrative. In fact, Callahan hints at this trope when he mentions the Bible's form—text: "As a written text, it greeted [African Americans] with silence."[6] In fact, the Bible "greeted" the captain in the same manner. Gronniosaw did not realize it, but the Bible gave him no more and no less than it had given to the Dutch captain. So when he spoke *for* the book, Gronniosaw did exactly as the Dutch captain had done. Both took up the book, both interpreted its silence, and both left the encounter with meaning. To be sure, each apprehended the book differently: Gronniosaw interpreted the book's iconic power, while the captain read the book's letters.[7] But the difference between the two encounters cannot be reduced to their modes of apprehension. Even after Gronniosaw learned to read, he and the captain still spoke differently in the book's silence. The politics of their respective subject positions led them to fill the silence with differing intentions. Gronniosaw spoke from the position of the vanquished, while the captain spoke from the position of the conqueror. As Charles H. Long describes, such is the irony of this silence. "Silence forces us to realize that our words, the units of our naming and recognition in the world, presuppose a reality which is prior to our naming and doing."[8] In the silence, what Gronniosaw took for granted—in a world totalized by his subjugation to white power—immediately came to consciousness and to articulation. From his viewpoint, even the book of God had nothing for him. Along with everyone and everything in this new world, it despised him because he was black.

Textuality, History, and Resistance

Textuality has therefore . . . become the exact antithesis and displacement of what might be called history. Textuality is considered to take place, yes, but by the same token it does not take place anywhere or anytime in particular. It is produced, but by no one and at no time. It can be read and interpreted, although reading and interpreting are routinely understood to occur in the form of misreading and misinterpreting. The list of examples could be extended indefinitely, but the point would remain the same. As it is practiced in the American academy today, literary theory has for the most part isolated textuality from the circumstances, the events, the physical senses that made it possible and render it intelligible as the result of human work. Even if we accept (as in the main I do) the arguments put forward by Hayden White—that there is no way to get past texts in order to apprehend "real" history directly—it is still possible to say that such a claim need not also eliminate interest in the events and the circumstances entailed by and expressed in the texts themselves. Those events and circumstances are textual too (nearly all of Conrad's tales and novels present us with a situation—giving rise to the narrative that forms the text), and much that goes on in texts alludes to them, affiliates itself directly to them. My position is that texts are worldly, to some degree they are events, and, even when they appear to deny it, they are nevertheless a part of the social world, human life, and of course the historical moments in which they are located and interpreted.

—Edward Said, *The World, the Text, and the Critic*, 1983

Like other West Africans, Gronniosaw entered the Western world from a position of security and centeredness.[9] They were the subjects of their own rich and venerable oral tradition that was precise in both word and inflection from one generation of griots to the next. But he also entered as one whose people had been "sentenced" (both condemned and textualized) to silence by modernity. Indeed, modernity rendered its harshest judgment upon people with no history that the Western investigator could recognize.[10] Hegel stated the issue clearly, "What we properly understand by Africa, is the Unhistorical, Undeveloped Spirit, still involved in the conditions of mere nature, and which had to be presented here only as on the threshold of the World's History."[11] First, Hegel and his contemporaries' reference to history meant the modern world's accounts of each "people's" contributions to humankind's evolutionary progress. Second, for the various European nations, these stories were discursive exercises in self-construction, but they proceeded dialectically. The accounts self-reflexively constructed the European against their projection of some "other." Third, such history was written. It obtained in books, newspapers, and other print media. Fourth, it is self-referential—texts refer only to other texts. History produced in the new American Republic derived from a larger tradition that referred to British texts, which referred to Latin texts, which referred to Greek texts. Each referred to an earlier text, which is how language creates history and how history scripts a past.

In the Western tradition, this past represented people of African descent only in their silence.[12] This second silence, like the silence Gronniosaw encountered, was neither an absence nor a void. Africans were present but only as projections of the Western gaze. Its tradition took up the "African" as an empirical and religious "other," not as a human subject. Scientific discourses, particularly biology and anthropology, signified the African as a vacuous body and wrote their theories upon it. At the same time, Christianity viewed the African body as an empty canvas and wrote the religion of the heathen upon it. Both religious and scientific discourses constructed the white body as human and Christian, and simultaneously constructed the black body as savage and heathen. History's silence fell upon people of African descent with crushing violence. From the eighteenth century forward, savage and heathen operated as concrete structures against which Euro-American "civilization" and its "Christianity" constructed themselves.

African Americans had few resources to resist the discursive force of written history and to determine their own lives, but their religious imagination held transformative power. They deployed religious discourse to reclaim black bodies as human bodies and to reconstruct them in the *Imago Dei* with the firm conviction that they also were created in the likeness of the Divine. For most African Americans, the Bible's stories, particularly exodus, grounded their religious knowledge.[13] African Americans readily transferred its themes of bondage and freedom to their own context. Black religious imagination endowed Moses, Pharaoh, the Egyptians, and the Children of Israel with iconic status. Such imaginations summoned the Bible's stories to mediate the textuality of Western history with their own counter-history.[14] Their captors' world may claim that descendants of Africa were enslaved because they were despised, but Africans and their descendants in the American Republic mediated their identity with the exodus story and knew a different truth. *Because* they were enslaved, they knew God would deliver them. God had chosen them and God's election would be manifestly evident when freedom came. They refused to be engrafted into the Western tradition as the conquered ones, whom the enlightened Euro-American civilized. They read the Bible's stories onto themselves and, by doing so, they signified themselves into history (that is, into the Western tradition) and re-signified themselves as subjects in the present. When they preached about the "band of Israelites," they inscribed new meaning upon their past and trafficked in the Bible's discursive power. They conferred upon themselves the standing that the Israelites possessed within the Western tradition. These activities constitute the politics of African American biblical interpretation, which consists of successive attempts from the antebellum period onward to reclaim black bodies from Euro-American discourses and their epistemologies.

When African Americans appealed to biblical authority, they sought the Bible's signifying power. For much of the new republic's history, the Bible was singularly suited for this form of resistance. Through the nineteenth century, most Protestants in the American Republic saw the Bible as the Urtext of the Western tradition. Because other histories were interpreted in view of the Bible's presentation of a transcendent history, the Bible's interpretation could disrupt the signifying processes of the Western historical tradition. For example, by claiming an identity with the Israelites in the story, Africans and their descendants re-signified the story's symbols in the American Republic's religious imagination. As early as the seventeenth century, Anglo-American settlers imagined themselves mimetically performing the Israelites' conquest. They pacified New England and rid it of so-called abominations just as the Israelites had done in Canaan. However, African Americans identified with the story's presentation of the Israelites as an enslaved people whom God delivered, rather than as an instrument of God's military will. Eventually, their interpretation informed the nation's self-understanding through the Civil War where U.S. troops sang about freeing Israel from Egypt as they marched through Confederate territory.

Pillars of Cloud and Fire as Political Forms and Biblical Precedent

The Lord went in front of them in a pillar of cloud by day,
to lead them along the way, and in a pillar of fire by night,
to give them light, so that they might travel by day and by
night. Neither the pillar of cloud by day nor the pillar of fire
by night left its place in front of the people.
—Exodus 13:21–22

In the exodus narrative, God uses two distinct beacons—a pillar of cloud and a pillar of fire—to lead the Children of Israel to Canaan. Each sign appears when its form was most visible—a cloud during the day and fire at night. During the day, clouds appear in fluid forms, blending almost seamlessly with sky. Their subtle, quiet movement recalls those more conservative leaders, whose interpretive activity sought civic reform, using measures legitimated by civil society. However, a raging column of fire pressing urgently against the silent, dark nightscape is at once a brilliant and arresting spectacle; such a symbol invokes those more strident voices whose interpretive work radically challenged the social and political fabric of the nation. Although the respective beacons of cloud and fire appeared in vastly different forms, they both led the Children of Israel in the same direction, from slavery toward the Promised Land, and were necessary components of a liberatory project.

In the same manner, black interpreters summoned the exodus story with differing politics. Their positions resist the traditional dichotomous categorization of "radical" and "conservative."[15] Kelly Miller's 1908 essay, "Radicals and Conservatives," clarifies my correlation with cloud and fire politics.

> When a distinguished Russian was informed that some American Negroes are radical and some conservative, he could not restrain his laughter. The idea of conservative Negroes was more than the Cossack's risibilities could endure. "What on earth," he exclaimed with astonishment, "have they to conserve?"[16]

More than a century ago Miller used these categories to describe the political landscape between William M. Trotter, Booker T. Washington, and W.E.B. Du Bois. They still aptly frame a particular character of the politics of African American Biblical Interpretation. In the essay, Miller rethinks these categories to describe the tactics that African Americans deployed as a part of larger strategies to resist racial repression in the United States. His categories attend to difference in form, while holding ends in common. For Miller, "Radical and conservative Negroes agree as to the end in view, but differ as to the most effective means of attaining it. The difference is not essentially one of principle or purpose, but point of view."[17]

What Miller calls "point of view," I take up as cloud and fire performances over a changing political economy. First, the pillar of cloud performance appears as the ironic doubling described in Paul Lawrence Dunbar's classic poem, "We Wear the Mask":

> We wear the mask that grins and lies,
> It hides our cheeks and shades our eyes,–
> This debt we pay to human guile;
> With torn and bleeding hearts we smile,
>
> And mouth with myriad subtleties.
> Why should the world be overwise,

In counting all our tears and sighs?
Nay, let them only see us, while
We wear the mask.

We smile, but, O great Christ, our cries
To thee from tortured souls arise.
We sing, but oh the clay is vile
Beneath our feet, and long the mile;
But let the world dream otherwise,
We wear the mask![18]

In Dunbar's poem, the mask conceals the existential alienation that African Americans experience as a part of everyday life. But mask*ing* possesses an ironic doubling. One does not simply hide behind the mask; one simultaneously publicizes something as well. In the poem, the mask obscures the *wearer's* "cheeks" and "eyes," but simultaneously announces the *mask's* "grin" and "smile." Its annunciation calls attention to the mask *itself* and *its* disposition. The pillar of cloud performances entail this doubling that simultaneously *conceals* and *advertises*. Metaphorically, the "grin" and "smile" advertise contentment with the social arrangements. The mask diverts the viewer's attention from what it hides and directs attention to what it advertises. Thus, the mask's power lies in its ability to distract—not only by concealing (the mask is not simply a blank cover)—but by advertising something *different*. The greater the incongruity between the mask's self-expression and that of the wearer, the greater the mask's diversion. African Americans take up the mask in forms such as a mastery of civic and social behaviors. They exemplified model citizenship, moral virtue, and intellectual acumen. For pillar of cloud politics, these performances were not ends unto themselves. They *fit* their lives within the contemporaneous social arrangements so that the mask showed congruity with the social world.[19] For example, Absalom Jones displayed a mastery of exemplary citizenship to become a pillar in his Philadelphia community. He used his social and political capital to fortify the free black community against increasing white animosity in the early decades of the nineteenth century. Race notwithstanding, Frances E. W. Harper mastered the presentation of Victorian womanhood while orchestrating a program to undermine its complicity with racial hierarchies. Martin Luther King, Jr., deployed republican rhetoric and Christian theology—representing ideal models of citizenship and religious virtue respectively—while he and his lieutenants at SCLC strategized nationally and internationally broadcasted conflicts between violent southern segregationists and unarmed African Americans engaging in the virtue of civil disobedience. For each pillar of cloud performer, the mask's expression differed from the wearer's activities.

On the other hand, those figures who represent pillars of fire reject the mask in order to advertise themselves. They are unwilling to fit within the unjust social arrangements. In fact, their politics proceed by advertising their unwillingness to fit as both a source of resistance and a show of power. For example, even though they lived in different centuries and under divergent circumstances, both David Walker and Adam Clayton Powell, Jr., made their emancipatory intentions explicit. Their capital accrued not from *fitting in*, and enacting performances of congruence, but from remaining steadfastly *out of place*. They testify to the power of alienation.

Opposing Pillars but Converging Moral Ends

Although their politics differed, the various interpreters presented herein each took up exodus to articulate a shared and emancipatory hope—to reach a Promised Land. They adapted their prevailing politics, both cloud and fire, to meet the challenges of the nation's changing political economy and its ever-changing forms of racialization. From the end of the slave regime to uplift in the nineteenth century to civil rights and Black Power eras in the twentieth century—in each era "Promised Land" took on new meaning—black biblical interpreters in each generation reoccupied emancipatory language and imbued it with new meaning in hopes that they might realize fulfillment some day.

Description and Outline

Over the course of six chapters, this book, a study of "pillars of cloud and fire," develops a typology for the biblical interpretive activity in black religious leadership as it has informed social transformation in the United States. After introducing the project and its methodological considerations, the book lays out a method for interrogating the relationship between scripture and interpreter that attends to three dimensions of each figure's lived experience: biography, cultural context, and political context. Each of the remaining chapters is structured in two moves: contextual and textual. The first frames the historical context for the interpretive activity at three levels: It identifies prevailing debates in black communities; second, it draws in broad outline the wider national socio-historical context of black political, social, and economic life; third, it locates each interpreter within the broader historical context. The second move, the lion's share of each chapter, analyzes particular examples of ecclesial and popular sources of black interpretive activity and its effect in transforming black social reality.

Chapter 1 takes up the antebellum period. The chapter describes the political and social contexts of two African American interpreters: Absalom Jones and David Walker. Their works exemplify the robust and diverse political discourse occurring within African American communities in northern cities such as Philadelphia and Boston. In 1808, Absalom Jones delivered his celebrated "Thanksgiving Sermon" based on Exodus 3 to a well-established congregation at Philadelphia's African Episcopal Church. He deploys a pillar of cloud politics that balances his ecclesial community's commitments to justice for enslaved African Americans with concerns for their own survival and social uplift. Two decades later in Boston, David Walker, a Methodist layperson, published the first edition of his *Appeal to the Coloured Citizens of the World*. Using references to the exodus story throughout, Walker's missive is a display of his pillar of fire politics of the first order. It is oriented toward emancipation through nothing less than open rebellion. From radically different vantage points, both figures take up the exodus story to transform black social reality.

Chapter 2 takes up black biblical interpretation between 1865 and the Nadir. The chapter analyzes the interpretive activity of two prominent figures: Frances E. W. Harper and John Jasper. In the wake of the Civil War's radical disruption of the South's slave economy, and amid the promise of Reconstruction, Harper's *Moses: Story of the Nile*, published in 1869, shows optimism about the possibilities for black life. Her pillar of cloud politics proceeds by locating her rhetoric of racial uplift within the wider concurrent conversation of national character. In the epic poem she fashions a Moses with virtues of the politics of respectability and commends him to the black community as the key to racial uplift. The chapter will show how Harper's depiction of Moses—a critical integration of the biblical character, Moses, and the life of her friend, Harriet Tubman, a real-life Moses—raises important questions about the status of black women following slavery.

Nine years later, after any hopes of the promise of Reconstruction had been eroded, John Jasper, the towering pastoral figure of Richmond, Virginia, takes Exodus 13:5 and preaches his renowned sermon, "The Sun Do Move." Defiant rather than optimistic, Jasper's pillar of fire politics rejects the truth claims of the new scientific discourses from which African Americans have been barred access. Rather, he affirms the truth claims of his community's liberating God to sustain them amidst the rapidly unraveling protections and broken promises of Reconstruction. Unlettered, he leverages hermeneutical sophistication, political savvy, and unwavering faith to offer his community a powerful counter to the onslaught of southern repression. Both Harper and Jasper, from radically different social and political milieus and with divergent interpretive moves, turn to the exodus to negotiate the politics of early post-slavery America.

Chapter 3 turns to the New Negro Movement, particularly as the Harlem Renaissance manifests it. The chapter studies the work of Zora Neale Hurston as emblematic of the Harlem Renaissance intellectual tradition. In 1939 Hurston published *Moses, Man of the Mountain*. It is the first novel-length treatment of the exodus story. In the aftermath of the Great Depression, Hurston is suspicious of the black community's reliance upon divine activity to resolve social ills. She focuses her pillar of fire politics on questions of African American self-reliance and human agency and offers an important critique for black ecclesial biblical interpretation.

Chapter 4 focuses on the Civil Rights Movement both as an ideological trajectory and a chronological rubric. The marches, boycotts, and sit-ins characterized a type of black resistance oriented toward reforming institutions that had denied access to African Americans. Much of the interpretive activity of the time appropriated biblical texts for the purpose of civil attainment. Within that frame, the chapter analyzes the interpretive work of two figures: Adam Clayton Powell, Jr., the U.S. congressional representative from Harlem and pastor of Harlem's Abyssinian Baptist Church; and Martin Luther King, Jr., the civil rights leader from the South. The chapter begins with Powell's sermon on Exodus 32 entitled, "Stop Blaming Everybody Else," delivered in 1953 at a critical juncture in his career and in the formation of black political identity. His pillar of fire politics takes up the exodus story to focus the black community on both the ravages of McCarthyism and the responsibilities of citizenship. Powell's interpretive lens serves as a natural bridge between the thinkers of the Harlem Renaissance and the activists of the Civil Rights Movement proper, beginning in 1954. The chapter then examines two sermons of Martin Luther King, Jr., "Death of Evil Upon the Seashore," and "Birth of a New Nation," delivered in 1955 and 1957 respectively. Both sermons take the book of Exodus to deploy King's pillar of cloud politics. Together, they serve as examples of interpretive activity during the civil rights era. King's sermons gain a visibility that shapes the national discourse while Powell's political and social excesses diminish his impact on public life. Ironically, each needed the other's work. Powell's legislative influence benefitted from King's ability to energize the public. For King, many of the real material gains of the Civil Rights Movement depended upon Powell's hardball politics and his legislative prowess. Taken together, their work, oriented toward reform, not only served as a catalyst for drastic changes in the black public sphere, but participated in transforming American identity as well.

Chapter 5 turns to the era of the Black Power Movement. The chapter probes the contours of the Black Power Movement as the ideological heir to the Civil Rights Movement. Within that frame, the chapter examines the interpretive work of Albert Cleage. Delivered in October 1967, his sermon "What Can We Give Our Youth" interprets the exodus narrative both as an exercise in radical race politics and Cleage's own pillar of fire politics. While most figures of the Black Power Movement abandoned the Black Church for what they perceived to be its accommodationist orientation, Cleage constructed a theology and a politics that maximized the best insights of the Civil Rights and the Black Power Movements, while remaining grounded in the history and traditions of the Black Church.

The conclusion makes overtures to the contemporary world and the ongoing deployment of exodus within a politics of freedom. From the Antebellum period through the Black Power Movement, *Pillars* attempts to expand the field considered proper to biblical studies and to show that analyzing such interpretations requires sustained attention to the cultural and historical forces from which it arose.

1

Exodus: Israelite Deliverance and Antebellum Hope

The cry of the Israelites has now come to me; I have also seen
how the Egyptians oppress them. So come, I will send you to
Pharaoh to bring my people, the Israelites, out of Egypt.
—Exodus 3:9–10

The book of Exodus tells the Bible's ancient story of a people's slavery
and their struggle for emancipation. In the early nineteenth century,
many communities took the Bible's story of slavery and emancipation
and made it black people's story of faith. Anguished black souls, both
enslaved and free, angry and hopeful, adopted it as their own. In brush
harbors and tall steeple churches, they preached its message. In cotton
fields and choir lofts alike, they glorified its vision of justice in spirituals.
And everywhere, they prayed to realize its emancipatory hope. Among
that chorus arose two voices from two of the largest, most politically
active, and financially viable free black populations in the nation. From
the reservoir of black religious imagination, these two voices summoned
this ancient, archetypal narrative of slavery and freedom. With it, they
told their own people's story. In Philadelphia, Absalom Jones climbed
from slavery to become a pillar of the community and the father of black
Episcopalians. In 1808 he preached his celebrated "Thanksgiving Sermon" on Exodus 3. With a mild-mannered disposition that belied his
burning indignation, he articulated the politics and aspirations of the
black Philadelphia community that had formed him. While others at
that time spoke differently, Jones was optimistic about the possibilities
for African American life in the first decade of the nineteenth century.

Two decades later in Boston, David Walker, a clothing merchant who
had emigrated from the South, took up the same book of Exodus and
fired off his strident *Appeal to the Coloured Citizens of the World*. Its
message was urgent; its tone was defiant. News of the pamphlet's contents ignited so much fear throughout slaveholding states that south-

ern planters offered a price for his head. Jones and Walker were among the earliest to deploy the exodus narrative to articulate black struggles against repression. Their politics and interpretations differed so radically that neither would have had much regard for the other. Yet both would come to the same exodus narrative to express their shared emancipatory hope.

The Black Problem and the Philadelphia Experiment

In 1684, slavery came to Philadelphia when the Bristol firm's ship *Isabella* docked at the city's port. In its hold, 150 Africans lay chained.[1] On the whole, such events were normal occurrences along North America's Atlantic coast. But Philadelphia was the City of Brotherly Love. In 1681, when William Penn received the charter for the territory that would become Pennsylvania, he hoped to establish it as a haven for persecuted Quakers. Writing about the land grant, he vowed, "I would not abuse His love, nor act unworthy of His providence, and so defile what came to me clean."[2] Penn dreamed of a society where Quaker values of love and justice would guide the colony's ethos. He named its capital—Philadelphia, City of Brotherly Love—to be a beacon for the territory. That dream ended the day the *Isabella* arrived. By week's end, the city's approximately 1,000 residents had purchased the entire cargo of human chattel.[3] Thereafter, white Philadelphians were caught between two competing priorities: the anti-slavery commitments entailed in their Quaker heritage and their appetite for human chattel. Over the next century, two wars, shifts in the economy, a politically robust free black community, and a coalition comprised of Quakers and other abolitionists, including the Philadelphia Abolition Society, worked to end slavery in the City of Brotherly Love. The 1780 Abolition Law mandating the gradual manumission of enslaved Africans had all but ended the institution in Philadelphia by 1800. Of the 6,381 blacks in the city, only fifty-five remained enslaved. The 1810 census showed that out of the black population of 9,656 persons, only three were held in slavery.[4]

For the Philadelphia Abolition Society, the Society of Friends, and other white abolitionists, the end of slavery in the city meant that the Philadelphia Experiment had been a success. Their work depended upon the efforts of abolitionists such as Anthony Benezet, a Huguenot who published a series of anti-slavery pamphlets beginning in 1759 and continuing until his death in 1784. After establishing a school for the instruction of black children, Benezet argued publicly that they were not intellectually inferior to white children.[5] Others such as Benjamin Rush, a Presbyterian physician, and Thomas Paine, who later wrote *Common Sense*, aimed pointed critiques at the hypocrisy of slaveholders in America who demanded freedom from Britain.[6] In 1787, the Philadelphia Abolition Society, touting its good work to its British counterpart, the London Society for the Abolition of the Slave Trade, reported that men and women emerging from slavery could indeed be "industrious, orderly, and of moral deportment."[7]

Despite emancipation, however, black Philadelphians continued to suffer racial hostilities. The Commonwealth of Pennsylvania enacted new laws suppressing their freedoms. Often, local authorities manumitted persons only to force them into decades of indentured servitude. Nonetheless, the free black community of Philadelphia knew that, as the subjects of the Philadelphia Experiment, the hopes and possibilities of sisters and brothers still chafing under the yoke of chattel slavery rested in part on their ability to ensure the Experiment's continued success.

For most white Philadelphians, the Experiment's success was not a fait accompli; its status always remained contingent upon the free black community's behavior at that particular time, a situation black Philadelphians understood all too well. From 1726 until 1780, the colonial assembly's "Act for the Regulation of Negroes in the Province" checked their freedom. Channeling the prejudices of their constituents, the legislators made the spirit of the Act clear in its disparaging preamble: "Whereas, free Negroes are an idle and slothful people and often prove burdensome to the neighborhood and afford ill examples to other Negroes."[8] It meant that free black Philadelphians lived under constant suspicion and the regulating gaze of their white counterparts. Among its provisions, the Act levied fines for free black persons who harbored those escaping enslavement, required slaveholders to post a bond with the county if they released a person held in slavery, and fined them if they allowed any enslaved person to "hire out his own time."[9] Free black persons were always subject to enslavement, since the act empowered magistrates to bind out annually black persons of "slothful" behavior to work for whites. Black women were subject to this provision until the age of twenty-one, while black men remained subject until the age of twenty-four.[10] When any law was broken, one person's minor infraction cast doubt upon the entire black community. Every day, free black Philadelphians knew their behavior would be used to judge the character of the entire race, slave and free. Furthermore, they had little recourse to address the insults and injuries they received as a part of daily life. Black Philadelphians lived with a mitigated freedom. But for them, such freedom was not too heavy a burden if it meant that the Philadelphia Experiment might be replicated in other cities throughout the new Republic. They believed—as had those children of slavery who preceded them and adopted the exodus story—that perhaps one day, all of their sisters and brothers would be free.

Absalom Jones: Pillar of Cloud as Pillar of the Community

Growing up in Philadelphia's black community, Absalom Jones understood its social world and its political economy configured by slavery and freedom, education and illiteracy, wealth and poverty, and enfranchisement and marginalization. His response to the challenges facing its newly freed members took the form of a "pillar of cloud." Jones's politics proceeded by advertising a diversion, namely, his willingness to *fit* within the social and racial strictures of Philadelphia's social world. His display, a mastery of the moral and civic virtues prized by his community, masked his efforts to free enslaved Africans and build wealth and political capital among the city's black residents. With this politics, he believed that he could raise his station and that of others without agitation.

Jones developed the components of his politics organically. From the beginning, Calvinist virtues shaped Absalom Jones's world.[11] The social options available to him reinforced the ultimate economic and theological significance of work as a spiritual discipline rationalized into a system.[12] Born in 1746 in Sussex, Delaware, Absalom Jones, along with his mother and siblings, was held in slavery by Benjamin Wynkoop, a wealthy planter from a prominent Dutch family. Wynkoop's Calvinist leanings and strong ties to the Episcopal Church would influence the young Absalom. As a child, Absalom worked in the Wynkoop home. He taught himself to read using books that he purchased by saving the occasional pennies he received in tips.[13] Absalom probably did not share Wynkoop's Calvinist understanding that his work, frugality, book purchases, and achieved literacy were signs assuring his salvation. Nevertheless, deploying some portion of his labor for his own benefit rather than for the slave system at such an early age must have been gratifying. Moreover, to be a literate black child in the mid-eighteenth century only magnified the importance of his achievement because Absalom had permanently raised his own social status.

In 1762, Wynkoop traded his quiet, rural Delaware planter's life to become a merchant in Philadelphia. That year, without regard for the family, he sold Absalom's mother, sisters, and brothers, but took the fifteen-year-old Absalom to Philadelphia. In the city, Absalom had ample opportunity to run away and to lose himself in densely populated black Philadelphia neighborhoods. However, the prospects for a boy to provide for his safety and other basic necessities on his own in the unfamiliar urban world were almost as dismal as under the slave system. Moreover, there would have been little chance of reuniting with his mother and siblings since escaping meant crossing state lines. Even more difficult, passing himself off as a free person at such a young age would have been virtually impossible. Instead, the maturing Absalom Jones employed the lessons he had learned as a child. He had seen Wynkoop's devotion to his mercantile vocation and how his shrewd business acumen led to financial security. For Wynkoop, these rewards were material signs of his status as one of the Elect. While one could neither know nor affect one's status in the world to come, one's success in this world was indicative of one's status among the Elect. Success in this world was not assurance of salvation, but it was one among many signs. Thus, Calvinists were not to enjoy the natural fruits of such success. Rather, frugality, moderation, and temperance emerged as virtues. Jones's work would return for him signs of salvation as well.

However, Jones, like many other blacks held in chattel slavery, followed Gronniosaw and interpreted the silence differently. Salvation for them was polyvalent; it meant emancipation here and life with Christ in the world to come. At least for the next sixteen years, Jones labored in Wynkoop's store beyond the time imposed by his enslavement, saving the money he earned.[14] In 1770, Jones married Mary King and, by continuing to labor beyond his enslavement, he purchased her freedom eight years after their marriage. Working another six years, he saved enough to secure his own freedom.[15] By 1779, Jones had amassed enough wealth to purchase property in Philadelphia's southern Dock Ward. His neighbors included Cyrus Griffen, a delegate to the Continental Congress from Virginia, and Thomas Mekean, chief justice of Pennsylvania.[16]

Jones's Calvinist political ethics accounted not only for his financial position, but also for his survival and subsequent rise to prominence amid an increasingly racially polarized city. He blended with the social landscape as a cloud blends with the sky. Jones survived by performing a mastery of exemplary citizenship. Succinctly put, Jones modeled the "orderliness, industry, and moral deportment" that the Philadelphia Experiment demanded of the free black community. He understood well the black community's vulnerability to violent forms of white backlash. The end of slavery in Philadelphia had not brought the long hoped-for Jubilee. When the legislature repealed the 1726 Act, it only rendered more visible the smoldering hatred and fear of the small number of free black residents. As their numbers grew, so did white fear. From 1780 to 1800, Philadelphia's white population grew from 30,900 to 63,242.[17] During the same period, its black population grew from 1,100 to 6,436.[18] Whenever news of some small insurrection, individual act of resistance, or rebellion, such as the one that took place in Santa Domingo, frightened the white public, the Philadelphia Abolition Society made it a practice to warn the black community of its obligation "to do credit to yourselves, and to justify the friends and advocates of your colour in the eyes of the world."[19] Repeatedly, the Society held the black community accountable for the white backlash they experienced. On one occasion, the Society went so far as to issue rules admonishing the black community toward "churchgoing, educating the young, temperance, frugality, respectful behavior, and avoidance of 'frolicking and amusements.'"[20] In the politically charged environment, Jones believed that his survival depended upon his ability to perform these virtues idealized by the white public sphere—a *mastery* of exemplary citizenship. By showcasing these values, Jones believed he could leverage whatever spheres of power his society made available to him to achieve his political ends. First, this meant *fitting* in his place as prescribed by his social world and raising his station only by those means acceptable in the white public sphere. Second, Jones believed he could convince white Philadelphians, even those hostile toward blacks, that there was some mutual benefit in achieving those ends. At every opportunity Jones wore the mask that *advertised* these values as constituting not only his character but that of the black community as well.

Nine years before he preached his celebrated "Thanksgiving Sermon," Jones petitioned Congress on December 30, 1799 to end slavery. He began with the following:

> That, thankful to God, our Creator, and to the Government under which we live, for the blessings and benefits granted to us in the enjoyment of our natural right to liberty, and the protection of our persons and property from the oppression and violence which so great a number of like colour and national descent are subject to, we feel ourselves bound, from a sense of these blessings, to continue in our respective allotments, and to lead honest and peaceable lives rendering due submission unto the laws, and exciting and encouraging each other thereto, agreeable to the uniform advice of our friends of every denomination. [21]

His opening sentence foregrounds the behaviors included in his "pillar of cloud" politics; they constitute his display of exemplary citizenship. By "lead[ing] honest and peaceable lives," Jones signals his intent *to fit* in his place as an upstanding member of the Philadelphia community. By "render[ing] due submission unto the laws," Jones commits to the role of citizen and the prevailing social order. By foregrounding or *advertising* this commitment to such a politics, Jones masks his community's efforts toward achieving material, social, and political equality. His strategy intended to deflect racist reprisals that might be triggered by growing white resentment toward the free, but vulnerable, black community as they worked toward political and economic parity.

Jones had practiced such a politics throughout his life. Years earlier, he had re-imagined his dehumanizing relationship with Wynkoop, the man who profited from the sale of his mother and siblings. He decided to maintain the relationship as a necessary evil and even re-envisioned it as a potentiality from which he would amass the resources to free himself and build a family. Doing so required more than the discipline of hard work and delayed gratification of his Calvinist formation. He represented his own advancement as coinciding with Wynkoop's goals. Jones persuaded Wynkoop that they shared more interests by relating under a labor economy rather than a slave economy. Only then could he have convinced the merchant to pay him overtime for work beyond that required of his slave status. Jones accomplished this political feat while he modeled the values that Wynkoop's Calvinist faith prized.

By 1787, Jones had emerged as a pillar of the Philadelphia community. Borne by his hard work, financial success, and deep faith, he earned the admiration of the racially mixed congregation of the prominent St. George's Methodist Church, which appointed him as their lay minister. For several reasons, Jones, like so many blacks in the Philadelphia community, was drawn to the Methodist church. First, the anti-slavery views of Methodism's founder, John Wesley, were well known. Second, Methodism's style of worship was far more stirring and participatory than other denominational traditions. Third, membership depended on testimony and experience rather than catechism. Fourth, Methodists did not demand that its clergy possess a theological education, only a converted heart, disciplined character, and the gift of preaching. Fifth, Methodists also ordained black ministers where it was legal and licensed them in other places to lead congregations.[22] Jones, along with Richard Allen, another Methodist layperson, evangelized together. Allen's preaching increased black membership dramatically. The rapid increase in black congregants unnerved white members at St. George's. In 1792, after contributing financially to an expansion of the St. George edifice, black members, who thought that they would be able to sit in the general seating area, were told that they were restricted to the balcony. Soon Allen and Jones decided to test the new rule by leading a group of black parishioners to pray at the altar. When a white deacon forcibly pulled them from their knees, instructed them to leave from praying, and directed them to retire to the balcony, Allen and Jones promptly marched the black members out of St. George to form a new congregation.[23] Both men wanted to remain in fellowship with the Methodist church, but the congregation voted overwhelmingly to join the Episcopal church. Jones served as their new minister and Allen went on to establish the African Methodist Episcopal Church. Although the congregation forced a professional split between the two men, their deep friendship remained intact and they continued to work together in other arenas throughout their lives.

Nowhere is Jones's political ethics more clearly deployed than in his work with Richard Allen and the Free African Society (FAS). On April 12, 1787, Jones and Allen formed the society to aid members of the Philadelphia black community.[24] Publicly, the society showcased the free black community's civic participation and moral deportment. It emphasized to their members and advertised to the wider community the virtues of frugality, abstinence from alcohol, simple living, and fidelity in marriage that represented both Calvinist values and Methodist holiness. At the same time, the Society amassed ample funds that were used to aid its members and to establish those persons newly freed from slavery. The Society's work during the devastating yellow fever epidemic of 1793 is an example of the civic participation that Jones and Allen publicized. By the summer, nearly 20,000 white residents had deserted the city. Despite the humiliating treatment they had received at St. George's, Jones and Allen responded to white officials' urgent requests for their assistance. They mobilized the FAS to minister to both black and white residents throughout the city. When Benjamin Rush, who had been an advocate of manumission, pleaded with Jones and Allen to enlist members of the FAS to respond to the epidemic, they offered care to more than 800 persons.[25] During that time, the society raised funds to bury any black person who could not afford the expense. After the epidemic, the organization's enhanced reputation enabled it to work more effectively in political and judicial arenas on behalf of the black community. With the FAS's raised status, Jones and Allen worked more diligently to fortify the organization and focus its efforts on supporting the black community. Jones continued to embody the political temper of the free blacks in the Philadelphia society that shaped him. As part of this endeavor, he interpreted the exodus story out of his Calvinist political ethics and his pastoral concerns for the free black Philadelphia community.

Exodus as Pillar of Cloud: Building Pillars of the Community

On January 1, 1808, Jones ascended the African Episcopal Church pulpit to celebrate what he believed was God's providence upon the U.S. Congress. That morning, he delivered his best-known oration, the "Thanksgiving Sermon." The sermon commemorated the Congressional Act of 1807 criminalizing the importation of human chattel from the African continent to the United States. Jones began with a common technique, a strategy that combined intercontextual and figural interpretation as he "took his text" from Exodus 3:7–8: "And the Lord said, I have surely seen the affliction of my people which are in Egypt and have heard their cry by reason of their task-masters; for I know their sorrows; and I am come down to deliver them out of the hand of the Egyptians."[26]

Jones's figural interpretive work correlated biblical history's trajectory with historical forces in his own world. It was probably not by coincidence that Jones chose the Exodus 3 passage, the theophany at Midian where God declares to Moses the intent to deliver God's people from Egyptian bondage, as the scriptural basis for his sermon. At this juncture in the narrative, God had not yet accomplished the emancipation of the Children of Israel. So when Moses returned to the Israelites, he had little evidence to confirm the promise of freedom—only his own report of an encounter with an unfamiliar deity. Jones understood himself to be in a similar position. With no evidence for the end of the slave regime, Jones saw the congressional act as his burning bush theophany. He believed the new law signaled God's intent to act on behalf of suffering blacks in North America. Long suffering and faithfulness had activated God's intervention for the Children of Israel and he believed the same now brought justice for Africans. The congressional act was but the latest instance in a long trajectory of divine justice. In contradistinction to David Walker, whom I shall discuss next, Jones took the opportunity to commend to his congregation the pillar of cloud politics and the continued labor that had served him. With both, he believed he would encourage progress toward emancipation.

That morning, the sermon's effectiveness depended upon Jones's rhetorical ability to describe the ancient Hebrews' world, where the symbols of good, evil, bondage, emancipation, sorrow, and hope are readily identifiable, and to transfer them to the life-world of his congregation. Jones's exegetical approach correlated the biblical world and the antebellum world that his congregation knew. That is, his sermon wove the biblical text and the contemporaneous context together into a seamless whole, so that each gave meaning to the other. As a nuanced instrumentalist deploys blue notes and thirteenth chords to evoke rich and complex emotions, Jones deployed the plot, symbols, and themes of the exodus story to interpret meaning for the unique situation of American slavery. In so doing, Jones brought his congregation to the place where biblical history's horizon fused with the contemporaneous world. Jones exhorted:

The history of the world shows us, that the deliverance of the children of Israel from their bondage, is not the only instance, in which it has pleased God to appear in behalf of oppressed and distressed nations, as the deliverer of the innocent, and of those who call upon his name. He is as unchangeable in his nature and character, as he is in his wisdom and power. The great and blessed event, which we have this day met to celebrate, is a striking proof, that the God of heaven is the same *yesterday, and to-day, and for ever.* Yes, my brethren, the nations from which most of us have descended, and the country in which some of us were born, have been visited by the tender mercy of the Common Father of the human race. He has seen the affliction of our countrymen, with an eye of pity. He has seen the wicked arts, by which wars have been fomented among the different tribes of the Africans, in order to procure captives, for the purpose of selling them for slaves. He has seen ships fitted out from different ports in Europe and America, and freighted with trinkets to be exchanged for the bodies and souls of men. He has seen the anguish which has taken place, when parents have been torn from their children, and children from their parents, and conveyed, with their hands and feet bound in fetters, on board of ships prepared to receive them. He has seen them thrust in crowds into the holds of those ships, where many of them have perished from the want of air. He has seen such of them as have escaped from that noxious place of confinement, leap into the ocean; with a faint hope of swimming back to their native shore, or a determination to seek early retreat from their impending misery, in a watery grave. He has seen them exposed for sale, like horses and cattle, upon the wharves; or, like bales of goods, in warehouses of West India and American sea ports. He has seen the pangs of separation between members of the same family. He has seen them driven into the sugar; the rice, and the tobacco fields, and compelled to work—in spite of the habits of ease which they derived from the natural fertility of their own country in the open air, beneath a burning sun, with scarcely as much clothing upon them as modesty required. He has seen them faint beneath the pressure of their labours. He has seen them return to their smoky huts in the evening, with nothing to satisfy their hunger but a scanty allowance of roots; and these, cultivated for themselves, on that day only, which God ordained as a day of rest for man and beast. He has seen the neglect with which their masters have treated their immortal souls; not only in withholding religious instruction from them, but, in some instances, depriving them of access to the means of obtaining it. He has seen all the different modes of torture, by means of the whip, the screw, the pincers, and the red hot iron, which have been exercised upon their bodies, by inhuman overseers: overseers, did I say? Yes: but not by these only. Our God has seen masters and mistresses, educated in fashionable life, sometimes take the instruments of torture into their own hands, and, deaf to the cries and shrieks of their agonizing slaves, exceed even their overseers in cruelty. Inhuman wretches! Though you have been deaf to their cries and shrieks, they have been heard in Heaven.[27]

The homiletic performance brought text and context together in a reciprocating relationship; each colored the other with vivid meanings. Drawing artfully from both the Bible and tragic scenes in North America, Jones signified upon the condition of Africans held as slaves and constructed a particular meaning for the strange, foreign, and ancient world of the Hebrews. His carefully chosen rhetoric transformed the biblical story about the practice of conscripting labor in the ancient world[28] to a contemporaneous story of chattel slavery expressly addressed to the descendants of Africans residing in North America. Jones contextualized the calamity of North American slavery by mapping it upon the exodus narrative. As his rhetoric led the congregation into the biblical world, whose signs Jones shaped in the sermonic moment, his congregation came to shared vision about the contemporary world they inhabited.

Combining figural with intercontextual interpretive strategies proved particularly effective for Africans living in the United States during the antebellum period. The Trans-Atlantic Slave Trade had disrupted both their social world and those structures of meaning necessary to apprehend their circumstances in North America. The former religious, intellectual, social, and political structures no longer held the cohesion of a society and could not offer Africans a coherent worldview.[29] In other words, these meanings did not make "sense" in the context of North

American chattel slavery. Slavery on the African continent generally maintained coherence with cultural meanings that were already in place. To be captured in war could mean that one's God had been conquered by the victor's deity. Servitude as a prisoner of war often meant living with a neighboring people—perhaps even becoming one of them. Even so, the former social and religious structures remained intact. In the Bible's silence, Jones used these two strategies to bring the congregation to hermeneutical understanding as they experience the tragic rupture in meaning and the evil of slavery in North America.

The sermon begins by expounding upon the word, "affliction," interpreting it as the "privation of liberty."

> These words, my brethren, contain a short account of some of the circumstances, which preceded the deliverance of the children of Israel from their captivity and bondage in Egypt. They mention, in the first place, their *affliction*. This consisted in their privation of liberty: they were slaves to the kings of Egypt, in common with their other subjects; they were slaves to their fellow slaves. They were compelled to work in the open air, in one of the hottest climates in the world; and, probably, without a covering from the burning rays of the sun.[30]

His connection of "affliction" and "privation of liberty" can be found in two contemporaneous intellectual traditions that were familiar to Jones and his congregation: first, the black spirituals, whose lyrics extolled the moral virtue of the kinship and equality of all humankind; and second, rights philosophy. In both, Jones was reaching for justice, which he saw as egalitarianism. With respect to the black spirituals, three examples will suffice: In lyrics such as "I got shoes/ You got shoes/All God's children got shoes," the spirituals advocated the equitable distribution of wealth in God's economy. In the lyrics of another spiritual, "Weeping Mary/you got a right to the tree of life," religious communities on John's Island, South Carolina claimed a particular solidarity with those who had suffered loss, affirming that they also had a right to justice.[31] In the third stanza of "Swing Low, Sweet Chariot," the lyrics "If you get there before I do, tell all of my friends that I'm coming too" alludes in double entendre to emancipation both in heaven and in the North, claiming the hope that all would reach fulfillment someday.[32]

The African American spiritual tradition, whose vision of equity testifies against the horrifying background of American slavery, guided Jones's deployment of the term "affliction." He wove descriptors of the inhumane conditions in which Africans suffered under slavery in the plantation South and those the Bible uses to describe the Israelites; he took up both groups as referents to the subject pronoun "they" and its possessive form, "their."

> *They* were compelled to work in the open air in one of the hottest climates in the world; and, probably, without a covering from the burning rays of the sun. *Their* work was of a laborious kind: it consisted of making bricks, and travelling, perhaps to a great distance, for the straw, or stubble that was a component part of them. *Their* work was dealt out to *them* in tasks, and performed under the eye of vigilant and rigorous masters, who constantly upbraided them with idleness. The least deficiency in the product of *their* labour, was punished by beating.[33]

Jones concluded with an allusion to Pharaoh's infamous plot to kill all infant Hebrew boys, again with effective use of double signification: "*their* huts and hamlets were vocal at night with *their* lamentations over *their* sons; who were dragged from the arms of *their* mothers, and put to death by drowning."[34]

The description evoked memories of countless stories of the loss of family members to brutality or the auction block and the powerlessness of their kin who could do nothing but be a witness to the horror. While many in Jones's congregation may have remembered slavery personally, others had only heard of the horrors of the institution whose center had by then moved to the South. Some may have read of the brutality in matter-of-fact newspaper descriptions. A few heard the stories from the lips of men and women brave enough to escape, skilled enough to make the journey north, and fortunate enough to survive. But here, in the sermonic moment, Jones inscribed the terrible scenes upon their imaginations in the most sensuous detail. The vicissitudes of chattel slavery took on meaning as Jones mapped them onto the exodus template. His descriptions of injustice and suffering drawn from the symbols of the biblical world landed upon the congregation with the full weight of biblical authority. As Jones's congregants recognized their own history in the exodus narrative, the biblical authority that grounded the Hebrews' story now legitimated their struggle and affirmed their humanity as a people chosen by God.

The second tradition arises out of a North American trajectory of rights philosophy. Constructed against the background of eighteenth-century British colonialism, it holds that there is no right more basic to humanity than that of individual liberty. So fundamental was such a right that by 1776 it was asserted to be "inalienable" in the Declaration of Independence. Jones would have been familiar with the appropriation of the concept of human rights in both the Declaration of Independence (1776) and the Declaration of the Rights of Man and of the Citizen (1789) because he had lived in Philadelphia through the commonwealth's rebellion and had seen the city lead the birth of the new American Republic. Fourteen years after he arrived, the American Revolution engulfed the city and British soldiers occupied the city streets. As white Philadelphians weighed their pragmatic concerns against their political options and ideological commitments, so did black Philadelphians. Many white Philadelphians fled the city. Others fought as loyal British subjects. Still others fought with Washington's army to free themselves from the tyranny of the British Crown. Black Philadelphians saw the war as an opportunity to free themselves from the tyranny of the slave system. When General Howe offered manumission to any person held in slavery in return for service to the British army, many blacks reported for duty. Later, when General Washington was forced to extend a competing offer, blacks joined the Continental Army as well. Still others simply passed as free persons in the chaos of military occupation. However, Jones and others like him did not flee, but remained in bondage. Again, by obeying the law, Jones adhered to his politics of exemplary citizenship.

In 1781, Jones saw the third Continental Convention meet in Philadelphia. While writing into the Constitution the basic liberty that white Philadelphians enjoyed, that historic convention also enshrined the institution of chattel slavery. In 1787, those enslaved were relegated to three-fifths of a person in the new Republic. In the city where both the Declaration of Independence and the U.S. Constitution were penned and ratified, both would have been familiar to Jones's black Philadelphia congregation. The irony of a document ratified in the City of Brotherly Love that codified freedom and simultaneously legitimated slavery was not lost on black Philadelphians.

Finally, Jones moved the sermon from contextualizing slavery to a constructive mode. He takes hold of the Bible's silence and composes a counter-narrative that gives meaning to his congregation's social circumstance as well as a counter-identity for members of a race enslaved. They are not destined to be tools whose labor God determined to enrich the American planter aristocracy. Rather, Jones declares that they are ends unto themselves—the very subjects of God's providential activity. With the symbols of the exodus as his idiom, Jones foretells the end of the slave experience. He gives the cultural meanings that had been uprooted from the social world of Africa a new hermeneutical context in North America that makes "sense of the senselessness" of chattel slavery.

For Jones, American slavery's historical trajectory would follow the exodus metanarrative written long ago. The story of Africans held in slavery will parallel that of the children of Israel. With the authority signified by the Bible in his nineteenth-century world, Jones mediates the textuality of Western history that has landed upon Africans in North America with crushing force. In each description, Jones rewrites history for a people whose absence from Western annals rendered them dehumanized. He makes his bold assertion decades before the first salvo of the Civil War and, with pastoral authority, assures his congregation that their circumstance has already been prefigured; it has a beginning, middle, and a glorious end—God comes down.

By turning to the last phrase of his biblical text, "I am come down," Jones interpreted the Act criminalizing the capture and forced importation of black people from the continent of Africa as divine action, a sign that divine justice will ultimately triumph over repression. Although his interpretation participates in the long tradition of African American religious optimism, it differs from God's emancipatory activity in the book of Exodus. In the biblical story, God calls the Hebrews to be primary agents who agitate and demand their own liberation—Moses and Aaron first, then the entire community. On the surface, it appears that Jones locates God's presence among the slaveholders—in an act of congress. He proclaims:

He has heard the prayers that have ascended from the hearts of his people; and he has, as in the case of his ancient and chosen people the Jews, come down to deliver our suffering country-men from the hands of their oppressors. He came down into the United States, when they declared, in the constitution which they framed in 1788, that the trade in our African fellow-men, should cease in the year 1808: He came down into the British Parliament, when they passed a law to put an end to the same iniquitous trade in May, 1807: He came down into the Congress of the United States, the last winter, when they passed a similar law, the operation of which commences on this happy day.[35]

Ostensibly, Jones's interpretive work excludes Africans held as slaves from a primary role as agents in their own liberation. So, by extension, following the example of Moses and Aaron would be contrary to his own politics. Rather, Jones grounded his constructive vision of freedom in his own life experience; his vision was pragmatic, Calvinist, and fore-grounded God's providence. Jones affirmed that it was not Congress acting on its own volition, but rather it was *God* who "came down" and directed the course of human affairs by prevailing upon the legislative process.

For Jones, God's intervention was a sign of compassion affirming the moral good of his abolitionist position and commending the community to continued work.[36] In response, he exhorts his congregation to five duties: to offer "gratitude to God for his late goodness and mercy to our countrymen"; to offer "prayer to Almighty God, for the completion of his begun goodness to our brethren in Africa"; to "conduct ourselves in such a manner as to furnish no cause of regret to the deliverers of our nation, for their kindness to us"; to "be grateful to our benefactors"; and to "let the first of January, the day of the abolition of the slave trade in our country, be set apart in every year, as a day of public thanksgiving."[37] His instructions are practical and Calvinist. They returned his congregation to the pillar of cloud politics of exemplary citizenship—the values to which Jones owed his own advancement. Jones calls upon the congregation to blend with the social world as he had done. In other words, not through radical politics, but rather through the quotidian drudge of hard work and vigilant frugality, Jones had earned his freedom, taught himself to read, and elevated himself in black Philadelphia society. Likewise, his instructions call the congregation to leverage the spheres of power their society made available to them. Jones himself had done exactly that: he had worked for Wynkoop and saved his money to purchase his freedom rather than run away; he had advanced his financial position by continuing to work for Wynkoop even after being manumitted; and he had raised his social status by modeling exceptional civic behavior, even engaging in extraordinary acts of courage during the yellow fever outbreak.

In his instructions to the congregation, Jones exhorted them to the same cloud-like politics. By showing displays of gratitude, he believed that they would encourage progressive attitudes among their "benefactors." By modeling virtues of temperance, frugality, and hard work, they would give evidence of their worthiness for full inclusion into civil society. By building wealth and political capital, Jones believed the community could fortify itself against the worst racist excesses of his society. Even if they never gained the acceptance of their "benefactors," it did not matter. They would continue to work toward emancipation. For now, however, it was enough for Jones that God had come down.

Massachusetts Bay Colony: Puritan Promised Land

By the time Philadelphia experienced its fateful encounter with the *Isabella*, Boston had long participated in the slave trade. As early as 1638, Massachusetts Bay Colony governor John Winthrop documented the presence of slaveholders among the colonists. Winthrop's interest in slavery was more than a curious matter of fact; for the New England Puritan, it was both a matter of faith and a matter of commerce. As governor, he was responsible to administer the Puritan colony by the laws of God as contained in the Old and New Testaments. As the principal of the Massachusetts Bay Company, he needed to make the venture profitable for his investors. Like many of the other colonists, Winthrop believed that a strict Puritan faith could achieve both. Its doctrines would organize them as a religious society pleasing to God. Its discipline would make its adherents productive and their endeavors profitable. For the next 140 years, slavery proved important for both New England Puritanism and the success of the Massachusetts Bay Colony.

Early on, Massachusetts Puritans saw no inconsistencies between their faith and their slaveholding practices. By 1641, the Body of Liberties, the colony's first binding legal agreement, codified the enslavement of "such strangers as willfully sell themselves or are sold to us." The basis for such was grounded in "the law of God established in Israell [sic] concerning such persons."[38] Cotton Mather, a slaveholder and the colony's most prominent minister, believed slavery was morally redemptive and encouraged fellow colonists to make every effort to convert Africans held in chattel slavery from their Traditional African Religions to Christianity. He entreated his fellow colonists, "O all you that have any Negroes in your Houses; an Opportunity to try, Whether you may not be the Happy Instruments, of Converting, the Blackest Instances of Blindness and Baseness, into admirable Candidates of Eternal Blessedness."[39] Mather and other New England Puritans saw slavery through their "presentist" biblical interpretations. They read the Bible and applied the Israelite story to themselves. They told themselves that they were God's chosen people in the New World. North America was a "New Canaan," which they were called to pacify just as the Children of Israel had been instructed in the Promised Land.

However, the Massachusetts colony was not a Canaan conquered by a wandering band of Israelites; rather, it was a business venture in an early capitalist society. The land charter granted by the British Crown came at a price. There were investors back in England who expected a sizable return on their risk. Winthrop and other principals of the company knew that meeting these expectations required labor. The colonists first attempted to enslave Native Americans, but their superior knowledge of the territory enabled frequent escapes. Edward Dunning, Winthrop's brother-in-law, maintained that African slavery was essential to the colony's growth. In a 1645 letter he lamented, "The colony will never thrive, untill we get . . . a stock of slaves sufficient to doe all our business."[40] By 1676, Massachusetts's colonists turned to the Trans-Atlantic Slave Trade and were actively trafficking in human chattel. Boston merchants sailed ships built in Massachusetts Bay to Madagascar, where they captured Africans and transported them to the West Indies. Upon arriving, the merchants exchanged them for persons who had been "seasoned" by violent processes that subjected them to relentless brutality and inhumane conditions until they "submitted" to captivity. The colonists considered these "seasoned" Africans to be suitable for enslavement and transported them to Massachusetts and other ports in North America.

Puritan religious doctrine only legitimated slavery, but Massachusetts's industries and its robust demand for labor fueled the growth of its slave population. By 1700, England had vacated the Royal African Company's monopoly rights to the Trans-Atlantic Slave Trade and effectively opened the enterprise to any subject of the Crown. The decision was a boon for slave traders.[41] Speculators and other would-be entrepreneurs long barred from competing now raced to profit from newly opened markets. Massachusetts's shipbuilding industry supplied demand for both North American and British trading companies. As the industry expanded, the colony's appetite for slave labor grew. By 1715, 10 percent of the population of Boston comprised Africans held as slaves.

Gradually, however, public sentiment turned against the institution. Religious influences and legal structures, which had initially legitimated slavery, began to view the institution as incompatible with its commitments. In 1781, Massachusetts Supreme Court chief justice William Cushing delivered a ruling on the Quock Walker case that signaled the end of slavery's reign in the state:

> And these sentiments led the framers of our constitution of government—by which the people of this commonwealth have solemnly bound themselves to each other—to declare—that all men are born free and equal; and that every subject is entitled to liberty, and to have it guarded by the laws as well as his life and property. In short, without resorting to implication in constructing the constitution, slavery is in my judgment as effectively abolished.[42]

The facts of the case concerned one James Caldwell who, along with his wife, held Quock Walker, a Massachusetts resident, in slavery. The couple promised to free Walker, who was ten years old at the time, when he reached twenty-five years of age. In the intervening years, Caldwell died and the widow Caldwell married Nathaniel Jennison. She, in turn, died, leaving Walker with Jennison. After Jennison refused to honor the promise of manumission, Walker fled and took refuge with John and Seth Caldwell, brothers of the late James Caldwell. When Walker refused to return, Jennison found him and beat him severely. In return, Walker promptly sued Jennison for 300 pounds. The jury awarded Walker fifty pounds and found that he was indeed a free person. After subsequent litigation between Jennison and the Caldwells, the State Supreme Court found slavery itself unconstitutional. The ruling led to the eventual end of slavery in Massachusetts by 1795.[43]

Long after slavery had disappeared in Boston, black Bostonians, like black Philadelphians, continued to suffer economic and political marginalization. Unlike in Philadelphia where blacks and whites of varying classes lived within the same quarters of the city, black Bostonians cloistered themselves in the second, fifth, sixth, and seventh wards of the city.[44] These closed neighborhoods offered some measure of protection against the onslaught of racial insults and indignities that blacks suffered constantly. In these enclaves, African Americans developed their own political discourses unchecked by the dominant white gaze. This was the city that David Walker found when he established himself in the Beacon Hill neighborhood, a district known for its politically robust and intellectually active African American residents.

David Walker: A Pillar of Fire "Unfit" for This World

Two decades after Jones delivered his "Thanksgiving Sermon," Walker deployed the exodus story and its narrative antecedent, the Joseph novella, with a vastly different politics in mind. Walker issued a strident call for black self-determination that meant nothing less than open rebellion against the slave regime. Like Jones, Walker believed strongly that God's providence destined Africans and their descendants in America for emancipation. But, unlike Jones, Walker did not believe that a slow and inconspicuous progression would achieve the goal. Instead, Walker's vision took the form of a public and direct confrontation with the forces and representatives of racial repression.

> But has not the Lord an oppressed and suffering people among them? Does the Lord condescend to hear their cries and see their tears in consequence of oppression? Will he let the oppressors rest comfortably and happy always? Will he not cause the very children of the oppressors to rise up against them, and ofttimes put them to death? "God works in many ways his wonders to perform." I will not here speak of the destructions which the Lord brought upon Egypt, in consequence of the oppression and consequent groans of the oppressed—of the hundreds and

thousands of Egyptians whom God hurled into the Red Sea for afflicting his people in their land.[45]

Jones's politics mastered a "pillar of cloud" form that seamlessly blended into the Philadelphia social world, but Walker's politics burst upon Boston as a pillar of fire. Rather than *fitting* into his place as Jones's politics had modeled, Walker's politics relied upon being *out of place* in Boston's racialized world. Where Jones accepted "his place" within the contemporaneous social and political arrangements of Philadelphia, Walker refused to acquiesce to the current social and political configurations that he saw as fundamentally unjust. He believed any capitulation to them shamefully diminished black humanity. Where Jones advertised his *willingness* to *fit* into Philadelphia's social world, Walker advertised his *refusal* to *fit* into a social world where people of African descent were second-class. Both his persona and his interpretive activity in exodus challenged contemporaneous notions about the deficient nature of African Americans. As Walker understood himself, he was a self-educated Negro in the antebellum South whose self-construction challenged slavery's rationale as a civilizing institution. Walker advanced his interpretation of exodus by brandishing his own existence as much as the document's fiery content. In the *Appeal*, Walker shows (as in showing off) that he "knows" what nineteenth-century modernist discourses claim a Negro could not know. By invoking complex logical constructions along with erudite literary and historical allusions, he defied the scientific discourse of his day to account for his existence.

The politics of Walker's interpretation of the exodus narrative germinated in a life marked by proximity to black resistance—examples of Africans in North America who refused to fit quietly into a repressive social landscape. Walker was born in Wilmington, North Carolina, in 1796.[46] Because his mother was a free black woman, by law he inherited her status.[47] From his birth, Walker was out of place; he was a free black man in the antebellum South where slavery defined black life. Despite his legal status, the fundamental inequities and injustices of North Carolina's slave society shaped his formative environment.[48] The brutal slave system, however, could not totalize the Cape Fear social world where Walker spent his formative years. Rather, an opposing force—the incessant self-determinative impulses of black resistance—was ever-present to check white repression. In the Lower Cape Fear area, swamps and dense vegetation protected the proliferation of maroon camps, offered easy cover to those who dared run away, and served as a fertile breeding ground for conspiracies and episodes of organized resistance.[49]

As formidable as these emancipatory impulses may have been, resistance struggles that only existed in shadows did not satisfy Walker. Consonant with the pillar of fire politics that Walker would later display, he left North Carolina to seek a more public model of defiance that affirmed black humanity. Between 1817 and 1822, Walker lived in Charleston, South Carolina. The city's highly visible, free black community actualized the emancipatory impulses that existed only in the shadows of the Cape Fear swamps. Charleston's prominent AME congregation captured Walker's imagination. Perhaps he was drawn to the congregation because, like Walker, the church was itself out of place. Black Methodists in Charleston outnumbered white Methodists ten to one. They developed separate ecclesial conferences, managed their own finances, and adjudicated their own church trials. In 1815, when white Methodists attempted to exert greater control over their black counterparts, black Methodists left in the kind of self-determinative impulse that Walker would himself later display. By 1817, 6,000 black Methodists had withdrawn from the city's white church to form the Charleston AME congregation, with Morris Brown as its bishop. The church's presence *advertised* black resistance. Its prominent edifice shone as a public symbol of black achievement in the face of repression. Its existence testified to black self-determination.[50] For the next five years, Walker chose to associate with this congregation freshly constituted by an act of defiance.

During Walker's tenure at Mother Emmanuel AME Church, its congregation participated in planning the Vesey conspiracy.[51] The Vesey conspiracy was possibly the most significant episode of black resistance in Walker's experience. Hundreds of African Americans pledged to struggle together for emancipation. The plan began with Denmark Vesey, one of the church's founding members. Vesey, a Charleston resident, purchased his own freedom after witnessing rebellions in the Caribbean. He developed a network of African American resistance that stretched across the state of South Carolina; it included munitions, extensive supply lines, and participation from persons enslaved and free at almost every level of society. When white Charlestonians discovered the plan, news of its extent sent fear throughout the slaveholding South. Soon after the Vesey conspiracy, Walker, like so many others who escaped hanging, fled Charleston.[52]

Eventually, Walker settled in Boston, by that time a city known for its large and politically active black community. In 1826 he married Eliza Butler, a member of a prominent Boston family.[53] The couple settled in Beacon Hill, which served as home to a black community energized with intellectual activity fused with anti-slavery activism. There, he opened a clothing store and also became active in abolitionist circles.

Influenced by the political climate, Walker developed into an outspoken abolitionist, even writing articles for the New York–based *Freedom's Journal*, the nation's first black newspaper. His life had afforded him two experiences that most in Boston abolitionist circles did not have—he had grown up in close proximity to the repressive brutality of southern slavery, and he also had experienced the power of black resistance. In Boston's intellectual milieu, his first-hand observation of the suffering wrought by slavery took the shape of a clear, forceful invective that seized upon the exodus story, titled *Appeal, in Four Articles; Together with a Preamble, to the Coloured Citizens of the World, but in Particular, and Very Expressly, to Those of the United States of America*.[54] Between 1829 and 1830, Walker published three editions. He distributed the pamphlets by sewing them into the lining of clothing to be shipped by black sailors to the South. The powerful missive challenged enslaved Africans in the United States to take whatever measures were necessary to free themselves from bondage. Calling upon African Americans to reject subjugation, Walker's *Appeal* boldly exercised his "pillar of fire politics." So effective was his argument that it frightened slaveholders in several states. Planters in Georgia even prevailed upon their governor to send a letter of protest to the mayor of Boston. The letter demanded that Walker be punished. In effect, their request meant to punish Walker for being *out of place*. When these efforts failed, Southern slaveholders put a price on his head. If they could not force him to accept a Negro's *place*, then executing Walker would signal to others how far southern society would go to enforce white supremacy. A year later, Walker was found in his clothing store, presumably poisoned to death.[55] Although southern slaveholders had succeeded in targeting Walker, they could not quell his defiant voice. His enemies had made him a martyr. Walker's challenge now reverberated with each new copy of the *Appeal*. Long after the antebellum period, Walker and his writings remained a fiery beacon to those who refused to *fit*.

Walker's Appeal: Exodus as Radical Politics and Public Contest

It was not by accident that Walker structured his *Appeal* as a classical disputation or that it responded directly to Thomas Jefferson's *Notes on the State of Virginia*.[56] Although written almost fifty years earlier, Jefferson's taxonomy of the flora, fauna, and natural resources of his home state of Virginia remained one of the most influential publications of the early nineteenth century. In *Notes*, Jefferson showcases Virginia's natural resources and American life along with its fledgling institutions to demonstrate that they rivaled those of Europe. He even argued for a moral equivalence between the cultures of the United States and Great Britain. Walker took umbrage at Jefferson's disparaging appraisal of people of African descent. In his *Appeal*, he challenged two of Jefferson's claims: First, people of African descent were morally and intellectually inferior and aesthetically wanting in comparison to whites. Second, slaveholders in the United States treated Africans held as slaves humanely, given their innate capacities.[57] During the nineteenth century, these two claims fundamentally shaped self-understandings essential to white southern identity. As early as the mid-eighteenth century, the new sciences of biology and later anthropology legitimated popular claims of African American inferiority.

Walker knew that his counter-narrative for racialization would disrupt southern planter society's deeply entrenched values. He composed his *Appeal* specifically for such a challenge. With it, he performed his pillar of fire politics in the most ostentatious fashion. Walker set up the *Appeal* as if to orchestrate a public contest between a well-known champion and an insurgent. The idea of a public challenge fit Walker's work well. In *Notes*, Jefferson had publicly disparaged African Americans as a race. The appropriate response had to be as public as Jefferson's display.[58]

In the *Appeal*, Walker presents himself as the exemplary representative of his race able to take up Jefferson's tossed gauntlet and meet the former president man to man.[59] By choosing Jefferson as his nemesis, Walker knew he was challenging the most celebrated American intellectual of his day. For Walker's purposes only a response to Jefferson would suffice. To aim at a lesser figure would be as if David had declined Goliath's challenge in favor of some unknown Philistine infantryman. To be sure, Jefferson had played a taunting Goliath with his dismissive assertions. In a particularly provocative passage, Jefferson wrote: "Comparing them by their faculties of memory, reason, and imagination, it appears to me, that in memory they are equal to the whites; in reason much inferior, as I think one could scarcely be found capable of tracing and comprehending the investigations of Euclid; and that in imagination they are dull, tasteless, and anomalous."[60]

In his *Appeal*, Walker's response takes the form of a grand display of his intellectual superiority and, by extension, black intellectual potential. He calls Jefferson out publicly as if to a fisticuffs: "Has Mr. Jefferson declared to the world, that we are inferior to the whites, both in the endowments of our bodies and of minds?" With that opening salvo, the challenger's grievance is clear; he will not countenance a second-class status. Walker advertised his manhood by addressing Jefferson by name at a time when blacks held in chattel slavery could be beaten for initiating conversations with whites. His response signals that he will not play the dull, bestial object of Jefferson's ethnographic description; he is equally human and he refuses to *fit*. With the sarcasm and effusive praise that recalls a Socratic dialogue, Walker's language baits and goads Jefferson as if the two were champions on the field of battle: "It is indeed surprising, that a man of such great learning, combined with such excellent natural parts, should speak so of a set of men in chains." As Socrates to Thrasymachus, Walker's sarcasm intends to embarrass Jefferson for the pleasure of an onlooking audience. For Walker, the audience *is* the entire world:

> It is expected that all coloured men, women and children (Who are not too deceitful, abject, and servile to resist the cruelties and murders inflicted upon us by the white slave holders, our enemies by nature) of every nation, language and tongue under heaven, will try to procure a copy of this Appeal and read it, or get some one to read it to them, for it is designed more particularly for them.[61]

Walker's contest is not merely with Jefferson, but with Jefferson as the champion of the white planter class and, by extension, the "white race."[62]

Walker, in turn, performs the role of the champion for black people enslaved in North America.

While Walker crafts the *Appeal's* language to provoke his audience, he uses the form of his discourse to meet Jefferson's challenge. He organizes his *Appeal* in successive articles in mock replication of Jefferson's Declaration of Independence.[63] His classical logical construction for each argument offers one proposition after another. Each premise builds upon a previous and leads to the next; each final premise leads to a conclusion. To Jefferson's Euclid, Walker produces Josephus and Plutarch from classical antiquity. As Jefferson raises Euclidian geometry against the conceptual limits of the African American intellect, Walker responds by claiming the "wretchedness and miseries" that African Americans suffer "are so very numerous and aggravating, that I believe the pen only of a Josephus or a Plutarch, can well enumerate and explain them."[64]

In the opening volley, Walker signaled a daring hermeneutical strategy: he intends to leverage a close, literal reading of the Scripture against the Christian tradition. First, he questions a common notion found in nineteenth-century sermons on exodus, that the ancient Egyptians were a morally reprehensible people, "a gang of devils."[65] Walker was well aware that the Christian tradition understood the Egyptians as symbols of national depravity and paganism. But he claimed that those who adhere to this part of the Christian tradition do so "not knowing any better." He intended to show that the Old Testament describes them differently.[66] Next, Walker places his audience in a moral quandary by identifying them with the ancient Egyptians. He points out that these "Africans were colored people, such as we are—some of them yellow and others dark—a mixture of Ethiopians and the natives of Egypt—about the same issues as we see in the colored people of the United States at the present day."[67] Prima facie, the identification appears to work against Walker's purposes. However, by disrupting his audience's acceptance of the interpretive tradition, he positions his readers to reappraise the moral standing of the Egyptians, despite the Christian tradition. Walker's claim of a common identity between Egyptians and people of African descent in North America is a sophisticated hermeneutical move that becomes central for his argument. In effect, Walker brackets the interpretive tradition and instead relies upon the Protestant interpretive principle (*solo scriptura*), and the Enlightenment belief that the legitimate interpretation of scripture is grounded in one's intellectual capacity as much it is a product of divine revelation.

By presenting a "plain reading" of the Bible to his audience, Walker does not have to contradict the Christian tradition. He leaves his readers to see the contradictions themselves; when they do, Walker knows how they will interpret the silence. In the new American Republic, a "plain reading" of the Bible will trump the long and complex tradition. His takes a critical orientation to the Christian tradition and stakes his intellectual prowess against a long history of church fathers. But Walker believes that by relying upon a "plain reading" of the biblical text, he can show that in three areas of civil life, namely, political enfranchisement, social relations, and economic inclusion, the ancient Egyptians displayed a more evolved humanity than Christian slaveholders. Ultimately, Walker believed his argument would persuade his audience to reject the Church tradition in favor of what he believed to be his audience's emancipatory interests.

Turning to the Joseph novella in Genesis, Walker gradually builds his case, beginning with the question of political enfranchisement. The story narrates the background conditions that brought Israel to Egypt. After having been betrayed by his brothers and sold into slavery, Joseph finds himself in the service of an Egyptian patriarch and, later, the Crown. In each circumstance, Joseph uses his administrative prowess in Egyptian service. He ultimately enriches the Crown—and, sadly, impoverishes the people of Egypt—with a strategy that speculates on the supply of grain ahead of an upcoming famine. In return for Joseph's service, the Pharaoh promotes him to the position of vizier over the entire country. Walker highlights three illustrative passages where the Egyptian pharaoh recognizes Joseph's capacity for civic leadership and offers him the opportunity to deploy his skills irrespective of his ethnic difference. Each example demonstrates the range of political access that the Egyptians extended to the Hebrew sojourners.

> And Pharaoh said unto Joseph, thou shalt be over my house, and according unto thy word shall all my people be ruled: only in the throne will I be greater than thou. 49:40

And Pharaoh said unto Joseph, see, I have set thee over all the land of Egypt. 49:41

And Pharaoh said unto Joseph, I am Pharaoh, and without thee shall no man lift up his hand or foot in all the land of Egypt. 49:44[68]

Walker takes the story and points to the level of political power placed in the foreigner's hands. Then, dramatizing the absence of any correlating treatment of Africans by North American slaveholders, Walker addresses his audience with a rhetorical plea, "Now I appealed to heaven and to earth, and particularly to the American people themselves, who sees not to declare their condition is not hard, and that we are comparatively satisfied to rest in wretchedness and misery, under them and their children. . . . show me a coloured President, a Governor, a Legislator, a Senator, a Mayor, or an Attorney at the Bar."[69] The rhetoric intends to embarrass his opponent. Walker already knows that the American Republic has offered no such position to any of its residents of African descent. Finding no satisfactory response, of course, Walker returns to his opening proposition that the ancient Egyptians were not the barbaric nation claimed by the Christian tradition. Having shown them to be otherwise, he delivers a parting shot in a wry and facetious tone and refers to the Egyptians as "that heathen nation."[70]

Second, Walker takes up social relations. He returns to the Joseph novella and points to Joseph's state-supported marriage to an Egyptian woman: "And Pharaoh called Joseph's name Zaphnath-paaneah; and he gave him to wife Asenath, the daughter of Potipherah, priest of On. And Joseph went out over all the land of Egypt" (41:45).[71] By juxtaposing the Egyptians' inclusive disposition toward foreigners against that of American slaveholders, Walker dramatizes the disparity between the Christian tradition and his plain reading of the biblical story. He asks his audience to "[c]ompare the above, with the American institutions. Do they not institute laws to prohibit us from marrying among whites?"[72] Walker sufficiently established his point with the rhetorical question above, but he cannot ignore another of Jefferson's particularly inflammatory claims:

Is it not the foundation of a greater or less share of beauty in the two races? Are not the fine mixtures of red and white, the expressions of every passion by greater or less suffusions of colour in the one, preferable to that eternal monotony, which reigns in the countenances, that immoveable veil of black which covers all the emotions of the other race? Add to these, flowing hair, a more elegant symmetry of form, their own judgment in favour of the whites, declared by their preference of them, as uniformly as is the preference of the Oran-ootan for the black women over those of his own species. The circumstance of superior beauty, is thought worthy attention in the propagation of our horses, dogs, and other domestic animals; why not in that of man?[73]

Intermarriage was so volatile that Walker takes pains to clarify to his audience that he has no personal interest in the matter. Rather, in response to Jefferson, he assures them:

> I would wish, candidly, however before the Lord to be understood that I would not give a pinch of snuff to be married to any white person I ever saw in all the days of my life. And I do say it, that the black man, or man of colour, who would leave his own colour (provided he can get one, who is good for any thing) and marry a white woman, to be a double slave to her, just because she is white, ought to be treated by her as he surely will be, viz: as a NIGER!!![74]

His invective drips with disdain. Those who succumb to notions of black inferiority and attempt to mitigate their status through cultural hypergamy engage in an exercise in futility. Walker warns further that the man will continue to be viewed as inferior by society, and now will suffer the same insult in his own home from the wife whom he hoped would raise his status.

Third, Walker turns to economic inclusion. In Boston, as in Philadelphia, even skilled African Americans were barred from work in many trades. Life meant a meager existence. Again, Walker turns to the Egyptians: "The land of Egypt is before thee: in the best of the land make thy father and brethren to dwell; in the land of Goshen let them dwell: and if thou knowest any men of activity among them, then make them rulers over my cattle" (47:6).[75]

His audience is familiar with the story. But Walker highlights this verse to emphasize what the Christian tradition obscured, namely, the

Egyptians' generosity. The Egyptians in the story offer this foreigner the best land while they grant his compatriots administrative positions corresponding to their individual potentials. Walker juxtaposes the stark contrast between the Egyptians and Christian slaveholders of the plantation South.

> Need I mention the very notorious fact, that I have known a poor man of colour, who laboured night and day, to acquire a little money, and having acquired it, he vested it in a small piece of land, and got him a house erected thereon, and having paid for the whole, he moved his family into it, where he was suffered to remain but nine months, when he was cheated out of his property by a white man, and driven out of door! And is not this the case generally? Can a man of colour buy a piece of land and keep it peaceably? Will not some white man try to get it from him, even if it is in a mud hole?[76]

The anecdote in and of itself exercises Walker's pillar of fire politics. Its form is as poignant as the content. Walker prefaces his delivery with the rhetorical feint, "Need I mention the notorious fact . . ." No, of course not. Walker already knows that his anecdote states the obvious to his audience. His report alludes to countless episodes where the law failed to guarantee property rights for Native Americans, Latinos, and people of African descent. Laws that ostensibly protected property rights did not. In many cases, these laws conspired with unscrupulous citizens and local government officials to alienate real property and other forms of wealth from people of color. But the anecdote is showcased in order to set up the three questions that follow, which Walker poses in rapid succession. The first question, "And is not this the case generally?" establishes the "case" in point of this "notorious fact" as a general condition. The second question, "Can a man of colour buy a piece of land and keep it peaceably?" maintains the case categorically. The third question, "Will not some white man try to get it from him, even if it is in a mud hole?" indicts the racialized political economy that suppresses any effort for black life to flourish.

The anecdote's content exposes the political economy's regulative work in barring African Americans from participating in the nation's most celebrated virtues: diligent labor, careful fiscal management, homestead investment, and responsible provision for one's family. When African Americans reap the benefits from their own work and fiscal management, their efforts do not accrue to their stature in the new republic. Rather, black lives structured by the practice of these virtues render the "man of colour" in Walker's example *out of place*—at least for a Negro. Only nine months pass before "some white man" confiscates the man's wealth and returns him *to* his place—that is, destitute and at the mercy of whites. Walker's language is also telling. He laments that the man "was *suffered* to remain but nine months."[77] Even that short tenure of financial well-being placed undue burden on the social world. As Walker described the social economy, the one who cheated the landowner removed the burden and returned the society to its proper order.

Walker takes up Moses biographically to respond to Jefferson's second claim concerning the intellectual capacities of people of African descent. Although a Hebrew, Moses was raised as a member of the royal house. Jefferson, along with many other slaveholders and even some Northern abolitionists, held in common the notion that in the economy of human diversity, blacks possessed the lesser share of moral, intellectual, and aesthetic virtue.[78] It followed that people of African descent did not have the capacity to participate fully in civic life. Thus for Jefferson, slavery was a benevolent institution that made the best use of African American talents and capacities. Jefferson located his argument in the new biological determinism of the day. Walker responds by demonstrating that what Jefferson believed was ontological in fact owes to the social conditions under which black life existed. In other words, the place that Jefferson believed was *fit* for black life only deformed it. In one analogy, Walker compares such a place to a cage, writing that Jefferson's expectation was like placing "one wild deer in an iron cage, where it will be secured and hold another by the side of the same, then let it go, and expect the one in the cage to run as fast as the one at liberty."[79] For Walker, the social arrangements themselves were unjust; the fundamental conditions offered no possibility of flourishing. So Jefferson's comparison was itself illegitimate. Worse for Walker were Jefferson's disparaging assessments based on contemporaneous social arrangements. They only compounded slavery's injury and offended any basic sense of humanity.

Walker saves the most passionate argument for last. With it, he challenges Jefferson's claims that in imagination, African Americans were a tasteless, dull, and anomalous people. He responds by imagining a human inclusiveness far beyond the horizon of his nineteenth-century world: "So far, my brethren, were the Egyptians from heaping these insults upon their slaves that Pharaoh's daughter took Moses, a son of Israel for her own."[80] In fact, the Egyptian princess recognizes Moses' ethnic identity upon their first encounter as "one of the Hebrews' children."[81] Walker takes up her recognition through his nineteenth-century liberalism:

> And Pharaoh's daughter said unto her, [Moses' mother] take this child away, and nurse it for me and I will pay thee thy wages. And the woman took the child [Moses] and nursed it. And the child grew, and she brought him unto Pharaoh's daughter and he became her son. And she called his name Moses: and she said because I drew him out of the water. (Exodus 2:9–10)[82]

He concludes by claiming, "in all probability, Moses would have become Prince Regent to the throne."[83] Indeed, in exodus, the stories of Joseph and Moses bear out his analogy. Both rise to prominence without regard to their ethnic identity. Walker's interpretation envisions a society where both sojourner and native recognize a common humanity in the other and work for each other's mutual enhancement. In Walker's vision, one's state was limited only by one's potential.

With the cumulative weight of these biblical episodes, Walker demonstrated that even the Egyptians, whom the Christian tradition considered reprehensible, treated the Israelites more humanely than Christian slaveholders treated African people in the United States. Second, he showed that African Americans held in slavery lived a far more wretched existence than even those depicted in the exodus story, which was often used during that era as a paradigmatic example of degradation. Third, he showed that those differences between blacks and whites that Jefferson assigned to natures and capacities were due to the social conditions of black life.

In each case, Walker played biblical authority against Jefferson's "observations." In Puritan New England as well as the evangelical South, biblical history was inviolate. At the time, the Bible's historical presentation held more authority than books of Western history, which often based their own contents on some version of biblical history. For Walk-

er's readers, black and white, his arguments, arising from biblical interpretations, were both provocative and dangerous. For most slaveholders,
the Christianity derived from their biblical interpretations justified the
slave institution. But Walker's *Appeal* disrupted their fundamental understandings of the Christian faith and, more importantly, their foundation for justifying the slave regime. Not unlike the Puritans, many
slaveholders believed slavery possessed a civilizing function and was a
social good. However, Walker showed that the conditions themselves
did just the opposite insofar as they deformed black life. Jefferson's observations, which reflected black life under those conditions, gave self-
serving affirmation to white supremacy. By identifying his audience
with ancient Egypt, Walker gestured obliquely toward an example of
black life absent slavery's crippling effects. In other words, by connecting
Africans in North America to the ancient Africans in the Book of Exodus, Walker signaled that the very people whom Jefferson disparaged
are more civil than those who hold them in bondage. Ultimately, Walker
laid bare the Christian slaveholder's hypocrisy. Their Christianity had
made them more depraved and barbaric than the "heathen" Egyptians,
who did not know Christ.

Unlike Jones, Walker believed that Africans and African Americans
held in slavery should exercise directive agency rather than take a supportive role in their own emancipation. Walker's hermeneutic reflected
the political and social currents within his life-world. First, Walker came
of age during the years between the struggle that forged the nation's
identity and the subsequent War of 1812, which solidified the American Republic as a sovereign state. Both conflicts tested the legitimacy of
individual liberty over the divine right of kings and a republican over
a monarchic form of government. The new Republic claimed individual liberty as a human right by virtue of one's creation, but the wars
suggested to Walker that human subjects themselves were obligated to
struggle to ensure these rights. More importantly, their outcomes suggested that mass resistance could overcome repression.

Walker's formative experiences revealed more than the emancipatory
examples of the American Revolution and the War of 1812. The same
North Carolina patriots who had overthrown British tyranny could not
subdue black resistance in the Cape Fear swamps. Although the Vesey
conspiracy was uncovered before its work could be accomplished, its

discovery did more to heighten the fears of Charleston's white citizenry than to allay them. If Walker took any lesson from the episode, it was not that black struggles for freedom end in failure. Rather, Walker learned that attaining freedom was a moral obligation. He believed "[t]he man would not fight under our Lord and Master Jesus Christ, in the glorious and heavenly cause of freedom and of God—to be delivered from the most wretched, abject and servile slave, that ever a people was afflicted since the foundation of the world, to the present day—ought to be kept with all of his children or family, in slavery, or in chains, to be butchered by his cruel enemies."[84]

Clearly, Walker believed in divine Providence. But so did Jones. Where Jones emphasized God's providential intervention and called his congregation to a supportive role, Walker came to believe that human effort had to activate divine Providence. Even as he warned his readers not to take rash or imprudent action in gaining freedom, he immediately clarified that he does not "mean for us to wait until God shall take us by the hair of our heads and drag us out of abject wretchedness and slavery, nor do I mean to convey the idea for us to wait until our enemies shall make preparations."[85] For Walker, as for Jones, divine Providence had already assured them victory. However, Walker, unlike Jones, believed that even an assured victory did not preclude a precipitating struggle. Appropriating the apocalyptic depiction of the *parousia* to convey his vision, Walker boldly exhorted his audience to battle, "when that hour arrives and you move, be not afraid or dismayed; for be you assured that Jesus Christ the King of heaven and of earth who is the God of justice and of armies, will surely go before you."[86]

On the whole, Jones and Walker did not disagree on ends; both desired emancipation and full inclusion for people of African descent in the United States. In the two decades following Jones's celebratory sermon, the capture and enslavement of people from the African continent had not abated but had increased. Congress did not have the resources to enforce the ban, which left profiteers free to satisfy the southern appetite for human chattel.[87] Whenever the law could be enforced, ship captains often ordered captured people to be thrown overboard rather than pay the fines levied against them.[88] The congressional action that had inspired Jones's hope and his vision of divine activity could not hold the same possibilities for Walker. By 1829, he had too few signs to inspire any realistic hope. Rather than advocate for moderate action within the limits legitimated by his society, Walker believed that the social arrangements of his society were illegitimate.

The Antebellum period would not be the last time that hope and despair gave rise to cloud and fire politics in black biblical interpretation. In successive eras, African Americans reincarnated both Jones's politics that built the FAS and Walker's politics that provoked black radicalism. As African Americans built institutions to fortify themselves against the everywhere present forces of racialization, they continued masking performances along the lines Jones had embraced. Where repressive forces shaped the Republic's political economy more than they could stand, new iterations of Walker's radicalism struck blows of resistance.

Nonetheless, the open rebellion that Walker hoped to incite never occurred. Arguably, it was defeated by one vote at the National Negro Convention in 1843. Neither Jones nor Walker lived to realize the emancipation to which each had devoted their lives. But thirty-five years after Walker's death the slave regime that he and Jones had fought to end was no more. Even so, chattel slavery's demise did not bring the emancipatory reality for which Jones and Walker had hoped. New forms of racialization emerged to present challenges that neither could have imagined. It required new ways of speaking for the Bible in its silence. In response to the shifting political economy and its evolving processes of racialization, this tradition of black activists returned to the same exodus story that had inspired Jones and Walker and developed new iterations of the politics of cloud and fire that they had performed.

2

Exodus in the Wilderness: Making Bitter Water Sweet

I will sing to the Lord, for he has triumphed gloriously;
horse and rider he has thrown into the sea. The Lord is my
strength and my might, and he has become my salvation;
this is my God, and I will praise him, my father's God, and I
will exalt him. The Lord God is a Man of War; the Lord is his
name. Pharaoh's chariots and his army he cast into the sea;
his picked officers were sunk in the Red Sea. The floods covered them; they went down into the depths like a stone. Your
right hand, O Lord, glorious in power—your right hand, O
Lord, shattered the enemy. In the greatness of your majesty
you overthrew your adversaries; you sent out your fury, it
consumed them like stubble. At the blast of your nostrils the
waters piled up, the floods stood up in a heap; the deeps con-
gealed in the heart of the sea. The enemy said, "I will pursue,
I will overtake, I will divide the spoil, my desire shall have
its fill of them. I will draw my sword, my hand shall destroy
them." You blew with your wind, the sea covered them; they
sank like lead in the mighty waters. Who is like you, O Lord,
among the gods? Who is like you, majestic in holiness, awesome in splendor, doing wonders? You stretched out your
right hand, the earth swallowed them.
—Exodus 15:1–12

In exodus, slavery ended for the Hebrews at the far shore of the Red
Sea. They looked back across the water and saw chariots and riders, the
military apparatus of the Egyptian regime, tossed into the sea, and they
were amazed. The tide settled. Spontaneously, Moses and the Children
of Israel were overtaken with jubilation and they sang a song of victory.
In that moment of celebration, they knew they were free, for they had
encountered the God of their ancestors, the Man of War, who defeated

the most powerful nation on earth and delivered them from four hundred years of bondage. Their celebration, however, did not last long. Soon after Miriam raised her triumphant hymn, the Hebrews discovered a painful reality: emancipation was only the absence of slavery and not the presence of freedom. They had defeated Pharaoh, but escape from Egypt was not liberty in the Promised Land. Rather, the Hebrews found themselves in the Wilderness (*be-midvar*).[1] Three days after their victory at the sea, their journey nearly ended in the Wilderness of Shur. Thirsty and exhausted, they complained that the waters were undrinkable. In Egypt they depended upon Pharaoh's fleshpots, but the wilderness journey meant becoming a self-sustaining people. Moses led the way. He found a piece of wood and transformed the bitter water and all the people drank sweet and potable sustenance. Even so, they named the place Marah (bitter), to remind themselves of the first test after slavery. They learned that freedom was not an event, but a journey toward liberty. So the Hebrews continued their exodus, for they believed that the Lord committed to deliver them from the house of bondage *and* to bring them up "to a good and broad land, a land flowing with milk and honey," not to abandon them in the desert. For what value could freedom hold in the wilderness?

Unlike the dramatic scene at the Red Sea, emancipation came gradually for African Americans. Even though the Civil War ended on April 9, 1865, slavery persisted. The Union Army could not fully enforce the Emancipation Proclamation until two months later. On June 18–19, 1865, General Gordon Granger and 2,000 U.S. troops stormed into Galveston, Texas. At gunpoint, they closed the last plantation and ended chattel slavery in the American South. With no sea nearby in which to bury the evidence of the war, newly freed Africans could not watch as the symbols of their enslavement disappear, nor could they celebrate a single decisive victory. The wreckage of the South's slave economy remained scattered around them. The apparatuses that once held them in slavery lay prostrate before the feet of federal troops, and southern bitterness festered like an open sore. But across the South, seemingly mundane episodes aggregated to signal freedom's arrival. When newly freed Africans walked away from cotton fields and the slave driver's whip remained dormant, or when they fed their own children with no thought of the "master's" house, or left plantations for territories north and west and overseers did not pursue, they knew they were free. In one chorus after another, from Maryland to Texas, they shouted, danced, and sang to the "Man of War" who delivered them from bondage. But, while their melodies rose to heaven, a crushing reality came down upon them—only their shackles had been broken, and nothing more. With the rise of share-cropping and new laws restricting black life, the South's plantocracy had already mobilized to reinscribe the racial system. A post-slavery society notwithstanding, Africans and their American descendants realized that their journey was far from complete. They had heard the exodus story in hush harbors and churches, cotton fields and maroon camps, and they knew that it did not end at the Red Sea, but continued to the Promised Land. There was a long wilderness path between the two, but they were willing to follow it to get there.

Along the way, the post-slavery political economy demanded that freed Africans transform old symbols to meet new challenges that faced black life. Themes and symbols from the exodus story that had so easily transferred to black life under the chattel system would now have to be reinterpreted to make "bitter water sweet." To be sure, activists in both the North and South had already anticipated the dilemma. They offered new significations to make sense of this strange freedom in the wilderness where they were no longer enslaved but continued to be denied liberty. They projected emancipation from the immediate end of slavery into a new ideal—uplift. For most black activists, uplifting the masses from slavery's degradation meant inscribing upon them markers of refinement such as literacy, cultural attainment, and economic independence. By reaching toward uplift, they set out to recover what slavery had stolen and to "raise up" a generation that would show the world the unrealized genius that God had given to humanity's darker sibling.

In both the North and South, black biblical interpretation transformed exodus from a story of slavery and freedom to a story of uplift and empowerment. As early as 1869, Benjamin "Pap" Singleton realized that black life after slavery meant a constant struggle against discrimination. Tennessee laws prevented him from purchasing land to establish a settlement for formerly enslaved African Americans, so soon after Singleton led waves of African Americans, called "Exodusters," to settle in Kansas. By moving west, they enacted their own "exodus" and constructed a life just outside of the orbit of Confederate politics. Most African Americans could not pull up stakes and move west. They took up exodus politics in other ways to aid their communities to negotiate the vicissitudes of life after slavery. Two of the more prominent examples were Frances Ellen Watkins Harper and the Reverend John Jasper. Their politics vastly differed. In the North, Harper, the first African American woman of letters, articulated her vision for uplift in successive interpretations of the biblical Moses. Her politics emerged as a pillar of cloud as she mastered the aesthetic form of Victorian womanhood and performed it for the masses as a beacon through the wilderness to the "Promised Land" of respectability. However, just 120 miles south of Harper's native Baltimore, respectability was not the priority of the Reverend John Jasper. In Richmond, Virginia, the former Confederate capitol, Jasper, pastor of the Sixth Mount Zion Baptist Church, took the opening line of Moses' song of Jubilee, "The Lord God is a Man of War, the Lord is his name," and, with a pillar of fire politics, taunted an already defeated Confederacy. Jasper took pleasure in reminding the citizens of Richmond that in the moral economy, they were on the wrong side of the Divine Actor, who was the source of the South's defeat.

Harper and Jasper never met. For Harper, Jasper was "uncultured" and ignorant of the world of humane letters. Indeed, for Harper, Jasper's unlettered preaching exemplified the South's desperate need for formal education. For Jasper, Harper insisted too much on cultural refinement as the key to uplift. The pastor of a black congregation in the Reconstruction South, Jasper attended to more immediate concerns such as caring for his flock who were daily assaulted by southern racism. Uplift through the "niceties" of respectability would have to wait. To be sure, the two spoke differently in the Bible's silence; nonetheless, both Harper and Jasper returned to the same narrative that inspired their people since the antebellum period. Couched in different politics that constituted Harper as a pillar of cloud and Jasper as a pillar of fire, both performed miraculous transformations in the post-slavery wilderness. By doing so, both made bitter water sweet and moved their people one step farther in the wilderness.

Every Round Goes Higher: Harper, Uplift, and the Politics
of Respectability

In 1869, Harper published her blueprint to uplift the race. Entitled
"Moses: Story of the Nile,"[2] the epic poem integrated her biblical scholarship, autobiography, and themes from the life of her friend, Harriet
Tubman, to refashion the biblical Moses into a paradigm of uplift. In
lyrical form, Harper depicts a bright future for the race. With the Republican Reconstruction in full swing, she had good reason to be optimistic
in the early post-slavery years. As she and other activists looked toward
the South, they saw apocalyptic change. The federal government that
once codified Africans in the American South as three-fifths of a human
being now sent troops to protect black life and pacify former Confederates. The Freedman's Bureau, the centerpiece of the nation's efforts to
rebuild a new South, distributed more than 21 million rations to emancipated blacks and displaced whites, established forty-six hospitals, and
relocated more than thirty thousand people from the South's most devastated areas.[3]

In Washington, congressional Republicans passed the Civil Rights Bill
of 1866 and a Reconstruction Act of 1867.[4] They extended the franchise
to every male citizen. As a result, black men and most white men had
the right to vote for the first time. Markers that had distinguished black
from white, such as mobility and literacy, were quickly disappearing.
Without the plantation system to restrict mobility, African Americans
migrated west and north in large numbers. Blacks were moving quickly
from chattel to property owners. Black and white families took advantage of the 1866 Homestead Act and took ownership of real property
in similar numbers. By 1875, black farmers owned more than 3 million
acres of land.[5] Literacy had been a significant marker for race. Indeed,
immediately after slavery, black literacy hovered at 2 percent. But by
1870, the number had increased tenfold. To Harper and African Americans throughout the nation, it must have appeared that, finally, the political economy was shifting toward equality between the races.

But Harper saw the most impressive change when the Fourteenth
Amendment granted citizenship and the franchise. During this period,
formerly enslaved African Americans elected some of the South's most
intelligent and forward-thinking men to southern legislatures. However,

this time these legislators were black. Despite racist opposition, they proposed homestead measures to offer new starts for both blacks and whites, relief for Native Americans, and public buildings for common use. Black legislators in North Carolina fought to establish a system of public schools, while others fought for the first free labor laws.[6] These men of character inspired black social reformists. They governed with a broad progressive vision and avoided corruption in a scandal-ridden congress.[7]

To be sure, there had been setbacks. Black Codes in the South mirrored the Slave Codes of a few years earlier. Labor unions in the North discriminated against African Americans who hoped for better job prospects beyond the Mason-Dixon line, and intransigent former Confederates continued attempts to undermine the nation's progress. But Harper and other reformers believed that if the Republic had overcome slavery, its greatest threat thus far, it could meet whatever challenges lay ahead.

Optimism notwithstanding, new and difficult questions about national character worried Harper and other black activists. The American Republic survived the trials of war and the Union stood firm, but cultural differences between the North and the South as well as between the millions of newly freed African Americans and immigrant groups from Europe complicated its demography. Generally, Americans accepted essentialized notions of race that characterized these groups, but in the national conversation these understandings possessed disturbing consequences, regulating access to authentic American identity despite the Thirteenth and Fourteenth Amendments. When nineteenth-century Oxford historian Edward Freeman reflected upon the nation's impulse to purge those whom it could not see as "white," he remarked, "The United states would be a grand land if only every Irishman should kill a Negro and be hanged for it."[8] Black activists were no doubt troubled by this new signification between race and national character. As the republic reimagined its character, the shifting political economy had little room for African Americans now that they were no longer enslaved.

Harper refused to accept essentialized notions of race. Orphaned at age three, the young Frances grew up under the care of her uncle, William Watkins, a northern activist and a staunch nineteenth-century liberal. He mastered English, Latin, Greek, and much of nineteenth-century medicine. In northern abolitionist circles, Watkins was well known for his "radical antislavery speeches and incendiary essays."[9]

He gave Frances a rigorous classical education at his popular school, the William Watkins Academy for Negro Youth, where the curriculum emphasized "biblical studies, the classics, and elocution. The Bible was read daily, Greek and Latin were a major part of the curriculum, and discipline was strict."[10] Her experiences taught her to see character differently. First, classical studies gave her an Aristotelian understanding of character as a function of *habitus*. The sum of one's deliberate and voluntary actions determined character. She refused to accept so-called natural racial dispositions. Second, her uncle's life defied claims of the racialized discourses to which African Americans were subjected. Frances saw him train black students to read the classics in Greek, to subject themselves to the Christian faith, and to be intolerant of the slave system. At the academy, Watkins worked to form his students' character lesson-by-lesson—through discursive engagement—he taught and, in return, students *chose* to develop themselves. If Harper's uncle's students could rise to markers of literacy and refinement, then so could any of her people, if given the opportunity.

Harper saw the state of black life in the United States as degraded rather than natural. In 1857, she vehemently refuted notions to the contrary.

Born into an inheritance of misery, nurtured in degradation, and cradled in oppression, with the scorn of the white man upon their souls, his fetters upon their limbs, his scourge upon their flesh, what can be expected from their offspring, but a mournful reaction of that cursed system which spreads its baneful influence over body and soul; which dwarfs the intellect, stunts its development, debases the spirit, and degrades the soul? Place any nation in the same condition which has been our hapless lot, fetter their limbs and degrade their souls, debase their sons and corrupt their daughters, and when the restless yearnings for liberty shall burn through heart and brain—when, tortured by wrong and goaded by oppression, the hearts that would madden with misery, or break in despair, resolve to break their thrall, and escape from bondage, then let the bay of the bloodhound and the scent of the human tiger be upon their track;— let them feel that, from the ceaseless murmur of the Atlantic to the sullen roar of the Pacific, from the thunders of the rainbow-crowned Niagara to the swollen waters of the Mexican gulf, they have no shelter for their bleeding feet, or the resting-place for their defenseless heads;—let them, when nominally free, feel that they have only exchanged the iron yoke of oppression for the galling fetters of the vitiated public opinion;—let prejudice assign them the lowest places and the humblest positions, and make them "hewers of wood and drawers of water;"—let their income be so small that they must from necessity bequeath to their children an inheritance of poverty and a limited education,—and tell me, reviler of our race! Censurer of our people! If there is a nation in whose veins runs the purest Caucasian blood, upon whom the same cause would not produce the same effects; whose social condition, intellectual and moral character, would present a more favorable aspect then ours?[11]

Harper was determined to show that slave society and its deforming technologies, rather than any essential racial character, produced the subjects that the nation despised. Without agency there is no character. Since African Americans had just broken free from the slave system, Harper believed that any evaluation of so-called racial character rightly should be deferred until her people removed slavery's imprint. In a letter to her friend, William Still, a conductor of the Underground Railroad, she articulated her hope:[12]

> I am giving all my lectures with free admission; but still I get along, and the way has been opening for me almost ever since I have been South. Oh, if some more of our young women would only consecrate their lives to the work of upbuilding the race! Oh, if I could only see our young men and women aiming to build up a future for themselves which would grandly contrast with the past—with its pain, ignorance and low social condition.[13]

Harper took the model that formed her and she envisioned character pedagogy as a primary tool to uplift the race and, by extension, the nation. Slavery had robbed her people's dignity, and she emphasized education structured by a Christian morality to restore it. In another speech, she expressed these same core values.

> How shall we educate? And a line of action was finely mapped. And alongside the suggestions of that paper arise the query, How can we best

utilize this education? The culture of the moral and spiritual faculties is destined to play the most important part in our future development. Knowledge is power, the great mental lever which has lifted up man in the scale of social and racial life; but a towering intellect, grand in its achievements, and glorious in its possibilities, may, with the moral and spiritual faculties held in abeyance, be one of the most dangerous and mischievous forces in the world.[14]

Harper committed herself to a thoroughly modernist liberalism.[15] She rejected traditional sources of authority but believed that if each person were granted the opportunity to raise her station, humanity would rise. She believed that those like her, who had been afforded the privilege of study, should teach toward enlightenment, that is, *Wissenschaften*, governed by moral principle. For Harper, this meant instructing black people in practical knowledge, politics, and cultural refinement with the virtues of individual sacrifice and mutual uplift.

Liberal ideology alone was insufficient to realize Harper's vision. She needed an appropriate politics to actualize her hopes. As Jones and Walker had done before her, Harper structured a politics that proceeded by performances of masking. First, her presentation *advertised* her ability to *fit* in the politest circles where black women on the whole were viewed too unrefined to gain access. She moved comfortably within elite activist circles populated by the most prominent reformers of the nineteenth century. Enthusiastic critical reception to her public lectures evidenced her mastery:

> She spoke for nearly an hour and a half, her subject being "The Mission of the War, and the Demands of the Colored Race in the Work of Reconstruction;" and we have seldom seen an audience more attentive, better pleased, or more enthusiastic. Mrs. Harper has a splendid articulation, uses chaste, pure language, has a pleasant voice, and allows no one to tire of hearing her. We shall attempt no abstract of her address; none that we could make would do her justice. It was one of which any lecturer might feel proud, and her reception by a Portland audience was all that could be desired. We have seen no praises of her that were overdrawn. We have heard Miss Dickinson, and do not hesitate to award the palm to her darker colored sister.[16]

Of a speech in Philadelphia, another critic, Grace Greenwood of the *Independent* opined:

> Next on the course was Mrs. Harper, a colored woman; about as colored as some of the Cuban belles I have met with at Saratoga. She has a noble head, this bronze muse; a strong face, with a shadowed glow upon it, indicative of thoughtful fervor, and of a nature most femininely sensitive, but not in the least morbid. Her form is delicate, her hands daintily small. She stands quietly beside her desk, and speaks without notes, with gestures few and fitting. Her manner is marked by dignity and composure. She is never assuming, never theatrical. In the first part of her lecture she was most impressive in her pleading for the race with whom her lot is cast. [17]

Critics praised both Harper's form—displayed by her "chaste language, pleasant voice," and economy of gestures—and her rhetorical force—displayed by her intellect and persuasiveness. Harper carefully crafted both—form and rhetoric. Indeed, her subject position demanded it. She was an educated, unmarried, black woman whose profession was public speaking at a time when women rarely spoke in public and certainly not to a mixed or "promiscuous" audience, as it was called. The matrix of Victorianism and capitalism that structured the nation's political economy required Harper to be vigilant as she managed her public presentation. Every time she ascended a podium, she risked public rebuke as both a "failed and fallen woman."[18] But Harper mitigated threats of censure by infusing her rhetoric with a high moral tone and by anchoring her arguments for racial uplift to high moral character.

When Harper encountered those in the women's movement who did not share her concern for matters of race, she deployed a second act of masking and showing. She masked her racial uplift rhetoric by *fitting* it within the larger national dialogue. Situating her rhetoric in this manner, Harper seized the larger conversation on national character and deployed it as a strategic vehicle for her rhetoric of racial uplift. She argued that the nation that repressed any of its members, disabled the whole. In a speech entitled "We Are All Bound up Together," delivered before the Eleventh Woman's Rights Convention in 1866, Harper pressed her position as she shared the stage with other equally well-known activists such as Susan B. Anthony, Lucretia Mott, and Elizabeth Cady Stanton.[19]

We are all bound up together in one great bundle of humanity, and society cannot trample on the weakest and feeblest of its members without receiving the curse in its own soul. You tried that in the case of the Negro. You pressed him down for two centuries; and in so doing you crippled the moral strength and paralyzed the spiritual energies of the white men of the country. When the hands of the black were fettered, white men were deprived of the liberty of speech and the freedom of the press. Society cannot afford to neglect the enlightenment of any class of its members. At the South, the legislation of the country was in behalf of the rich slaveholders, while the poor white man was neglected. What is the consequence today? From that very class of neglected poor white men, comes the man who stands to-day, with his hand upon the helm of the nation. He fails to catch the watchword of the hour, and throws himself, the incarnation of meanness, across the pathway of the nation. My objection to Andrew Johnson is not that he has been a poor white man; my objection is that he keeps "poor whits" all the way through. That is the trouble with him.[20]

Before a packed auditorium, Harper claimed a sad equality between the statuses and the interests of newly emancipated African Americans and the nation's president. She had made a bold and risky assertion, but the comparison was essential to Harper's strategy. Convinced that both Andrew Johnson's administrative ineptitude and the poor state of African American life reflected the nation's larger educational and character deficiencies, Harper attributed Johnson's "poor whits" to the same malaise that plagued African Americans emerging from chattel slavery. When the audience burst into laughter, it signaled that her gamble had paid off. She had successfully presented her rhetoric of black uplift veiled as a common good. By doing so, she expanded the nation's conversation on the boundaries of social reform.

Similar to Absalom Jones and Richard Allen, Harper masked those activities that may have provoked white retribution. As she captivated abolitionist circles with her rhetorical skill and Victorian presentation, she concealed her more subversive activities. In his archives, Stills wrote of Harper:

> Mrs. Harper was not content to make speeches and receive plaudits, but was ever willing to do the rough work and to give material aid wherever needed. From another letter dated Lewis Centre, Ohio, we copy the following characteristic extract:
>> Yesterday I sent you thirty dollars. Take five of it for the rescuers (who were in prison), and the rest pay away on the books. My offering is not large; but if you need more, send me word. Also how comes on the Underground Rail Road? Do you need anything for that? You have probably heard of the shameful outrage of a colored man or boy named Wagner, who was kidnapped in Ohio and carried across the river and sold for a slave. . . . Ohio has become a kind of a negro hunting ground, a new Congo's coast and Guinea's shore. A man was kidnapped almost under the shadow of our capital. Oh, was it not dreadful? . . . Oh, may the living God prepare me for an earnest and faithful advocacy of the cause of justice and right![21]

Harper did not publicize the material aid she directed to an illegal cause, but she committed so much of her honoraria to the Underground Railroad that one might claim that she intended her speeches and popular writings to fund these other endeavors in the cause of emancipation. So robust was her commitment that Still admonished her to care for her own needs.[22] Undeterred by these insistent admonitions, Harper persisted, "Well, I am but one, but can do something, and, God helping me, I will try."[23] For Harper, the value of her material wealth was its ability to lift the yoke of slavery from her people.

Harper's response to Still belied her ambitions. Perhaps it was another act of masking. Even for a man like Still, who committed himself to subverting societal order, Harper's efforts led her far afield of a "woman's place." Nonetheless, she knew that the kind of transformative work she imagined required more than her singular effort. Despite her self-deprecating response, Harper knew that she represented more than "but one." She planned to build a broad network of women working collectively to lift the race. Unfortunately, matters of racial uplift were the property of men. The nineteenth century relegated black, and other, women's voices to domestic spaces. Since she could not bring black women themselves into the public sphere, she strategized a means to bring black, and other, women's influence into public spaces. Harper early on recognized that ordinary human relationships connected domestic and public spaces. Men with public authority related to women in the privacy of the domestic sphere. So Harper took full advantage of domestic and other everyday spaces along with the resources that ordinary black women had at hand. She focused on the home, the primary site for women's agency, and on motherhood, its primary authoritative role. In her celebrated speech, "Enlightened Motherhood," Harper emphasized the power of the home and envisioned expansive influence for mothers who attended to character development:

> The school may instruct and the church may teach, but the home is an institution older than the church and antedates schools, and that is the place where children should be trained for useful citizenship on earth and a hope of holy companionship in heaven . . . The moment the crown of motherhood falls on the brow of a young wife, God gives her a new interest in the welfare of the home and the good of society.[24]

In the speech, Harper took the traditional language of the cult of domesticity and republican motherhood, which affirmed women's domestic authority,[25] and emphasized women's roles in forming the Republic's national character respectively, and reimagined the home as a site for black women's social agency. In the home, mothers trained their children for "useful citizenship," while motherhood itself vests women with an interest in "the good of society." For Harper, both connected the domestic and the public.

Harper taught women to exploit these spaces by using routine conversations. She often modeled character pedagogy in her lectures. In small towns throughout the South, she stayed with black families for days after a lecture and she taught women the art of character conversations. These teaching sessions "model[ed] a general theory of rhetoric that formulate[d] human relations as an ever-expanding circuit of addressor-addressee." Harper pointedly taught the quotidian art of conversation as a vital political resource.[26] Every ordinary space and routine conversation was an opportunity to catalyze social reform. Ultimately, she believed that black and other women's voices, properly directed, could transform their social world and the men with whom they inhabited it.

Indeed, the private sphere trumped public space as Harper re-envisioned maternal authority. She claimed that from the home mothers might even direct public policy:

> And has not every prospective mother the right to ask for the overshadowing of the same spirit, that her child may be one of whom it may be truly said, "Of such is the kingdom of heaven," and all his life he shall be lent to the Lord? Had all the mothers of this present generation dwelt beneath the shadow of the Almighty, would it have been possible for slavery to have cursed us with its crimes, or intemperance degraded us with its vices?[27]

For Harper, even the slave trade's horrific mark upon the Republic's history might have been prevented had enlightened mothers strategically and collectively deployed their agency to influence men who eventually entered the realm of public authority. Harper entertained no double standards regarding gender; she claimed a mother's authority over her sons as well as her daughters.

> I hold that no woman loves social purity as it deserves to be loved and valued, if she cares for the purity of her daughters and not her sons; who would gather her dainty robes from contact with the fallen woman and yet greet with smiling lips and clasp with warm and welcoming hands the author of her wrong and ruin. How many mothers to-day shrink from a double standard for society which can ostracise [sic] the woman and condone the offense of the man? How many mothers say within their hearts, "I intend to teach my boy to be as pure in his life, as chaste in his conversation, as the young girl who sits at my side encircled in the warm clasp of loving arms?"[28]

She admonished women to take responsibility for their sons' moral instruction with the same zeal as that of their daughters. She claimed that the sons and daughters raised by enlightened mothers would grow up to embody Harper's ideal race men and women.[29] Harper's vision of fulfillment called black women and men to produce an entire generation who sacrificed for the race. They would exemplify black moral and industrial genius and lift the race to its rightful place among the wider human family.

For Harper, the ideal race woman and man was as much a part of her nineteenth-century liberalism as her commitment to uplift. She derived her exemplary race woman and man from prevailing sensibilities that idealized the emerging middle class and its primary organizing unit, the nuclear family. A rising class of male professionals, one of the more visible by-products of the new Industrial Age, made possible a family unit that no longer required each member's labor to sustain it. A corresponding class of white women no longer worked outside of home. The nineteenth century idealized these women as the core constituency of the cult of domesticity who focused their lives on subservience to men, Christian virtue, and the domestic sphere. The correlate for men, the cult of masculinity, understood authentic manhood as modeling industry along with the provision for and defense of their families, particularly women.[30]

However, African Americans generally found both Victorian ideals unattainable. The slave institution and its regimens prevented African American men from attaining the social, political, and economic markers that constituted the "true manhood" of the new middle class. By extension, black women could not achieve "true womanhood" by replicating markers of domesticity in their own lives. Nonetheless, Harper pressed her firm conviction to the rarified few who could rise above subsistence. She challenged her audiences to devote themselves to raising black life to this ideal. She exhorted women to develop their daughters and sons into her vision of a "true womanhood and manhood," for whom uplift of the race was a singular life purpose.

When we have a race of men whom this blood stained government cannot tempt or flatter, who would sternly refuse every office in the nation's gift, from a president down to a tide-waiter, until she shook her hands from complicity in the guilt of cradle plundering and man stealing, then for us the foundations of an historic character will have been laid. We need men and women whose hearts are the homes of a high and lofty enthusiasm, and a noble devotion to the cause of emancipation, who are ready and willing to lay time, talent and money on the altar of universal freedom. . . . If this government has no call for our services, no aim for your children, we have the greater need of them to build up a true manhood and woman-hood for ourselves. The important lesson we should learn and be able to teach, is how to make every gift, whether gold or talent, fortune or genius, subserve the cause of crushed humanity and carry out the greatest idea of the present age, the glorious idea of human brotherhood.[31]

Ultimately, Harper believed that if she and other black activists could remain faithful to the task of uplifting the masses of African Americans, then her people would reap the fruit of a generation of "true" race women and men. They would show the world black moral and industrial genius, and sacrifice privilege to uplift their people.

To be sure, Harper's expansive idea of the authority that society vested in mothers overreached. Clearly, she underestimated some of the real impediments of nineteenth-century patriarchy. Nonetheless, she refused to be cowed by the daunting social forces set against her. Instead, she modeled the pillar of cloud form by exploiting whatever valences of power her society made available to her. She earnestly hoped African Americans could produce persons possessed with Christian virtue and a willingness to sacrifice for the race. She commended these virtues universally into a national character and ultimately, to the greater human family. In her epic poem, "Moses: Story of the Nile," Harper takes the exodus story to signify these same values upon the nation's religious imagination.

Harper's Moses, the Politics of Motherhood, and True Manhood

Then they talk about this thing in the head; what's this they call it? [member of audience whispers, "intellect"] That's it, honey. What's that got to do with women's rights or negroes' rights? If my cup won't hold but a pint, and yours holds a quart, wouldn't you be mean not to let me have my little half measure full?

Then that little man in black there, he says women can't have as much rights as men, 'cause Christ wasn't a woman!

Where did your Christ come from? Where did your Christ come from? From God and a woman! Man had nothing to do with Him.

If the first woman God ever made was strong enough to turn the world upside down all alone, these women together ought to be able to turn it back, and get it right side up again! And now they is asking to do it, the men better let them.

—Sojourner Truth, 1851 at the Women's Convention, Akron, Ohio

I like the character of Moses. He is the first disunionist we read of in the Jewish Scriptures. The magnificence of Pharaoh's throne loomed up before his vision, its oriental splendors glittered before his eyes; but he turned from them all and chose rather to suffer with the enslaved, than rejoice with the free. He would have no union with the slave power of Egypt.

—From "Our Greatest Want," delivered by Frances Ellen Watkins Harper in 1859

From its ominous opening in 1:8, "There arose a Pharaoh who did not know Joseph," ethnic difference frames the exodus story. The cooperative relationship between Joseph and Pharaoh that David Walker celebrated is no more. The story picks up generations later when ethnic difference between Joseph's people and Pharaoh's people becomes politically and conceptually oppositional. Egyptian life depends upon Hebrew suffering and death. In the opening chapter, Pharaoh conscripts two Hebrew midwives, Shiprah and Puah, as imperial agents to carry out his policy to kill male newborns. Instead of fulfilling their duty to the state, the midwives subvert the imperial directive and save the Hebrew boys. When Pharaoh interrogates them, they respond by appealing to ethnic difference,[32] "'Because the Hebrew women are not like the Egyptian women; for they are vigorous and give birth before the midwife comes to them'" (Exodus 1:19). The midwives' response plays on essentialized notions of ethnicity by connecting ethnic difference to a basic biological function, namely, giving birth. Their ruse exposes Pharaoh's weakness and foreshadows his ultimate demise at the hand of the Hebrews.

Except for the episode between Pharaoh and the midwives, the exodus story plays out difference among men, such as Moses and Aaron, deities, such as Yahweh, the God of the Hebrews and Pharaoh, God incarnate of the Egyptians, and their displays of power in public spaces, such as the Egyptian throne room, the Red Sea, and Sinai. The deities compete to determine the Hebrews' fate, while male confrontations drive the plot toward its climax, Yahweh's victory at the sea. Women arise in supporting roles as they either affirm or subvert men's designs. In that schema, the Egyptian princess, and Jochabed, Moses's birth mother, show up only briefly, as the story portrayed the Hebrew midwives. Jochabed places Moses in the Nile and later raises him as his surrogate mother, while the princess appears long enough to rescue Moses by retrieving him from the river. Both women disappear after chapter two. With no mention of his upbringing, Moses appears as an adult by chapter three.

Harper revisits the first two chapters of Exodus and commits almost half of her poem to expanding them. Of the more than one thousand lines of the epic, she commits four hundred forty six to expanding the first two chapters of Exodus. She dramatizes the power of maternal agency and character pedagogy to show how the two work to produce Moses, Harper's model for the true race man. In place of the men who dominate the biblical story, Harper retrieves the two women, the princess and Jochabed, and places them in her vision of cooperation across racialized difference. She expands upon the women's appearances and roles in the story, and recasts them both as primary actors in their respective domestic spaces. Jochabed and the princess, whom she names Charmian,[33] take center stage as Harper transforms the narrative into a story of two mothers—one Hebrew and the other Egyptian, one a member of an oppressed people and the other a member of the ruling class and, by analogy, one black and the other white. Neither woman realizes the nature of the other's participation in God's plan, but each, independent of the other, becomes an agent in divine providence. Without the princess's surrogate motherhood, Moses may have drowned in the Nile. Without Jochabed's nurturing and instruction, Moses would not have learned of his Israelite heritage. In effect, Harper turns this story on its head. Displays of male power recede. Instead, the story's plot depends upon strategic and persuasive conversations that transform public arenas into two domestic spaces where maternal power becomes determinative. These conversations demonstrate the permeability of domestic and public spheres. Both women exercise Harper's politics of character pedagogy and enlightened motherhood. Neither intends cooperation with the other, but together their performances cooperate with divine providence and, in turn, participate in God's design to free the Hebrews by developing Moses into Harper's "true man."

Harper begins her epic with three rounds of "mother-son talk" between Moses and the princess, his adoptive mother. Each round of the conversation models women's power to transform public spaces into private spaces. In each of the three rounds, Moses expresses his intent to leave the Egyptian court and to take his "rightful place" among the Hebrews in their struggle for freedom. His language is formal and his attitude is distant.

> Kind and gracious princess, more than friend,
> I've come to thank thee for thy goodness,
> And to breathe into thy generous ears,
> My last and sad farewell. I go to join
> The fortunes of my race, and to put aside
> All other advantages, save
> The approval of my conscience and the need
> Of rightly doing.[34]

In the second round, Moses addresses Charmian similarly: "Let me tell thee, gracious princess . . ."[35] In both rounds, Moses frames the conversation as between a princess and a prince, two officials at court, where his gender carries greater authority than hers. For Harper, Moses' speech sets up a public space where the princess is at a political disadvantage.

In form, style, and content, Harper counters Moses' speech with Charmian's elegant Victorian presentation. Charmian performs Harper's conversational politics. She deploys her formidable intellectual powers and keen moral discernment in an everyday space with the intent to persuade Moses. Turning to her son, she responds:

> What means, my son, this strange election?
> What wild chimera floats across thy mind?

What sudden impulse moves thy soul? Thou who
Hast only trod the court of kings, why seek
Instead the paths of labor? Thou, whose limbs
Have known no other grab than that which well
Befits our kingly state, why rather choose
The badge of servitude and toil?[36]

Charmian's erudite speech sharply contrasts with Moses' direct but polite entreaties. The dialog dramatizes Exodus 4:10 where Moses laments his elocutive inadequacy for public speaking. In the Masoretic Text, Moses is literally "heavy tongued." Harper elaborates on the biblical characterization by giving the princess light, supple, and nuanced language that outstrips Moses at every turn. In the conversation, Charmian begins by addressing Moses as "my son. " Her language immediately remands the prince to a filial posture both in role and in relationship to her. Charmian uses Socratic form to reclaim a mother's role as pedagogue, and she instructs Moses by posing five successive interrogatives.

In style, Charmian speaks to her son in elevated language that draws literary references from classical antiquity, such as Homer's "chimera." With a thinly veiled reference to the Christian soteriological narrative, "but what king e'er cast his diadem in the dust, to be trampled down by every careless foot," she integrates practical and religious instruction with biblical allusions and admonishes Moses for rejecting his "diadem" and descending to a lowly state to redeem the Hebrews. Both allusions are glaring anachronisms for a second-millennium Egyptian princess. But Harper subordinates her historical consciousness for the sake of her model. In the princess, Harper intends an ideal that she constructs after her own instruction in proper rhetorical form, which included both classical and biblical allusions. The former signifies upon her intellect and class formation, while the latter signaled her moral constitution.

In content, each admonition exploits the connection between the domestic and public sphere. Rather than consigning her speech to domestic matters, Charmian freely instructs Moses concerning the politics of relinquishing his crown. After she transforms their conversational space, Charmian's authority over Moses extends to matters of state. By displaying this politics in Charmian's performance, Harper commends the same political strategy and erudition to the women who take up her program.

But Harper's political strategy is interested in more than performance. She wants to direct political action toward realizing appropriate moral ends. For example, Charmian performs Harper's conversational politics flawlessly, but she fails to convince Moses to remain at court. Her success meant convincing Moses to remain as her son, but the same "success" would thwart another moral good, namely, God's plan to free the Hebrews. Harper parses the two between Charmian and Moses. Charmian's subject position directs her to pursue the former good, while Moses' position leads him to pursue the latter.

In the opening dialogue, Charmian displays virtues appropriate to an Egyptian princess whose son must navigate life at court. She instructs Moses in proper behavior as a member of the royal house, encourages him to be loyal to their family, and to accept his role in the Egyptian court. When he confides his intent to renounce his royal status, she rightly tries to dissuade him from a foolish and rash decision. In fact, if Moses were an Egyptian prince and not a Hebrew whose family and people suffered to support his luxury, then his plans to leave the royal house would indeed be irresponsible. Conversely, Charmian's advice is remarkably prudent for guiding any Egyptian prince toward a successful rise at court. But Harper intends a transvaluation of value with regard to moral virtue. She adheres to the oppositional themes that structure Exodus. What is right for Egyptian royalty is patently wrong for the Hebrews. Unlike the exodus narrative, Harper treats their ethnic difference with political rather than biological significance. This is the hinge upon which Harper's moral reasoning hangs. Identity and station are determinate for discerning between virtue and vice.

Although oppositional, ethnic identities in the story are fluid for Harper. By the time Moses announces his decision to leave the palace, he has long understood himself as a Hebrew rather than an Egyptian. The princess is confused by his announcement, so she regards Moses' plan as "some strange election," a "chimera" summoned by youthful impulse. As the conversation continues, the "strangeness" of their ethnic difference leads to an estrangement between the princess and Moses that even their "mother-son" relationship cannot bridge. When Moses decides to abandon the royal house, he chooses an unnatural course for an Egyptian prince. Naturally, Charmian finds his moral reasoning unrecognizable.

> Sadly she gazed
> Upon the fair young face previous lit with its lofty
> Faith and high resolves—the dark prophetic eyes
> Which seemed to look beyond the present pain
> Unto the future greatness of his race.[37]

She searches his gaze for some sign of the young prince whom she thought she raised. Instead, she finds a stranger whose eyes "seemed to look beyond the present" toward a future and an ethnic identity that no longer includes her. Although Charmian tries earnestly to understand her "son," her political horizon cannot endow her with the moral and cultural sensibilities to appreciate Moses' decision.

> She had known life only
> By its brightness, and could not comprehend
> The grandeur of the young man's choice;[38]

Charmian stretches as far as her sensibilities can reasonably carry her; she only comes to acceptance but not *Verstehen*, or understanding.

Nonetheless, Charmian refuses to relinquish her claim to Moses. In an attempt to legitimate the mother-son relationship that she imagines, she appeals to a story of origins by telling Moses about the day she came to be his mother. As she begins her story with the simile, "like a dream," her language betrays the fiction that grounds her claim to motherhood.

> How like a dream the past floats back: it seems
> But yesterday when I lay tossing upon
> My couch of pain, a torpor creeping through
> Each nerve, a fever coursing through my veins.
> And there I lay, dreaming of lilies fair,
> Of lotus flowers and past delights, and all
> The bright, glad hopes, that give to early life
> Its glow and flush; and thus day after day
> Dragged its slow length along, until, one morn,
> The breath of lilies, fainting on the air,
> Floated into my room, and then I longed once more

To gaze upon the Nile, as on the face
Of a familiar friend, whose absence long
Had made a mournful void within the heart.
I summoned to my side my maids, and bade
Them place my sandals on my feet, and lead
Me to the Nile, where I might bathe my weary
Limbs within the cooling flood, and gather
Healing from the sacred stream.
I sought my favorite haunt, and, bathing, found
New tides of vigor coursing through my veins.
Refreshed, I sat me down to weave a crown of lotus leaves
And lilies fair, and while I sat in a sweet
Revery, dreaming of life and hope, I saw
A little wicker-basket hidden among
The flags and lilies of the Nile, and I called
My maidens and said, "Nillias and Osiris,
Bring me that little ark which floats beside
The stream." They ran and brought me a precious burden.
'Twas an ark woven with rushes and daubed
With slime, and in it lay a sleeping child;[39]

Charmian's story juxtaposes echoes of labor and birth with the comforts of the palace. Throughout the scene, Harper manages presences and absences to present Charmian's story as cruel farce. Each of Charmian's images turns in on itself and signals absence of Jochabed's authentic motherhood. The royal "couch" where Charmian experiences "pain" possesses the unsettling tension between luxury and agony.[40] But her aches are only shadows of the real labor pains that Jochabed experienced in Goshen. The princess's cries mock the screams of birth into oppression that rose from Jochabed's hut when Moses entered the world. Jochabed's cries reverberate as a backdrop even as Charmian describes the placid scene of the infant Moses floating among the lilies. As with much that the Egyptians consume, real Hebrew "labor" even produces the child that Charmian eventually claims. Charmian simply plucks the infant from the river as if he were a gift from the fertile Nile. At the story's climax, where a mother encounters her child face-to-face for the first time, Moses recoils.

> His little hand amid his clustering curls,
> And a bright flush upon his glowing cheek.
> He wakened with a smile, and reached out his hand
> To meet the welcome of the mother's kiss,
> When strange faces met his gaze, and he drew back
> With a grieved, wondering look[41]

The "strange faces" signal an estrangement so entrenched that Moses confirms it in his first encounter with Charmian. For Harper, Moses recoiled in the face of difference that could not be overcome given the political reality between Hebrews and Egyptians. Although Charmian tells the story as Moses' "birth narrative," Jochabed has already told Moses that he was born in Goshen. Harper's readers know the exodus story, so Charmian's narrative resonates as a desperate and empty ruse.

As Charmian attends to the responsibilities of motherhood, she continues the farce.

> but while I stood gazing upon
> His wondrous beauty, I saw beside me
> A Hebrew girl, her eyes bent on me
> With an eager, questioning look, and drawing
> Near, she timidly said, "Shall I call a nurse?"
> I bade her go; she soon returned, and with her
> Came a woman of the Hebrew race, whose
> Sad, sweet, serious eyes seemed overflowing
> With a strange and sudden joy. I placed the babe
> Within her arms and said, "Nurse this child for me;"
> And the babe nestled there like one at home,
>
> . . . .
> When many days had
> Passed she brought the child unto the palace;
> And one morning, while I sat toying with
> His curls and listening to the prattle of his
> Untrained lips . . .[42]

When Charmian comes face-to-face with Moses, meeting her child does not move her to nurture or instruct Moses as had Jochabed. Rather, she abdicates her responsibility and commits what is for Harper an unforgivable sin. Harper portrays the two mothers in stark contrast: Charmian places Moses in Jochabed's care and he "nestled" in her arms "like one at home."[43] While Jochabed nurtures Moses, the princess sits "toying with his curls."

Having contrasted the two women, Harper reverses their portrayals. This time Jochabed's presence fills the princess's absence. Again, Harper plays with irony when Moses reveals to Charmian how Jochabed, the nursemaid, became the legitimate mother.

> The Hebrew nurse to whom thou gavest thy foundling.
> That woman was my mother; from her lips I
> Learned the grand traditions of our race that float
> With all their weird and solemn beauty, around
> Our wrecked and blighted fortunes. How oft!
> With kindling eye and glowing cheek, forgetful
> Of the present pain, she would lead us through
> The distant past: the past, hallowed by deeds
> Of holy faith and lofty sacrifice.
> How she would tell us of Abraham,
> The father of our race, that he dwelt in Ur;
> Of the Chaldees, and when the Chaldean king
> Had called him to his sacrifice, that he
> Had turned from his dumb idols to the living
> God, and wandered out from kindred, home and race,
> Led by his faith in God alone; and she would
> Tell us,—(we were three,) my brother Aaron,
> The Hebrew girl thou sentest to call a nurse,
> And I, her last, her loved and precious child;[44]

Moses does not call upon the story of his birth to Jochabed to counter Charmian's "birth" narrative. Rather, he contrasts both women's roles in his life after his "birth" in the Nile. Moses tells Charmian how Jochabed instructed him in the history of his people. By doing so, she, unknown to Charmian, formed his character, and, by extension, his identity. With the exclamation, "How oft," Moses emphasizes *habitus*, the connection between repetition and a proper course of instruction.

Charmian's story notwithstanding, Moses rejects her claim and refers to himself as "her foundling," which Charmian "gavest" to a Hebrew woman. Harper's point would not be lost on her audience. Even the palace's wealth and privilege cannot undo Jochabed's enlightened motherhood. Jochabed did not rely only upon her biological relationship to Moses, because ontology (for Harper, this is ethnic or racial identity) insufficiently grounds any judgment about character. She nurtured him in his ancestral traditions and *made* him a Hebrew in consciousness as well as blood. For Harper, character rather than birth determines identity.

By emphasizing character over ethnicity, Harper plays with the tension between filial and affilial relationality to instruct African American women to whom white women have abdicated their maternal responsibilities. In this way, she encourages African American women to exercise both their transformative and subversive power upon the children in their care. By elevating Jochabed's role, Harper emphasizes both types of relationality. Both construct Moses. But his identity emerges from an affilial relationship with his Jochabed in her role as his *caretaker*. By analogy, Harper gives African American women license to exploit their own affilial relationships to "teach" white children in their care to appreciate the "strangeness" of the humanity of African Americans. She saw the utility for such instruction. By transforming children's moral sensibilities, Harper believed that these women could thwart the larger structures of repression that the children in their care would eventually be expected to uphold.

For Harper, this type of maternal work could not easily be undone. Since Jochabed, by daily instruction, nurture, and love, had fulfilled Harper's enlightened motherhood ideal, Charmian could not supplant the relationship. Charmian's conversational strategy, while adroitly performed with Moses, was ineffective nonetheless. However, when Charmian performed the same strategy in the throne room, her actions were both morally legitimate and politically effective. In the latter portion of her soliloquy, Charmian recalled Moses' first encounter with Pharaoh.

> My father, proud and stately,
> Saw me bending o'er the child and said,
> "Charmian, whose child is this? Who of my lords
> Calls himself father to this goodly child?

He surely must be a happy man."
Then I said, "Father, he is mine. He is a
Hebrew child that I have saved from death." He
Suddenly recoiled, as if an adder
Had stung him, and said, "Charmian, take that
Child hence. How darest thou bring a member
Of that mean and servile race within my doors?
Nay, rather let me send for Nechos, whose
Ready sword shall rid me of his hateful presence."
Then kneeling at his feet, and catching
Hold of his royal robes, I said, "Not so,
Oh! honored father, he is mine; I snatched
Him from the hungry jaws of death, and foiled
The greedy crocodile of his prey; he has
Eaten bread within thy palace walls, and thy
Salt lies upon his fresh young lips; he has
A claim upon thy mercy."
"Charmian," he said
"I have decreed that every man child of that
Hated race shall die. . . .

. . . Give me up the child, and let him die."
Then clasping the child closer to my heart,
I said, "The pathway to his life is through my own;
Around that life I throw my heart, a wall
Of living, loving clay." Dark as the thunder
Clouds of distant lands became my father's brow,
And his eyes flashed with the fierce lightnings
Of his wrath; but while I plead, with eager
Eyes upturned, I saw a sudden change come
Over him; his eyes beamed with unwonted
Tenderness, and he said, "Charmian, arise,
Thy prayer is granted; just then thy dead mother
Came to thine eyes, and the light of Asenath
Broke over thy face. Asenath was the light
Of my home; the star that faded out too
Suddenly from my dwelling, and left my life

> To darkness, grief and pain, and for her sake,
> Not thine, I'll spare the child."[45]

In the throne room, the most public of spaces in Egypt and the place of public authority, Charmian directs both transformative and subversive power. Her rhetoric transforms the Pharaoh to father and Charmian, the princess, to a daughter. At Charmian's request, her father exempts Moses from the mass killings. By legitimating Charmian's influence upon her father rather than upon Moses, Harper circumscribes the "proper" boundary of white women's politics and demonstrates where white women may rightly participate in the work of uplift. Nonetheless, Harper remains cautious about extending Charmian's relationship with Moses. Her willingness to sacrifice herself notwithstanding, Charmian cannot redeem the maternal relationship that she abdicated to Jochabed.

In the last portion of Charmian's soliloquy, Harper again emphasizes Charmian's illegitimate motherhood. Despite his daughter's performance, the Pharaoh's mind changes only as he recalls another *real* mother, Asenath, his wife, and Charmian's mother. Again, the princess, who has not taken up the hard work of Harper's enlightened motherhood, only signifies the absence of a more legitimate maternal figure. She ends the soliloquy with the emphatic but futile "claim" that she lays upon Moses.

> And thus I saved
> Thee twice—once from the angry sword and once
> From the devouring flood. Moses, thou art
> Doubly mine; as such I claimed thee then, as such
> I claim thee now.[46]

For the princess, rescuing Moses from the Nile and courageously protecting him in the throne room should inspire Moses' loyalty. In fact, she believes that she has done enough to claim him twice. But Charmian's double claim to Moses' life falls short. Jochabed's double claim, which is both filial (as birth mother) and affilial (as nursemaid), already trumped it.

The throne room scene fails to affirm Charmian's maternal relationship, but it does offer a clue to the place of divine providence within

Harper's schema. Charmian is unaware of any divine plan to deliver the Hebrews. Nonetheless, she participates in the divine plan by doing what Harper understands to be universally virtuous and, thus, transcends ethnic difference. Charmian's opening conversations with Moses modeled virtue only for an Egyptian mother, but her performance in the throne room modeled virtue for *any* mother. Through the princess, Harper demonstrates her own commitment to the universal human family. In this act, Harper's princess risked all—even her life—to save Moses from imperial policy. She demonstrated for Moses the virtue of resisting state repression for the sake of justice. Moses learns not from her wealth or position, but from her singular virtuous act. In a mimetic performance of his adoptive mother, Moses, in turn, sacrifices his position, and risks his own life for his people.

Finally, Harper brings the section to a climax. The setting shifts from the Egyptian court to Goshen, where the Hebrew people live. The two mothers' work in forming Moses comes to fruition when he finally leaves the palace. Moses sacrifices for the sake of the masses and demonstrates the cornerstone of Harper's ideal for black uplift.

> (Chapt 2) It was a great change from the splendor, light
> And pleasure of a palace to the lowly huts
> Of those who sighed because of cruel bondage.[47]

Harper is careful not to romanticize Moses' Goshen experience. Moses passes from the splendor of the Egyptian court to the scenes of desperate life in Goshen. She describes the scene in stark terms. For Harper, Moses' choice is not a glorious one, but ultimately a moral decision to which the true man or woman must commit absolutely. "[Moses] was leaving all."[48] There is no middle ground. Harper's Moses is resolute. As he forsakes the pleasures and possibilities of royal life, Harper uses war images to describe Moses' moral discernment as an ongoing battle between good and evil.

> Dark eyes which looked their parting on the scenes
> Of beauty, where his life had been a joyous
> Dream enchanted with delight; but he trampled
> On each vain regret as on a vanquished foe,

> And went forth a strong man, girded with lofty
> Purposes and earnest faith.[49]

When Moses resists the pleasures of the palace, he passes his final trial and becomes Harper's "true man." Moses "tramples" and "vanquishes" the "foes," which represent temptations to turn back and enjoy his own privilege. Harper sublimates the war as the individual's struggle to subdue baser desires of self-aggrandizement rather than communal identification. Moses' struggle is no less than a moral battle to master the natural masculine inclinations and to emerge the true man. Each decision advances Moses' own character formation. He overcomes each temptation and strengthens his moral fortitude, which for Harper is the measure of manhood.

The battle won, Moses enters Goshen as a fully developed "true man." Upon his arrival, the first scene offends his sensibilities:

> He journeyed on
> Till palaces and domes and lofty fanes,
> And gorgeous temples faded from his sight,
> And the lowly homes of Goshen came in view.
> There he saw the women of his race kneading
> Their tale of bricks;[50]

The first description of Goshen takes the reader's attention to a domestic space that is out of order. For Harper, upward progress demands true men and women to reorder this primary space. By analogy, Harper points to a similar disorder in African American life. The "lowly huts" signify a double inadequacy. The domestic space deformed by slavery prevented those enslaved in Goshen from developing into fully actualized women and men. In their enslavement, Hebrew men failed in their responsibility to their families and, consequently, Hebrew women could not actualize their own potentials. So disordered is the scene that when Harper directs her readers' gaze to the women who are making bricks, it is clear that they are doing "men's work." The indiscriminate treatment of women and men in a Victorian world where gender organizes labor roles horrifies Moses. To force women to perform "men's work" is, for Harper, dehumanizing. She states explicitly:

Beyond their strength—if neither age nor sex
Is spared the cruel smiting of their rods[51]

Moses acts as any fully formed man would and takes up the Hebrew cause. Harper's argument resonates clearly. The racialized system that devalued African American womanhood, along with the often violent assaults experienced by African American women, arise from the slave regime and the prevailing configurations of the political economy. Similarly, the men, "the sons of Abraham [c]rouching beneath their heavy burdens,"[52] have become so fearful and slavish that they cannot attend to the "natural" inclination to protect and provide for the family. Such a critique based in oppositional constructions as gender had come to be, turns upon authentic manhood as much as it does womanhood. Black women's degradation signifies mercilessly upon the black men's impotence, namely, their inability to defend their families, and thus, in a Victorian moral world, their ability to be authentically men.

Finally, the poem shifts from conversations between the princess and Moses to conversations between Moses and Jochabed. We see Jochabed instructing Moses, not as his surrogate, but this time as his mother. When Moses appears in Goshen with the announcement that opened the poem, "I've come to share the fortunes of my race," he surprises all of his Hebrew kin except Jochabed. She explains to Moses that they had heard a vicious rumor from other Hebrews.

> Two Hebrews, journeying from On to Goshen,
> Told us they had passed the temple of the Sun
> But dared not enter, only they had heard
> That it was a great day in On; that thou hadst
> Forsworn thy kindred, tribe and race; hadst bowed
> Thy knee to Egypt's vain and heathen worship:
> Hadst denied the God of Abraham, of Isaac,
> And of Jacob, and from henceforth wouldst
> Be engrafted in Pharaoh's regal line,
> And be called the son of Pharaoh's daughter.[53]

In sharp religious language, she describes the tragic sin that Moses avoided when he rejected the princess's maternal claim. Had Charmian persuaded Moses, he would have "foresworn [his] kindred" and thus abandoned his identity, both of which had been carefully constructed by Jochabed's faithful character pedagogy. But Moses is Harper's true man, he exemplifies the "race of men whom this blood stained government cannot tempt or flatter, who would sternly refuse every office in the nation's gift."

Jochabed continues the lesson and witnesses to the source of a mother's faith. Although Jochabed and Amram, Moses' father, heard the same news, they respond differently.

> When thy father Amram heard the cruel news
> He bowed his head upon his staff and wept.
> But I had stronger faith than that[54]

As Jochabed witnesses to Moses, her cadence appropriates the *Heilsgeschictliche* litany of Hebrews 11, but recast in blank verse.

> By faith
> I hid thee when the bloody hands of Pharaoh
> Were searching 'mid our quivering heart strings,
> Dooming our sons to death; by faith I wove
> The rushes of thine ark and laid thee 'mid
> The flags and lilies of the Nile, and saw
> The answer to that faith when Pharaoh's daughter
> Placed thee in my arms, and bade me nurse the child
> For her: and by that faith sustained, I heard
> As idle words the cruel news that stabbed
> Thy father like a sword.[55]

It is precisely the nature of her faith that compels her to act without assurance that her work would be fruitful. Because she acted faithfully, she has reason to believe despite the news that convinced Amram to lose faith. Harper affirms a theological connection between faithful practice and divine providence. In this climactic scene, Harper reaches to illustrate the core belief that has motivated her ongoing work: one's participation in God's providential design will be rewarded. With Jochabed, Harper calls African American women to muster their faith and to continue their struggle despite signs that their efforts might appear ineffective. She calls her readers to believe even when men lose faith, and to continue their acts of resistance. Although the journey from the Sea through the Wilderness was long and treacherous, she knows that black women who are committed to her politics will succeed because that journey leads to the Promised Land.

Harper believed that her program made God's will of moving her people toward the Promised Land discernable and attainable. All that was needed was faithful practice among the masses to pursue it. In 1869, Harper had every reason to be optimistic, so she lived out her model of the true woman and devoted the rest of her life to that purpose.

Promises Broken: Making Bitter Water Drinkable

In 1877, just eight years after Harper published her epic poem, Reconstruction officially ended and the last of its protections for black life in the South unraveled. Heartbreak replaced the grand optimism that black and other progressives shared at the end of the Civil War. Twelve years after the victory at Appomattox, a war-weary nation lost its appetite for fighting—even to protect its recently emancipated citizens. The coalition of Northern industrialists, congressional Republicans, and abolitionists who had been the driving force for reconstructing the South fell apart. Northern industrialists, anxious to exploit potential southern markets, reconciled with the Old South aristocracy. Together they formed a new alliance and claimed that further hostilities would harm prospects for transforming the South's outmoded agrarian economy. Congressional Republicans saw the handwriting on the wall. Without popular support, they could no longer justify continuing their Reconstruction program. Their political will waned, and they resigned from their grand aspiration of reconstructing the nation and settled instead for a sad compromise, namely, winning their party's bid for the presidency. In return for Rutherford B. Hayes's victory, Republicans were to remove all U.S. Army troops from the former Confederate states, appoint one southern Democrat to Hayes's cabinet, and enact policies to industrialize the South, including the construction of a transcontinental railroad through Texas. Only activists, such as abolitionists, continued the struggle. But without the political capital once held by Republicans in Congress or the financial backing of the industrialists, their moral persuasion had little influence.

Perhaps an astute prophet such as the biblical Amos might have read the signs leading to the compromise of 1877 and predicted its effects on black life thereafter. They were almost ubiquitous. Beginning in 1865 the South lurched between episodes of civil expansion for African Americans and attempts to return to an old racist regime. The first three years following the war brought a rapid succession of constitutional amendments that expanded rights for African Americans. The Thirteenth Amendment ended the slave regime. The Fourteenth and Fifteenth Amendments respectively provided for and protected citizenship and voting rights for African American men. However, backlash from southern states was swift and brutal. They enacted "Black Codes," shorthand for several laws that reinscribed racialized hierarchies within the political economy. These codes legislated labor relations and reinforced social hierarchies. Without the plantation system to ensure that blacks remained a readily available labor force, vagrancy laws imposed heavy penalties that reduced black labor to sharecropping and returned black workers to plantations. Quitting a job meant arrest or imprisonment and even absences from work were punishable by law. In effect, Black Codes granted white employers the same control over black labor that plantation owners possessed under the slave regime. The laws criminalized "seditious speech" and "insulting gestures" (which might mean anything, such as looking whites in the eye, forgetting to remove one's hat in the presence of a white man, failing to tip one's hat in the presence of a white woman, or failing to open a door for whites). Each provision reinforced the social hierarchy of the Old South. Finally, these codes made firearms possession illegal to ensure that blacks remained defenseless as the old regime resurged.

Where laws failed to enforce racialization, many southern whites turned to extra-legal measures in the form of violence. Just months after the Civil War, on Christmas Eve of 1865, former confederates and other southerners came together in Pulaski, Tennessee, to form the Ku Klux Klan. As southern bitterness intensified, other terrorist groups including the Black Horse Calvary, Knights of the White Camilia, Pale Faces, White Brotherhood, the Council of Safety, and The '76 Association, joined numerous local rifle and gun associations to root out any remaining U.S. Army troops and to attack African Americans in every form. Even before the nation could breathe a sigh to mark the close of the war, these groups forced a de facto second war upon battle-worn troops. They attacked American soldiers who were stationed in the South as peacekeepers. Using public displays of violence and intimidation, they destroyed or confiscated property owned by blacks and coerced them from exercising the franchise. But their most enduring legacy was inscribed on the mass of the lynched and raped bodies of black women and men that marked the South's landscape. Historians John Hope Franklin and Alfred Moss, Jr., summarize the situation well: "Depriving the Negro of Political equality became, to them, a holy crusade in which a noble end justified any means. Negroes were run out of communities if they disobeyed orders to desist from voting; and the more resolute and therefore insubordinate blacks were whipped, maimed, and hanged. . . . In 1874 a committee of the Colored Convention assembled in Atlanta informed the state legislature that they could not point 'to any locality in Georgia where we can in truth say that our lives and our liberties are perfectly secure.'"[56]

So when the Hayes-Tilden Compromise triggered the recall of the last of the U.S. Army troops garrisoned in the South, it was but the final episode in a long and disappointing decade that marked black life with steadily increasing repression. Losing federal troops meant that the southern aristocracy had finally won. For all of its promise, Reconstruction had neither guaranteed the security of African Americans, nor addressed the needs of poor whites, whom the southern aristocracy also exploited. With no federal troops to maintain law, former high-ranking Confederate officers and other officials disenfranchised black men and blamed the Republican Reconstruction and emancipation for the suffering poor whites experienced. The effect pitted poor whites against blacks. It heightened racial tensions and led the two groups to ignore their common class interests. In the end, poor whites sided with the aristocracy, which needed them to enforce the new repressive measures. As it had been before the Civil War, racial hierarchies returned punctuated by black vulnerability. Reconstruction, by and large, had failed.

The Reverend John Jasper: Man of War and Pastor to His People

Two celebrations occurred on July 4, 1812. First, the American Republic celebrated thirty-six years of freedom. Second, on a plantation in Flu-vanna County, Virginia, Tina and Philip Jasper celebrated the birth of their son, John, the last of their twenty-four children, all of whom were born into bondage.[57] Before Frances Ellen Watkins Harper delivered her first anti-slavery address in 1855, the Reverend John Jasper had lived the first forty-three years of his life under the brutal yoke of the slave regime. He accepted his call to ministry in 1839 and preached his most famous sermon, "The Sun Do Move," more than 250 times. Jasper developed his sermon on a type of theological reasoning that was not uncommon among North American clergy at the time. It included biblical inerrancy and a pre-Enlightenment stance on the order of the cosmos. On Sunday mornings, Jasper preached at Sixth Mount Zion, the Baptist church he founded in Richmond, Virginia. The sheer force of his personality electrified the congregation and his deep love for the people filled the pulpit. His sermons were a tour de force. At times, governors, legislators, and judges flocked to hear him. They sat side-by-side with Jasper's own congregation. On one occasion, Jasper delivered his sermon on the sun before the entire Virginia General Assembly.[58] Even those who disagreed with his positions were compelled by his charismatic personality and strong religious conviction.

In the sermon, Jasper affirmed his deep respect for knowledge despite his pre-Enlightenment positions on the sun. He had painstakingly learned to read while he was enslaved. At the same time, however, Jasper was deeply suspicious of scholarship. For good reason, he did not conflate the two. During the nineteenth century, academic discourses scrambled to ground their knowledge claims in methodological objectivity, the gold standard of the modern age. For most, the scientific method met this high watermark. Undergirded by empirical evidence, their claims exercised the power of objective truth. Unfortunately, these truths, formed in the cultural milieu of racialization, often distributed uninterrogated racialized understandings across academic disciplines. The impact was evident throughout post-Reconstruction society in law, politics, education, psychology, and religion. Increasingly, racialization became the common discursive formation across these disciplines. Each one developed its own rationale to affirm notions of black inferiority. Worse, African Americans could not participate in these discourses. They had no access to its conversations. Simultaneously, these knowledge claims migrated from academic conversations into the wider public. Through popular media such as magazine and newspaper articles, sermons, and lectures, they shaped the cultural milieu.

One area where the connection between race and academic discourse influenced the public sphere with devastating material consequences for black life was in the American Anthropological School's research in natural history. As early as 1839, ironically the same year that Jasper converted to Christianity, Samuel Morton published his classic *Crania Americana*. The study represented years of work in classifying human skulls to which he assigned differentiated intellectual capacities by race. Upon his death in 1851, the *Charleston Medical Journal* stated, "We can only say that we of the South should consider him [Morton] as our benefactor, for aiding most materially in giving to the Negro his true position as an inferior race."[59] The "material" nature of his aid, namely, the "truth" of black inferiority, now based in scientific fact, shaped racialized understandings for decades to come. During the 1840s, his student, Josiah Nott, from Alabama, published and lectured widely to aid proslavery advocates in their struggle against the abolitionist movement. Morton's research was also a primary influence for Louis Agassiz, who established a center for Natural History at Harvard University. Early on, Agassiz held a liberal view on racial origins, but upon encountering an African American for the first time, he cringed in visceral disgust and wrote in a letter to his mother:

> I could not take my eyes off their face in order to tell them to stay far away. And when they advanced that hideous hand towards my plate in order to serve me, I wished I were able to depart in order to eat a piece of bread elsewhere, rather than dine with such service. What unhappiness for the white race—to have tied their existence so closely with that of Negroes in certain countries! God preserve us from such a contact.[60]

For the remainder of the nineteenth century, Agassiz or one of his students would train every major scientist of natural history.[61]

The developments in natural history were only a part of a much larger phenomenon. Whether or not Jasper and his congregation knew it, the post-Reconstruction political economy was rapidly transforming race in the American Republic. Old moral and religious arguments for slavery slowly lost sway, and the whole slave institution came under increasing pressure from the abolitionist movement. Science offered another, more durable, justification to perpetuate the slave system. Unlike capacities that could be developed by education, behaviors that could be changed, or religious doctrines that southern planters and abolitionists interpreted differently, race—as a scientific "fact"—located empirical differences in black and white bodies. By doing so, race became an inescapable "truth" of nature. After the slave regime's demise, these arguments legitimized the cascade of legislation and violence necessary to maintain a racialized political economy.

With no recourse in the civil arena and no way to influence this rapidly increasing body of scholarship or the attitudes solidifying around it, Jasper relied upon the Bible. For most laypersons, black and white, the Bible remained the most authoritative source for truth in the nineteenth century. Throughout his life, Jasper maintained a staunch allegiance to the idea of Scripture's authority. Unlike scholarship, whose authority resided in academe where African Americans had little access, Jasper believed that the Bible's authority resided in a God who affirmed humanity irrespective of racialized distinctions. Its stories possessed power that he could direct. Its knowledge claims, at least, could be harnessed toward his people's fulfillment. So Jasper stepped into the silence of the biblical text and spoke such a word to his people. Jasper believed his pastoral role demanded that he protect the idea of Bible's authority because it was the only power upon which his people could rely. Even when scholars disagreed with Jasper over some point of fact, he doggedly refused to concede because their authority resided in institutions that assaulted black life. When they visited Jasper's congregation, their attire, speech, and institutional location visibly directed power. Even so, Jasper refused to be intimidated by their presentation. He believed the source of his authority was greater than those who challenged him. Before an appreciative congregation, Jasper would stand in the pulpit and deploy his critical sensibilities to unmask their racism.

At one point during his sermon on the sun, Jasper interjects an allegorical tale that clearly referenced the "scholars" who were visiting in the congregation that day. As he begins, he points to their outward status markers and remarked on their apparent well-meaning intentions, "Tother day er man wid er hi coler and side whisk'rs cum ter my house. He was one nice North'rn gemman wat think a heap of us col'rd people in de Souf. Da ar luvly folks and I honours 'em very much."[62] Unmoved by the scholar's appearance, Jasper related how the high-collared "gentleman" condescended to him and showed how the visitor's congenial approach was a façade, "He seem from de start kinder strictly an' cross wid me, and arter while, he brake out furi'us and frettid, an' he say: 'Erlow me Mister Jasper ter gib you sum plain advise. Dis nonsans 'bout de sun movin' whar you ar gettin' is disgracin' yer race all ober de kuntry, an' as a fren of yer peopul, I cum ter say it's got ter stop.'"[63] In the pastoral moment, Jasper takes the opportunity to instruct his congregation by making a startling comparison, "Ha! Ha! Ha! Mars' Sam Hargrove nuvur hardly smash me dat way. It was equl to one ov dem ole overseurs way bac yondur."[64] He warns his congregation with clear implications: These scholars may have no chains to constrain them, but their attitudes, directed through the institutional power of academe, did violence. They were no less destructive to black life than overseers under the slave regime. Less than thirteen years after the end of slavery, the congregation still remembered overseers and slave drivers who disregarded their lives and limbs and had contempt for their souls.

Although he might have thought about it, Jasper did not respond in kind to the visiting scholar. In the post-Reconstruction South, governed by the Black Codes and surveilled by the Ku Klux Klan, he knew the risks too well. Richmond's trees saw black men and women swing from nooses for less. Jasper knew his pastoral role made him even more vulnerable. White vigilante groups often exacted their retribution on black church members to control activist clergy. No, he could not afford a reckless comment. Instead, Jasper maintained a congenial tone. Ironically, he invited the gentleman to join him in the kind of open-minded inquiry that should have been the hallmark of the visitor's professional scholarly practice, "I tel him dat ef he'll sho me I'se wrong, I giv it all up."[65] At first the scholar appeared to agree to Jasper's proposition, but the man ended his response with an ad hoc and racially disparaging remark, "He sail in on me an' such er storm about science, nu 'scuv'ries, an' de Lord only knos wat all, I ner hur befo', an' den he tel me my race is ergin me an' po ole Jasper mus shet up 'is fule mouf."⁶⁶ In the scholar's mind, there is no hope for Jasper and, by extension, black people, because "his race is against him." Race, for the scholar, was a natural fact that could not be transcended. So, by condemning Jasper, the scholar intended to remand him, and, by extension, his people, to a Negro's place in any learned discourse, namely, silenced.

For the scholar, Jasper was an object to be taught rather than an opportunity for an intersubjective encounter. But Jasper saw the matter differently. He refused to fit in a Negro's place. Jasper knew that he could not compete with the visitor's scientific knowledge about "nu 'scuv'ries" and ideas that he "ner hur befo'"⁶⁷ So Jasper takes his stand by conceding *Wissenschaften*, but not moral authority. "I tel him John Jasper ain' set up to be no scholur, an' doant kno de ferlosophiz, an' ain' tryin' ter hurt his peopul, but is wurkin' day an' night ter lif 'em up, but his foot is on de rock uv eternal truff. Dar he stan' and dar he is goin' ter stan' til Gabrul soun's de judgment note."⁶⁸ As Jasper saw the matter, he uplifted his people toward a God who affirmed their lives. Then Jasper turns the conversation with the conjunction, "but" and a non sequitur "his foot is on de rock uv eternal truff." The phrase turns the debate from facts to foundations for the knowledge claims that they each held. Jasper asserted his source, Scripture, and his belief that its claims were true. While Jasper reveals the source of his own authority, he notes that the scholar has not been similarly transparent. With a coy tone for effect, Jasper remarks insightfully, "I ain' hur whar he get his Scriptu' from"⁶⁹ Nonetheless, Jasper's narrative has already revealed enough about the scholar for the congregation to make a judgment even without the scholar's "Script." If the scholar's behavior toward Jasper is any indication of the man's "Script" or the authority that grounded it, then Jasper's last remarks shows his keen discernment, "dat 'tween him an' de wurd of de Lord I tek my stan' by de Word of Gord ebery time."⁷⁰

Throughout his sermon, Jasper continues this trickster performance by masterfully managing personas, polyvalent language, and authority. First, he shifts strategically between two personas, namely, the man of war and the minstrel. The former confronts the interlocutors, while the latter parries or shields Jasper from the consequence of his rhetoric. As "man of war," Jasper stands in his pulpit and faces down the enemies of both the faith and his congregation. He goads and taunts to draw them into a confrontation where Jasper appears outmatched. He performs mimetically the scene of victory at the sea where the Lord hardened Pharaoh's heart and goaded him to attack the seemingly defenseless band of Hebrews only to drown in the Red Sea.

Jasper's "Man of War" worked dialectically with his "minstrel" persona. On any given occasion, Jasper's English could be as standard as the scholars he ridiculed, but he often chose to use a common artifice for blacks in the nineteenth century, the familiar sound of minstrel dialect.[71] Cultural critic Houston Baker describes the mask as "designed to remind white consciousness that black men and women are *mis-speakers* bereft of humanity."[72] The mask cobbles together components of black vernacular with a syntax that misrepresents African American sensibilities. Its performance is non-sense in black vernacular, but its meaning coheres in the white imaginary populated by black women and men as "carefree devils strumming and humming all day."[73] Jasper plays with the ambiguity of *mis*-speaking. It enabled blacks to speak their minds before whites where an otherwise straightforward conversation might be taken as "seditious speech." Indeed, as Baker claims, "For it was in fact the minstrel mask as mnemonic ritual object that constituted the *form* that any Afro-American who desired to be articulate—to speak at all— had to master during the age of Booker T. Washington."[74]

Act I of Ossie Davis's classic play, *Purlie Victorious*, presents a brilliant illustration of the minstrel's work. In the scene, a group of men enslaved by Cap'n Cotchapie participate in a plan with other enslaved members of the community to get the plantation owner to release the $500 needed to build a church that would serve as a center for the community. They do so by singing to him while the main character, Purlie, presents, unbeknownst to the Cap'n, a fictitious commendation that they call the "Great White Father of the Year Award." The award and their song leverage the "Great White Father" myth, which shaped the imagination of much of the white, southern, planter population. The myth assured planters that they were beneficent, paternal actors and that the slave regime's brutal work was necessary to civilize African Americans, who would always be as children to them. In effect, the myth valorized the white planter for shouldering the "burden" of grooming African Americans for nation. In the play, the song woos Ol' Cap'n. The early stanzas affirm Ol' Cap'n.

> On sacred hill above the Pine; in a hallowed hall
> There reigns a Dynasty Divine
> We pray shall never fall;
>
> And so we come from far and near
> To shed a sentimental tear,
> To raise our voice in song and cheer
> The Great White Father of the Year.
>
> Oh, we the humble haven't much
> But we do not mind
> The Lord has given you the Whip,
> And us, the Black Behind.
>
> And so we come from far & near
> To shed a sentimental tear
> To raise our voice in song & cheer
> The Great White Father of the Year.

However, the lyrics turn at stanza four. The wooing turns to disparaging.

> You so enrich the lives we lead
> we heed your every word,
> For we are like the Georgia soil
> And you're the Georgia turd
>
> Oh, we know your whippin's are but love
> Kisses in your mind;
> If it's love you want, then don't be shy;
> Come kiss our Black Behind.
>
> And so we come from far and near
> To shed a sentimental tear

> To raise our voice in song and cheer
> The Great White Father of the Year.[75]

It is clear by the end of the song that the chorus has deftly deployed southern cultural ideals to make fun of the plantation owner while still enlisting him to give the community the money they sought.

Jasper's minstrel mask operates similarly. With the mask, Jasper becomes the unlettered fool at will in order to appear intellectually outmatched by the northern scholars. Throughout his homiletic delivery, Jasper depends on the minstrel's claims upon the white imaginary: black speech is meaningless "*mis*-speak" particularly when it articulates a challenge to white authority. When he levels his harshest critiques, Jasper deploys the minstrel's style by signifying.[76] His grammar and diction recall the minstrel, but Jasper does not *mis*-speak. Rather, he makes perfect sense.

Second, Jasper stylized his sermon as a testimony, a common rhetorical form for the church, and one easily recognized by his congregation. The rules of form and syntax in church testimony differ from academic or popular lectures. Using polyvalent language, Jasper exploited the hermeneutical gap between his congregation and the scholarly visitors to convey distinct messages to both audiences simultaneously.

Third, Jasper grounded both his rhetorical form and language with two types of authority, namely, biblical and pastoral. Leveraging both, Jasper shifted the subject at hand from the nature and rotation of the sun, which is scientific knowledge (*Naturwissenschaften*), to the nature and character of the people in the room, which is moral knowledge, a faculty of the *Geisteswissenschaften*. Ultimately, Jasper offers a critique of the foundations for any knowledge claim. By the end of the sermon, the visitors skulk away. They realize that Jasper was preaching less about the sun as he was affirming three foundational hierarchies for determining the kind of knowledge upon which he believed his people could rely in his post-Reconstruction era, namely, moral knowledge over scientific knowledge, divine legitimation over the authority of institutions such as academe, and the Bible's authority over scholarly works.

The Sun Moves, or Signifying on the Sun and Affirming God's Sovereignty

Sunday, March 17, 1878 was not the first time Jasper delivered his "Sermon on the Sun." He had preached it many times before. However, this occasion was different; it was the first time he invited the public to hear his popular homily. White scholars visited among the congregation. They came to refute Jasper's position and show the old man up as a fool. From their perspective, altruistic intentions motivated them; they believed the congregation labored under a false consciousness and they hoped to enlighten the poor, black parishioners to what they saw as Jasper's demagoguery. They would not be the last of such "well-intentioned" visitors. In the ensuing years, Jasper's sermon gained a cult following and his renown spanned the Atlantic. His claims about the sun's movement perturbed many in the scholarly community for whom the Copernican Revolution was settled consensus. In each encounter, Jasper and his interlocutors contended amid an increasingly influential historical current. Modernism steadily shifted foundations for knowledge claims toward the scientific method, while revelation, an older pre-Enlightenment foundation, receded. In the long term, modernism's claims held sway and Jasper's arguments seemed passé and even ridiculous, but not on that Sunday in the spring of 1878, or for many Sundays thereafter. Jasper was always too well prepared for his guests. He knew these occasions required more than an eloquent sermon or a defense of biblical orthodoxy. These occasions required his Sunday best, namely, a pillar of fire performance that marked him as one of the greatest preachers in the nation's history. That morning, Jasper delivered.

Jasper began this and many sermons with the same provocative text, one verse, Exodus 15:3, "The Lord God is a Man of War. The Lord is his name." Its simple declaration framed the entire sermon. However, biographers disagree about the relevance of the choice. On one hand, Edwin Randolph sees no incongruity between Jasper's text and the remainder of his sermon, but Randolph does not show how Jasper's text connects to the sermon. In his biography on Jasper, Randolph gives it no more than a matter-of-fact mention, "After divine invocation, he announced as his text the 3d verse of the 15th chapter of Exodus: 'The Lord is a man of war: the Lord is his name.' He ably and minutely illustrated the text from the earlier history of the children of Israel."[77] On the other hand, in Jasper's better-known biography, William Hatcher is nonplussed and dismisses the scripture:

> The text for his sermon was a long cry from his topic. It was: "The Lord God is a man of war; The Lord is His name." He was too good a sermon-maker to announce a text and abandon it entirely, and so he roamed the Old Testament to gather illustrations of the all-conquering power of God. This took him over a half hour to develop, and as it took even much longer to formulate his argument as to the rotation of the sun it made his sermon not only incongruous, but intolerably long—far longer than any other sermon that I ever knew him to preach. The two parts of the discourse had no special kinship, while the first part tired the people before he reached the thing they came for. It was an error in judgment, but his power to entertain an audience went far to save him from the consequences of his mistake.[78]

For a preacher, the text frames the sermon and serves as the lens through which the congregation should refract the sermon's symbols, motifs, and theological meanings. Both biographers miss the Scripture's significance because they fail to consider both the milieu in which Jasper delivers his sermon and its connection to the exodus narrative. When Moses and the Israelites witnessed how God destroyed the mightiest army in the world, they looked back upon the watery battlefield and shouted the text that Hatcher disregarded. When Jasper announced the sermon's text, he relied upon contextual parallels with the capitol of the former confederacy. Richmond's streets and buildings still bore the marks of the Civil War. The city's former Confederate residents remained bitter after its devastating loss to the U.S. Army. During the conflict, both sides, Union and Confederate, claimed oppositional theologies of war. Each believed God was their Divine Advocate. Amid the South's havoc, Jasper spoke through his text to the former Confederacy. Richmondites heard his uncompromising clarity: During the war you claimed God's providence, now claim God's judgment. God is a Man of War. Jasper's message echoed the bellicose strains that became the Union Army's battle call and the leitmotif of their cause as they marched through the South.

Mine eyes have seen the glory of the coming of the Lord:
He is trampling out the vintage where the grapes of wrath are stored;
He hath loosed the fateful lightning of His terrible swift sword:
His truth is marching on.

It was not a message that Jasper needed to press hard. The stench of defeat and despair still hung over the South, so Jasper simply invoked it to his advantage. By announcing it as the sermon's text, Jasper delivered his condemnation using biblical authority. Perhaps Hatcher missed the significance because Jasper never intended for him or others like him to understand. In an increasingly hostile South, Jasper delivered his message from behind the mask.

Jasper began his presentation with a grand entrance. Dressed in a cape and beaver's hat, he brought together visual spectacle and linguistic performance to create the minstrel's persona, "Low me ter say," Hatcher reports, "He spoke with an outward composure which revealed an inward but mastered swell of emotion."[79] Jasper's entrance is overdone and out of place for a sermon. It is the minstrel's misjudgment of propriety. But Jasper's mis-steps and his exaggeration make the minstrel's performance more convincing. He continues, "when I wuz a young man and a slave, I knowed nuthin' wuth talkin' 'bout cosarnin' books. Dey wuz sealed mysteries ter me, but I tell yer I longed ter break de seal. I thusted fer de bread uv learnin.'"[80] The sound of Jasper's language lulls; it invites his interlocutors to become comfortable with the familiar image of the buffoon or darky. As they do, Jasper reinforces the image by recalling his experience with learning to read. He opens with testimonial language and appeals to two iconic images for the old South, namely, the ideal slave and the rebellious slave, respectively. First, he turns to the ideal slave. "When I seen books I ached ter git in ter um, fur I knowed dat dey had de stuff fer me, an' I wanted ter taste dere contents, but most of de time dey wuz bar'd aginst me."[81] For the ideal slave, this was the proper posture—desire for knowledge, but not fulfillment. Indeed, any attempt to satisfy such a desire was illegal and punishable by death. Under the slave regime, reading was the property of whites.

Initially, Jasper leaves the image of the ideal slave unchallenged even as he stands before the congregation as an example of black literacy. But, in trickster-like fashion, he resolves the ideal slave's unfulfilled hope by introducing a counter image, namely, the rebellious slave. But, before he does, Jasper invokes divine authority, a legitimating source recognized by both his congregation and the interlocutors. With the phrase, "By the mursy of the Lord," Jasper claims the power of God as motivation for the rebellious act.[82] Only then does he relate the remainder of the story.

> By the mursy of the Lord, a thing happened. I got er room-feller—he wuz a slave, too, an' he had learn'd ter read. In de dead uv de night he giv me lessons outen de New York Spellin' book. It wuz hard pullin', I tell yer; harder on him, fur he know'd jes' a leetle, an' it made him sweat ter try ter beat sumthin' inter my hard haid. It wuz wuss wid me. Up de hill ev'ry step, but when I got de light uv de less'n into my noodle I farly shouted, but I kno'd I wuz not a scholar. [83]

Jasper plays on "mercy's" polyvalence to glorify defiance under the slave regime. God's mercy emboldens his act of resistance, legitimates his actions by trumping human law in the Slave Codes, and it was only by God's mercy that Jasper did not pay the penalty for his act of resistance. From the pulpit, the pastor assures the congregation that God affirms their pursuit of knowledge and resistance to repression.

In the last sentence, Jasper qualifies two concepts, knowledge and resistance. Upon acquiring the ability to read, Jasper is so excited that he "fairly shouted," but assures the visitors that scholarship remains beyond his capacity. From the scholars' viewpoint, Jasper's statement recognizes the hierarchical distance between their status as "learned men" and Jasper's as an unlettered Negro preacher. The congregation, however, hears their pastor's claim as another device of testimonial rhetoric. Jasper's polyvalent language calls them into an insider conversation with their pastor, where they interpret another meaning. From the congregation's viewpoint, Jasper's testimony foreswore an identity that has been hostile to black life and whose discourses are predicated upon black inferiority. By articulating his avowal as "knowledge," as in "I *know* I was," Jasper signifies upon similar common ecclesial utterances such as "I know I've been changed," "I know the Lord has . . . ," and "I know what the Lord has done for . . ." Each affirms some *desirable* knowledge or an experience that a member relates within a community of believers. Taken together with the negative syntax in Jasper's statement, "I know I was *not*," claims knowledge of an identity *not* to be desired. In other words, stated positively, to be a scholar in that context is *undesirable*. By *knowing* how to learn for himself and by his choice *not* to "know" the political identity of the scholar, Jasper conveys his clear commitment to learning but his suspicion of ways that institutions structure and deploy knowledge.

Suspicion alone is not enough to be Good News. The Gospel in the Black Church tradition affirms something positive. So Jasper connects knowledge with his faith experience.

> 'Bout seben months after my gittin' ter readin', Gord cunverted my soul, an' I reckin 'bout de fust an' main thing dat I begged de Lord ter give me wuz de power ter und'stan' His Word. I ain' braggin', an' I hates self-praise, but I boun' ter speak de thankful word. I b'lieves in mer heart dat mer pra'r ter und'stand de Scripshur wuz heard. Sence dat time I ain't keerd 'bout nuthin' 'cept ter study an' preach de Word uv God. Not, my bruthrin, dat I'z de fool ter think I knows it all. Oh, mer Father, no! Fur frum it. I don' hardly und'stan myse'f, nor ha'f uv de things roun' me, an' dar is milyuns uv things in de Bible too deep fur Jasper, an' sum uv 'em too deep fur ev'rybody.[84]

Only after learning to read does Jasper evolve in the practice of his faith. In a time of low black literacy rates in the South, Jasper connects authentic Christian practice to a traditional tenet of uplift, namely, educational attainment. He commends this as a model of faithful practice to his congregation. Beyond knowledge, Jasper points his congregation to seek something more from the Bible, namely, understanding. With understanding, Jasper reaches beyond simple facts toward the ability to evaluate knowledge claims. For Jasper, understanding operates as a "meta-knowledge." It requires a critical posture toward particular knowledge claims, their sources, and their facts.

In this distinction, Jasper underscores the battle lines for the "man of war" performance later in the sermon. Foundations for knowledge, rather than the validity of any particular knowledge claims, guide his sermon. Far from some parochial assertion of facticity, Jasper petitions for understanding and claims the Bible for its iconic power. By appealing to its contents as the object of his understanding and the foundation for its knowledge, Jasper weakens his interlocutors' claims by subjecting their sources to his own. Finally, Jasper assures his congregation of the same truth that his sermon dramatized—namely God—the source of their power far exceeds that of the scholars in their midst, because as Jasper reminds them, some things about God are "too deep fur ev'rybody"—including these scholars.[85]

After shifting his topic to foundations, Jasper turns to the story of Joshua and the Gibeonites in Joshua 9–10 as a correlating account of God's sovereignty. The scholars expect Jasper to deliver biblical "proofs" of the sun's movement, but Jasper attends instead to the subject of his Scripture, namely, the authority of God who delivered the Hebrews. Focus on the sun's movement as an abstract fact recedes, and Jasper emphasizes the sun's movement only insofar as it demonstrates God's sovereignty as the Man of War, and the champion whom Israel encountered at the Red Sea. Again, Jasper invokes a text with historic resonance.

I got ter take yer all dis arternoon on er skershun ter a great bat'l feil'. Mos' folks like ter see fights—some is mighty fon' er gittin' inter fights, an' some is mighty quick ter run down de back alley when dar is a bat'l goin' on, fer de right. Dis time I'll 'scort yer ter a scene whar you shall witness a curus bat'l. It tuk place soon arter Isrel got in de Promus Lan'. Yer 'member de people uv Gibyun mak frens wid Gord's people when dey fust entered Canum an' dey wuz monsus smart ter do it. But, jes' de same, it got 'em in ter an orful fuss. De cities roun' 'bout dar flar'd up at dat, an' dey all jined dere forces and say dey gwine ter mop de Gibyun people orf uv de groun', an' dey bunched all dar armies tergedder an' went up fer ter do it. Wen dey kum up so bol' an' brave de Giby'nites wuz skeer'd out'n dere senses, an' dey saunt word ter Joshwer dat dey wuz in troubl' an' he mus' run up dar an' git 'em out. Joshwer had de heart uv a lion an' he wuz up dar d'reckly. Dey had an orful fight, sharp an' bitter, but yer might know dat Ginr'l Joshwer wuz not up dar ter git whip't. He prayed an' he fought, an' de hours got erway too peart fer him, an' so he ask'd de Lord ter issure a speshul ordur dat de sun hol' up erwhile an' dat de moon furnish plenty uv moonshine down on de lowes' part uv de fightin' groun's. As a fac', Joshwer wuz so drunk wid de bat'l, so thursty fer de blood uv de en'mies uv de Lord, an' so wild wid de vict'ry dat he tell de sun ter stan' still tel he cud finish his job.[86]

As in the exodus text, God champions the Israelites whom God liberated from slavery. The Joshua story presents God as so invested in
the war that God prolongs the day so that Joshua could completely an-
nihilate the Gibeonites, who were, as Joshua saw them, enemies of the
Lord. For Richmondites, the account resonated with fresh memories
of the Evacuation fire of 1865. It was the final humiliating episode of
the Civil War. After the U.S. Army successfully laid siege to St. Peters-
burg and Richmond, they forced the Confederates into retreat. Jefferson
Davis, president of the Confederacy, along with his cabinet, abandoned
Richmond on the last functioning rail line, the Richmond and Danville.
Retreating Confederate soldiers carried out orders to set fire to warehouses, the armory, and any bridges that the Union Army might use.
The fire spread uncontrollably far beyond its intended sites. Black soldiers filled the streets as they liberated the city. When African Americans held in slavery joined with the army, Richmondites were shocked
that their "slaves" could be so disloyal.[87] Only when the mayor and other
citizens surrendered the city did the U.S. Army extinguish the inferno.
Just as God held the sun until Joshua could complete his bloodletting
and completely pacify the Gibeonites, the Union troops allowed the fire
to rage until the city succumbed and the United States had its victory. As
the Union saw it, they also were fighting enemies of God, just as Joshua
had done.

When Jasper addresses the sun's movement, the matter is not Jasper's
primary concern. Jasper focuses on the sun only playfully, to show that
whatever motility it possessed was a function of God's authority. He
begins with a series of rhetorical questions to dramatize a humorous
dialogue between the sun and Joshua. "Wat did de sun do? Did he glar
down in fi'ry wrath an' say, 'What you talkin' 'bout my stoppin' for, Joshwer; I ain't navur startid yit."[88] The sun halts and proceeds as directed by
God's appetite for war. Then Jasper momentarily emerges from behind
the mask and anthropomorphizes the sun one last time, "Bin here all
de time, an' it wud smash up ev'rything if I wuz ter start'? Naw, he ain'
say dat."[89] With that statement, Jasper lingers between the two personas
long enough to show that he is aware of some of the general claims of
astrophysics. Doing so keeps the scholars off balance. He has read more
than he lets on. Immediately, Jasper changes his language. He no longer
personifies the sun. Instead, he invokes the source of authority—both

his and the sun's. "But wat de Bible say? Dat's wat I ax ter know. It say dat it wuz at de voice uv Joshwer dat it stopped. I don' say it stopt; tain't fer Jasper ter say dat, but de Bible, de Book uv Gord, say so."[90] Although Jasper begins his story by personifying the sun, he concludes it by grounding his claim in the "Book of God," and so reinforces his emphasis on foundations rather than knowledge claims.

Again Jasper declares his allegiance to the Bible. This time he calls it, curiously, "the Book of God." His language leaves an absence that begs a response from the scholars, "If God is the authority behind Jasper's Book, then what is the authority of their books?" With the language, the "Book of God," Jasper leverages biblical authority directly against his interlocutors and forces them into an untenable position. On the one hand, they can reject Jasper, but if they do so, they reject God's authority and lose the argument by abandoning any commonly recognizable expression of Christianity for that community. If they cannot reconcile their faith and their position on the sun, then Jasper has shown publicly that their studies have formed away from truth. On the other hand, the second option is worse; if they affirm Jasper, then they admit to an unlettered black preacher's intellectual superiority.

Finally, Jasper reminds the congregation of his point, "I toll yer dat I wud prove dis an' I's dun it, an' I derfies ennybody to say dat my p'int ain't made. I tol' yer in de fust part uv dis discose dat de Lord Gord is a man uv war. I 'spec by now yer begin ter see it is so. Doan't yer admit it?"[91] Contrary to Hatcher's interpretation, Jasper concludes the example by reasserting his subject, namely, the sovereignty of the God whom the Israelites named the Man of War when they celebrated on the far side of the Red Sea, not a moving sun.

Jasper turns from celebrating the Man of War to performing as the Man of War. He executes the confrontation that Walker's *Appeal* could only imagine.

> But I ain't dun wid yer yit. As de song says, dere's mo' ter foller. I envite yer ter heer de fust vers in de sev'nth chaptur uv de book uv Reverlashuns. What do John, und'r de pow'r uv de Spirit, say? He say he saw fo' anguls standin' on de fo' corners uv de earth, holdin' de fo' win's uv de earth, an' so fo'th. 'Low me ter ax ef de earth is roun', whar do it keep its corners? [92]

The learned men sitting among the congregation are silent. They offer no response to Jasper's question. By now, they know that Jasper has embarrassed them for sport. Perhaps emboldened by their silence, Jasper changes his tone to showcase for his congregation. White power totalized their lives, but Jasper demonstrated that such power is not absolute. Again, Jasper throws down the gauntlet:

> Er flat, squar thing has corners, but tell me where is de cornur uv er appul, ur a marbul, ur a cannun ball, ur a silver dollar. Ef dar is enny one uv dem furloserfurs whar's been takin' so many cracks at my ole haid 'bout here, he is korjully envited ter step for'd an' squar up dis vexin' bizniss. I here tell you dat yer karn't squar a circul, but it looks lak dese great scolurs dun learn how ter circul de squar. Ef dey kin do it, let 'em step ter de front an' do de trick.[93]

He taunts and challenges them. Jasper even plays with the language by inviting them to "square up" the problem by demonstrating earth's spherical geometry.

The unanswered challenge completes Jasper's masterfully orchestrated scene. His doubly signifying rhetoric invites the interlocutors to laugh at the minstrel's performance, while the congregation laughed at the interlocutors. In fact, the interlocutors have little choice but to interpret Jasper's performance as *mis*-speaking so that they *may* laugh at him. The alternative, to take Jasper's critique seriously, admits that a Negro preacher had publicly shamed them. Without warning, Jasper shifts the conversation from the momentary levity with a sobering pronouncement, "But, mer brutherin, in my po' judmint, dey karn't do it; tain't in 'em ter do it." For Jasper, the scholars lack the capacity and the constitution to meet his challenge. They may possess the intellectual ability, but Jasper refers to moral capacity. Rather, it is because, "Dey is on der wrong side of de Bible; dat's on de outside of de Bible, an' dar's whar de trubbul comes in wid 'em." With that claim, Jasper shifts the field of discourse from scientific reasoning to theological reasoning and the subject matter from their intellectual positions to their moral positions. He declares whatever knowledge they may possess is illegitimate because its sources are untrustworthy, and by extension, and so are the scholars. Jasper claims poignantly, "they are outside of the breeze works of the truth." For Jasper, truth refers to the scaffolding that structures their knowledge. So their knowledge can never lead to truth even if their facts are correct. For, as Jasper claims, "ez long ez dey stay dar de light uv de Lord will not shine on der path."[94]

As the drama in the congregation builds, Jasper moves the sermon from scientific fact (*Wissenschaft*) to truth and trivializes their topic of inquiry, "I ain't keer'n so much 'bout de sun, tho' it's mighty kunveenyunt ter hav it, but my trus' is in de Word uv de Lord. Long ez my feet is flat on de solid rock, no man kin move me. I'se gittin' my order f'um de Gord of my salvashun."[95] The sun is a convenience. In Jasper's cosmology, the interlocutors and, by extension, the objects of the interlocutors' inquiry reveal only mediate truths. As such, he compares the sun's temporality to God's ultimate authority.

> What I keer about de sun? De day comes on wen de sun will·be called frum his race-trac, and his light squincked out foruvur; de moon shall turn ter blood, and this yearth be konsoomed wid fier. Let um go; dat wont skeer me nor trubble Gord's erlect'd peopul, for de word uv de Lord shell aindu furivur, an' on dat Solid Rock we stan' an' shall not be muved. Is I got yer satisfied yit? Has I prooven my p'int? Oh, ye whose hearts is full uv unberlief! Is yer still hol'in' out? I reckun de reason yer say de sun don' move is 'cause yer are so hard ter move yerse'f.[96]

In the last sentence Jasper distinguishes between scientific knowledge and theological knowledge. It recalls St. Anselm's famous dictum, *fides quaerens intellectum* (faith seeking understanding). The scholar pursues scientific fact dispassionately with no personal investment.[97] However, theological claims demand one's investment. In other words, to claim theological knowledge *is* to be moved.

Undeterred by the scholar's resistance, Jasper continues with another mimetic performance.

> Truf is mighty; it kin break de heart uv stone, an' I mus' fire anudder arrur uv truf out'n de quivur uv de Lord. If yer haz er copy uv God's Word 'bout yer pussun, please tu'n ter dat miner profit, Malerki, wat writ der las' book in der ole Bible, an' look at chaptur de fust, vurs 'leben; what do it say? I bet'r read it, fur I got er noshun yer critics doan't kerry enny Bible in thar

pockits ev'ry day in de week. Here is wat it says: 'Fur from de risin' uv de sun evun unter de goin' doun uv de same My name shall be great 'mong de Gentiles . . . My name shall be great 'mong de heathun, sez de Lord uv hosts.' How do dat suit yer? It look lak dat ort ter fix it. Dis time it is de Lord uv hosts Hisse'f dat is doin' de talkin'.[98]

Where the "high-collared scholar" rendered Jasper silent in academic discourse, Jasper now orchestrates an amazing reversal to entertain his congregation. Born into slavery, legally barred from learning to read, Jasper now reads to publicly teach (as in formal instruction and teaching them a lesson) the white scholars as *they* sit in silence. The story forms an *inclusio* to Jasper's opening account of his struggle for literacy. In the sermon, Jasper comes full circle from a student gleaning bits of literacy from the *New York Spelling Book* at the beginning of the sermon, to instructing scholars in his midst.

In his penultimate act, Jasper moves from instructor to guardian of the faith. Again, Jasper returns to the question of knowledge. This time he focuses on the singularly important signifier of humanity in Western culture, namely, writing.

But I hears yer back dar. Wat yer wisprin' 'bout? I know; yer say yer sont me sum papurs an' I nevur answer dem. Ha, ha, ha! I got 'em. De differ-kulty 'bout dem papurs yer sont me is dat dey did not answer me. Dey nevur menshun de Bible one time. Yer think so much uv yoursef's an' so little uv de Lord Gord an' thinks wat yer say is so smart dat yer karn't even speak uv de Word uv de Lord. When yer ax me ter stop believin' in de Lord's Word an' ter pin my faith ter yo words, I ain't er gwine ter do it. I take my stan' by de Bible an' res' my case on wat it says. I take wat de Lord says 'bout my sins, 'bout my Saviour, 'bout life, 'bout death, 'bout de wurl' ter come, an' I take wat de Lord say 'bout de sun an' moon, an' I cares little wat de haters of mer Gord chooses ter say. Think dat I will fursake de Bible? It is my only Book, my hope, de arsnel uv my soul's surplies, an' I wants nuthin' else.[99]

Writing, the corollary to reading, held awesome power for African Americans. Documents that they could not decipher determined their lives. From their arrival in North America, they encountered notices of auction that put them on display, bills of sale that destroyed their families, court orders that alienated their real property, and death sentences that required of them their lives. African Americans living in the nineteenth-century South knew literacy was a marker that made white superiority real in the public sphere. To write was to master an awesome power. For Jasper, the academic treatises submitted by the scholars represented similar power over black life. The arguments contained in them intended to subject the knowledge claims within his community to the authority of the white academy. Jasper responds to them defiantly, calling them "some papers." His language devalues them and the sources of their content. By doing so, Jasper signifies that the written word, while an agent of power, is not always a carrier of truth. Although Jasper grounds his own faith in the written word, he claims understanding's meta-knowledge to discern the value of the written word for himself. Then, using warlike images such as an "arrow of truth," "quiver of the Lord," and the Bible as "the arsenal of my soul's supplies," Jasper frames his conflict with white scholars as a battle between two alternatives. The congregation can choose to place their faith in these men and their claims about black life. However, doing so conceded a second-class position in the political economy. Western discursive formations including history already judged them to be fit for captivity, enslavement, lynching, and Jim Crow. As if he had not made the choice clear enough, Jasper swells with disdain and announces the visitors as "haters of my God," no less than enemies of the Man of War.

In a final performance, Jasper reveals that the minstrel's mask is completely his artifice.

But I got ernudder wurd fur yer yit. I done wuk ovur dem papurs dat yer sont me widout date an' widout yer name. Yer deals in figgurs an' thinks yer are biggur dan de arkanjuls. Lemme see wat yer dun say. Yer set yerse'f up ter tell me how fur it is frum here ter de sun. Yer think yer got it down ter er nice p'int. Yer say it is 3,339,002 miles frum de earth ter de sun. Dat's wat yer say. Nudder one say dat de distuns is 12,000,000; nudder got it ter 27,000,000. I hers dat de great Isuk Nutun wuk't it up ter 28,000,000, an' later on de furloserfurs gin ernudder rippin' raze to 50,000,000. De las' one gits it bigger' dan all de yuthers, up to 90,000,000. Doan't enny uv 'em ergree edzakly an' so dey runs a guess game, an' de las' guess is always de bigges'. Now, wen dese guessers kin hav a kunvenshun in Richmun' an' all ergree 'pun de same thing, I'd be glad ter hear frum yer ag'in, an' I duz hope dat by dat time yer won't be ershamed uv yer name.[100]

From memory, he calls forth their calculations, articulates them precisely, and (re)presents them as guesses. He displays the uncertainty of their knowledge claims for the entire congregation. Race, speech, dress, and institutional identity can no longer mask it. Jasper no longer *calls* the visitors philosophers. Rather, Jasper *calls them out* as "guessers." With humor that both the visitors and congregation understand, Jasper continues by caricaturing their positions and adding his own outlandish proposal to their speculations:

Heeps uv railroads hes bin built sense I saw de fust one wen I wuz fifteen yeers ole, but I ain't hear tell uv er railroad built yit ter de sun. I doan' see why ef dey kin meshur de distuns ter de sun, dey might not git up er railroad er a telurgraf an' enabul us ter fin' sumthin' else 'bout it den merely how fur orf de sun is. Dey tell me dat a kannun ball cu'd mek de trep ter de sun in twelve years. Why doan' dey send it? It might be rig'd up wid quarturs fur a few furloserfers on de inside an' fixed up fur er kumfurterble ride. Dey wud need twelve years' rashuns an' a heep uv changes uv ramint—mighty thick clo'es wen dey start and mighty thin uns wen dey git dar.

Even in his humor, Jasper includes just enough of his knowledge of the sun's nature to play the trickster. Again, Jasper shifts abruptly from his humor to raise a serious matter: "Oh, mer bruthrin, dese things mek yer laugh, an' I doan' blem yer fer laughin', 'cept it's always sad ter laugh at der follies uv fools."[101] He shifts his language one final time—no longer guessers, but fools. Jasper delivers the final blow and the visitors who entered as respected scholars slink away as pitiful buffoons.

His public confrontation finished, Jasper returns to his primary concern, his "own brutherin." He addresses his congregation much like a conquering hero returning home after victory in battle. In the relationship between pastor and congregation, the scholars were inconsequential, so Jasper never bothered to respond to their questions directly. Throughout, Jasper's focus remained on his own congregation, for, as he affirms, "Dey is de people fer whose souls I got ter watch—fur dem I got ter stan' an' report at de last—dey is my sheep an' I'se der shepherd, an' my soul is knit ter dem forever."

Finally, in an incredible feat of faith, Jasper conjures his own vision of astronomical truth grounded in biblical authority. He challenges his people to see beyond their world.

> Our eyes goes far beyon' de smaller stars; our home is clean outer sight uv dem twinklin' orbs de chariot dat will cum ter take us to our Father's mansion will sweep out by dem flickerin' lights an' never halt till it brings us in clar view uv de throne uv de Lamb.

The laws, institutions, and racial hierarchies that repress black life are "the smaller stars." In 1878, such a request certainly stretched the limits of African American hope. But Jasper places his hope in context, "Doan't hitch yer hopes to no sun nor stars; yer home is got Jesus fer its light, an' yer hopes mus' trabel up dat way."[102]

He called the congregation to imagine a reality that was beyond their horizon. Jasper's statement is both damning and optimistic. It damned the world in which he lived and recalls the desperate sentiments that the 1874 Colored Convention expressed. It claimed no rest or fulfillment for his people in the post-Reconstruction era. To be sure, Jasper anticipated what historians would later call the "nadir of race relations," namely the period 1877–1920, which was marked by mass lynching and unprecedented violence toward blacks. To hitch one's hopes to the sun or the stars, the heavenly bodies that are readily apparent to the human eye was, for Jasper, not to imagine enough. There had to be more than death in the wilderness after slavery. Jasper did not want his congregation to accept the social and power arrangements that presently structured their world. Ultimately, Jasper only hoped that his people would seek out and evaluate for themselves sources of knowledge that affirmed black life in the wilderness and that would lead them to thrive in the Promised Land.

Within a few years, a cadre of intellectuals would come together in Harlem, New York. By recovering the voice of the New Negro, they took up Jasper's program. One of its members, Zora Neale Hurston, returned to the exodus story. In her novel, *Moses, Man of the Mountain*, she responded to Jasper's challenge. Ironically, her response was one that Jasper could not have expected and one he would never accept: Black people's deliverance lies neither in some transcendent Man of War nor within a single mosaic hero, but within the power, character, and humanity of black people themselves.

Exodus and Hurston: Toward a Humanist Critique of Black Religion in the Harlem Renaissance

I stepped in the water, and the water was cold
Chilled my body, but not my soul.
I looked at my hands, and they looked new
I looked at my feet, and they did too!
But Moses' hands grew weary; so they took a stone and put
it under him, and he sat on it. Aaron and Hur held up his
hands, one on one side and the other on the other side; so
his hands were steady until the sun set.
—Exodus 17:18

The Hudson River separates New York City from the U.S. mainland. In the early decades of the new century when African Americans crossed over, they found a land of milk and honey. Harlem! That four-square-mile swath of sweet urban heaven—from 110th Street to 129th Street—became a veritable Promised Land and the center of the New Negro Movement. Harlem nurtured a renaissance of black expressive culture in literature, visual art, music, intellectual activity, political activism, and even religion.

In the short few years that ended with the stock market crash of 1929, the Harlem Renaissance articulated a black aesthetic form. Its poets rendered the Negro soul human—capable of the full symphony of emotional expression, unlike the monotone trope of the happy-go-lucky darky who lived in popular stereotype. Its novelists narrated the rich and complex cultures of the Black world, not merely a stage whose cast was limited to minstrels and mammies, sapphires, and Uncle Toms. Its critics challenged the New Negro to speak for himself.[1] And he did—in literature, in song, and in the visual arts. But the road from Reconstruction in the South to a renaissance in Harlem began decades earlier.

War, Work, and Migration: Building a Critical Mass for the Renaissance

Both the Great Migration and World War I brought black populations westward and northward and contributed to the growing black communities that gave birth to the New Negro Movement. As early as the 1870s, just five years after the Civil War, Benjamin "Pap" Singleton led more than 7,000 African Americans from Kentucky and Tennessee into Kansas. Other waves followed. By 1910, blacks had established more than two dozen settlements in Oklahoma.[2] In successively increasing waves, black families escaped the South's racialized violence and deprivation. They abandoned its slower agricultural economies and joined the robust job markets of the industrial North: 170,000 from 1900–1910; 454,000 from 1910–1920; 749,000 from 1920–1930.[3]

World War I accelerated black migration. At first, the War Department enlisted primarily white men rather than African American men and thereby drained the pool of white, male laborers. Left to search for new workers, northern industrial barons sought black men who were eager to escape the racial brutality of the South and were hungry for the opportunity to finally earn better wages. The numbers of the black working class in northern cities steadily rose and finally produced a ready clientele for black professionals such as doctors, lawyers, teachers, accountants, and dentists. Both working and professional classes together formed the basis of the New Negro Movement.

New Negro, New Consciousness: Reconstruction to Renaissance

Beginning with the broken promises of 1877, African Americans in the post-Reconstruction period searched for the most advantageous political posture for a people no longer protected by federal troops. Two responses, economic achievement and civil inclusion as modes of racial uplift, predominated the black public sphere. Two towering figures, Booker T. Washington (1856–1915) and W. E. B. Du Bois (1868–1963), represented the positions, respectively. Du Bois's work gave the New Negro Movement political impetus and intellectual grounding for their grand project. However, in Washington the Harlem Renaissance found its anti-hero. He, and what the Movement considered his conciliatory politics, quickly became synonymous with an iconic "old" Negro still constrained by the previous era.

Renaissance politics notwithstanding, Washington dominated the U.S. political landscape during the late nineteenth and early twentieth centuries as its most prominent African American. He was a staunch advocate of industrial education and commercial endeavor for African Americans, but encouraged them to avoid direct confrontation with white power in response to repression. Naturally, his position gained support from conservative and liberal whites alike, particularly Southern whites.

Washington did not construct his politics simply to accommodate southern whites. He owed his political stance as much to his early experiences as to its obvious strategic advantages with Southern whites. Born into slavery and educated in the South, Washington had first-hand exposure to the slave regime's brutality and the violence that Southern whites could inflict upon blacks with impunity. Eleven years old at the end of the Civil War, Washington lived through slavery and Reconstruction. By the time he was twenty-one, he witnessed the heartbreaking compromise of 1877 and saw black civil advances dismantled in a political bargain. He knew the social, economic, and psychic devastation wrought in black communities throughout the South. For Washington such a context framed by southern white power and black vulnerability led him to defer publicly on social and civic advancement for African Americans. He wore his public posture as a mask. Privately, Washington funded some of the earliest civil rights litigation. Moreover, Tuskegee, the institution of higher education that he founded, was the most advanced in the state at the time. He hoped that blacks would first master agriculture, commerce, and industry before agitating for civil inclusion. By commanding these fundamentals of the South's economy, Washington believed that African Americans could build an economic base with which to sustain advances in the civic and social arenas. Laws could be easily changed, but he hoped that if African Americans made themselves indispensable to the nation's growing economy, their economic gains could not be erased as had been the case with the political gains under Reconstruction.

By the turn of the century, Washington's influence reached its apogee. It was said that he controlled the channels of funding and political access for all of black America. So prominent was his stature that President Theodore Roosevelt invited him to the White House as his adviser on all "Negro issues." To escape Washington's political reach, even Du Bois took his opposition movement to Canada for its formational meeting. For the most part, black churches and their rank-and-file congregants supported Washington's conciliatory stance over Du Bois's push for immediate civil inclusion.

Despite Washington's heroic efforts toward black fulfillment, the repressive demise of black life and culture in the South after Reconstruction lasted another generation.[4] In the face of Jim Crow in the South, the effects of *Plessy*, and later the deleterious ravages of the Red Scare purges of the 1940s, African American life experienced a cultural assault unlike any since the slave system. Nonetheless, Washington's brand of conservative uplift did not disappear. It resurfaced in another favorite nemesis of Du Bois and the New Negro Movement when the Honorable Marcus Mosiah Garvey resurrected Ethiopianism and adapted it to the new era. Garvey took the heart of Washington's program, commercial and industrial achievement, and integrated it with flamboyant shows of militarism, a philosophy of self-reliance, and a marvelous rhetoric of racial esteem to build his United Negro Improvement Association (UNIA). In the UNIA, Garvey envisioned a pan-African corporation that might free black people from economic exploitation across the globe.

Garvey's form of Ethiopianism galled members of the Harlem Renaissance. Garvey pointed black people to Africa as both a homeland and the geopolitical source of a culture that had been dirempted from them. As had others before him, Garvey framed his Ethiopianism with exodus and the Hebrew Bible's other foundation narrative, Exile—that is estrangement—which always entails Return. Exodus and exile bracket, in dialectical fashion, biblical Israel's identity. Both distinguish biblical Israel from the foreign "other," whether within their midst (such as those who worshipped the golden calf or those Israelites who polluted the Promised Land by following the practices of its inhabitants) or from another nation (such as the Egyptians or the Babylonians). When the book of Exodus claims that "all Israel" entered Egypt (Gen. 47:27) with Jacob and that after 430 years, "all Israel" left Egypt (Ex. 12:40), it deploys historical markers as requisites for claiming identity within the community. Only the descendants of those who meet the criteria can claim membership in "true Israel." The narrative further circumscribes Israel from any cultural residual by removing all who left Egypt, save Joshua and Caleb. So after crossing the Red Sea and the Jordan River, "true Israel" is the group who have been purged of any "foreign" element before entering a fallow Canaan. Exile, the second foundation story, begins where the exodus narrative ends. After hundreds of years, Israel had polluted the Promised Land with abominations (Numbers 26:27; Deut. 28:15–18). The Babylonians send "all Israel" into exile so that the guilty generation might be purged and a pure remnant may return. This remnant becomes the identity of "true" Israel.

Both narratives raised complex problems for African Americans. First, by claiming an identity as diaspora, African Americans emphasized their perpetual alienation both in the United States despite their foundational intellectual, civil, and economic contributions that shaped the republic, and from land of their African origins. Second, imagining Africa as a fallow homeland replicated the ideology that guided the Puritans to pacify indigenous peoples in North America. Ironically, such an ideology constructed African Americans as agents of Euro-American colonialism whose activity was turned toward the Continent. In this regard, exodus and exile positioned African Americans in an untenable dialectic and brought into crises prevailing interpretations of the exodus narrative. Nonetheless, Garvey's philosophy of self-reliance and racial esteem held sway even if his exodus paradigm did not. Garvey was a master of public spectacle. His flamboyant displays of militaristic and organizational power inspired black masses. Much to the dismay of his critics in the New Negro Movement, Garvey's work captured the imaginations of black people across the Atlantic world and even encouraged the ideologies that supported the New Negro project.

Meanwhile, Du Bois continued to pursue a different philosophy of black uplift. In the first years of the twentieth century, Washington's prominence diminished in many quarters of the African American community in part due to the industrial revolution and an infectious rising consciousness catalyzed by black soldiers returning from war, among other reasons, while Du Bois's competing philosophy steadily gained acceptance. In 1905 Du Bois, along with William Monroe Trotter, formed the Niagara Movement to emphasize the need for liberal arts education and civil and political attainment before pursuing industrial education and commercial endeavor. In their first position paper, "We Refuse to Allow the Impression to Remain that the Negro-American Assents to Inferiority," they reasserted claims to civil rights and decried what they saw as Washington's accommodationism. By 1909 the Niagara Movement developed into the National Association for the Advancement of Colored People (NAACP) and set the dominant political and social agenda and culture for African Americans through much of the twentieth century.

Ideological Convergences: Black Pride and Patriotism

Du Bois's urgent political posture found an affinity with a new figure in the public landscape—black soldiers returning from war. These men became visible shortly after the United States entered the growing conflict, when the War Department realized that it needed as many able-bodied men as it could muster—even black men. While overseas, black soldiers experienced increased civil freedom while they served as a part of the United States's fighting force in Europe. After the war, black soldiers came home, but with a new, confident spirit. In other words, black men returned as men, "not as boys." They were legally armed and would be subordinate to no one. The society that had deployed every legal mechanism to prevent them from bearing arms at home to protect themselves from the ravages of racism, had given them the authority to do so abroad. They were not about to relinquish such a right. Returning home did not mean returning to business as usual.

The South anticipated the problem that a black, armed, patriotic class of men might pose to their way of life. While black soldiers risked their lives overseas to protect freedom at home, groups of whites in southern states used that same freedom to prepare for their return. The Ku Klux Klan, which destroyed much of the social progress that the nation had made under Reconstruction, reactivated by 1915.[5] It grew slowly until the end of the war, when the South saw an increased number of black soldiers who no longer paid deference to old conventions. Within a year after the end of the war the Klan grew from a few thousand to in excess of 100,000 hooded white knights. It declared African Americans, Japanese Americans and other people of Asian descent, Mexican Americans, Jewish persons, and Roman Catholics, and all foreign-born persons, enemies of the state. Less than a year after war ended, the Klan made more than 200 public appearances in twenty-seven states. Beyond the South, cells of the organization flourished in several New England states, and in New York, Indiana, Illinois, Michigan, along with other northern and midwestern states. In many communities, candidates for public office faced defeat if they did not hold membership in the Klan.[6] In Texas, the Klan targeted both Mexican Americans and African Americans. They alienated tenure to thousands of acres of land held by Mexican American farmers and brought about a new black enslavement by forcing African Americans to work for wages that held them in debt.[7] In the West, Klan violence targeted Japanese American and Chinese American populations.[8] More than seventy African Americans were lynched during the first year after World War I. The same year at least ten black soldiers were lynched while still wearing their U.S service uniforms.[9] That summer, Longview, Texas witnessed a race riot like the nation had never seen.[10] The next summer saw the same scale of violence repeated in Chicago, Knoxville, Omaha, and Elaine, Arkansas. [11]

Despite the resurgence of racial violence throughout the country, New York City remained a beacon of hope. It was both the place from which Du Bois spoke to all of African America as editor of the NAACP's *Crisis*, then the largest black newspaper, and also the first port of return for most black troops. As they came home, first to Harlem, its stature as the shining city on a hill that radiated hope, freedom, and opportunity only increased. On February 17, 1919, Harlem celebrated the return of the 15th Infantry regiment with a heroes' parade. They had fought valiantly with the 369th regiment and had all been decorated.[12] Approximately one million people felt the sheer representational force of the spectacle of hundreds of armed and decorated black men in uniform with heads held high and backs straight as they marched in lock-step down Fifth Avenue from lower Manhattan to Harlem.[13] The scene of celebratory cheers (represented in newspapers and photographs across the nation was unheard of and sparked a "new militancy" around the country. When the 367th marched through Chicago, the city's businesses suspended activity to welcome them as they paraded through the Loop and into the Southside. At many junctures, the streets were so thick with spectators that troops could not maintain their formation.[14] In May of the same year, Du Bois wrote in the *Crisis*:

We are returning from war! *The Crisis* and tens of thousands of black men were drafted into a great struggle. For bleeding France and what she means and has meant and will mean to us and humanity and against the threat of German race arrogance, we fought gladly and to the last drop of blood; for America and her highest ideals, we fought in far-off hope; for the dominant southern oligarchy entrenched in Washington, we fought in bitter resignation. . . . We return from the slavery of uniform which the world's madness demanded us to don to the freedom of civil garb. We stand again to look America squarely in the face and call a spade a spade. We sing: This country of ours, despite all its better souls have done and dreamed, is yet a shameful land. . . . We return from fighting. We return fighting. . . . It *lynches us* . . . . And lynching is barbarism of a degree of contemptible nastiness unparalleled in human history. Yet for fifty years we have lynched two Negroes a week, and we have kept this up right through the war. It *disfranchises* its own citizens. . . . It *encourages* ignorance. . . . It *steals* from us. . . . It *insults* us. . . . This is the country to which we Soldiers of Democracy return. This is the fatherland for which we fought! But it is our fatherland. It was right for us to fight. The faults of our country are our faults. Under similar circumstances, we would fight again. But by the God of Heaven, we are cowards and jackasses if now that that war is over, we do not marshal every ounce of our brain and brawn to fight a sterner, longer, more unbending battle against the forces of hell in our own land. We return.[15]

Returning black soldiers had saved democracy in Europe. They were intent on doing the same at home by rejecting stereotypes of docile, slavish black men for an ostentatious display of a new black manhood, and renaissance writers were determined to do their part by representing the New Negro in letters.

Harlem Renaissance: Creating Black Authenticity

Alaine Locke and others seized upon the opportunity that the critical mass of black urbanites presented. They were educated, possessed disposable income, and leveraged both to produce aesthetic representations that affirmed black life. For them and for the world, Locke cultivated what he considered the voice of the "New Negro."[16] He sought young, artistic intellectuals whose work could stand in the tradition of James Weldon Johnson, Paul Lawrence Dunbar, and Charles Chesnutt, but could fully represent the *esprit du temps*. Among the most prominent of the group that Locke mentored were Langston Hughes, Countee Cullen, Nella Larse, and Zora Neal Hurston. Together, they recognized the first decades of the century as a critical moment in time when white publishers with vast resources and distribution networks were interested in black culture. In that moment, they self-consciously crafted a new image that they believed represented authentically the Negro as a full and equal participant among the races.

Along with others located across the nation, the small movement of intellectuals based in Harlem fashioned the dust of southern earth into the soul, culture, and voices of the New Negro freed from the manacles of slavery. They breathed into him the breath of life fresh with the strivings of the Great Migration and the cosmopolitan urgency of the urban North. Their creation was no less than a miracle, but their achievement was not without its own complexities. They had set out to recover the authentic New Negro absent the deforming forces of the slave regime.

However, two questions continued to spark robust debates among the collective: First, what was the standard of black aesthetic authenticity? Among even the collective, the quality of authenticity remained unresolved. They knew the forces of production, namely white publishers and patrons, mitigated it. Even if they did not have to produce art to sate white appetites, questions of identity plagued black bodies like no other. From their perspective, at least the German, the Irish, the Japanese, and even the Native American could recall some origin in which to ground an aesthetic ideal in art, music, and letters. That point of shared cultural recognition evaluated a group's progress toward assimilating into life in the New World. However, for African Americans, slavery was too amorphous a point of departure. Worse, to begin with, slavery rendered the logic of their project circular. Black life under the slave regime could not be both an aesthetic ideal and the same cultural formation from which they sought to rescue black cultural authenticity.

The second question, telos, divided the collective further. Alain Locke, Du Bois, and most Harlem Renaissance intellectuals claimed that black expressive culture fulfilled its purpose when it raised racial esteem. For them, authenticity and telos were synonymous. However,

Hughes saw the matter differently. Black cultural expression for its own sake was enough. In a defiant essay he opined:

> We younger Negro artists who create now intend to express our individual dark-skinned selves without fear or shame. If white people are pleased we are glad. If they are not, it doesn't matter. We know we are beautiful. And ugly too. The tom-tom cries and the tom-tom laughs. If colored people are pleased we are glad. If they are not, their displeasure doesn't matter either. We build our temples for tomorrow, strong as we know how, and we stand on top of the mountain, free within ourselves.[17]

Hurston agreed with Hughes and offered her own critique of Locke's program in the spirituals.

> There never has been a presentation of genuine Negro spirituals to any audience anywhere. What is being sung by the concert artists and glee clubs are the works of Negro composers or adaptors based on the spirituals. Under this head come the works of Harry T. Burleigh, Rosamond Johnson, Lawrence Brown, Nathaniel Dett, Hall Johnson, and [John Wesley] Work. All good work and beautiful, but not the spirituals. These neo-spirituals are the outgrowth of the glee clubs. Fisk University boasts perhaps the oldest and certainly the most famous of these. They have spread their interpretation over America and Europe. Hampton and Tuskegee have not been unheard. But with all the glee clubs and soloists, there has not been one genuine spiritual presented.[18]

Together, the two remained staunchly committed to presenting the beauty and nobility of black life as they found it rather than projecting it into a politics of respectability.

Hurston: Pillar of Fire Out of Place in the Renaissance

Hurston's position on the spirituals in particular and black art in general is rooted in her approach to race. Her perspective was so different from her colleagues' that arguably she pursued a program that was distinct from the mainstream renaissance artist. The gulf of difference rendered her a pillar of fire in a community of intellectuals who viewed their art as their race's vehicle to respectability. They celebrated black urbanites as products of the Great Migration refined by cosmopolitan life in the North and distanced their "New Negro" from the rural South because of its connection to the former slave regime. In their art they represented these modes of black life as an aspirational ideal for black folk and as an example that demonstrated for the world the worthiness of black humanity. But Hurston envisioned a blackness that need not be concerned with currying white folks' esteem, because for her, blackness was already as respectable as any other racialized identity.

Perhaps Hurston's training inspired such a position. Hurston had taken a Masters in Anthropology from Columbia University, where she studied under renowned scholar Franz Boas.[19] She honed her skills abroad studying religion in Haiti, and preserving southern folklore in the United States as a field supervisor in the Florida Division of the Works Progress Administration. She mined folk stories and cultural artifacts to understand the post-slavery Negro in the South. Hurston discovered an integral "Negro" presence in the real lives and stories of southern rural African Americans.

Unlike most of her counterparts, Hurston treated race with fluidity. In her celebrated 1928 biographical piece, "How It Feels to be Colored Me," she sounds a strong note of rebellion against the mainstream Harlem Renaissance thinkers. In the essay, Hurston recalls her life in the all-black town of Eatonville, Florida.[20] There, she tested social difference from the security of her parents' front porch. Hurston recalls performing for tourists passing by when she would "speak pieces," "sing," or "dance the parse-mela" in return for pocket change. Her counterparts shunned such presentations because they portrayed black people in familiar stereotypical roles. But Hurston remembered life as a girl with a robust sense of curiosity and adventure who explored difference untainted by any awareness of a world that had already over-determined her with race, gender, and stereotype. What they called stereotypes missed the deep complexity of the lives of the people she knew. She insisted on representing the rural southern life she remembered and its people unfettered by her colleagues' projects or by their politics. Only upon leaving Eatonville did she first feel "colored." She lamented:

But changes came in the family when I was thirteen, and I was sent to school in Jacksonville. I left Eatonville, the town of the oleanders, a Zora. When I disembarked from the riverboat at Jacksonville, she was no more. It seemed that I had suffered a sea change. I was not Zora of Orange County any more, I was now a little colored girl. I found it out in certain ways. In my heart as well as in the mirror, I became a fast brown warranted not to rub nor run.[21]

In the last phrase, "fast brown [as in colorfast] warranted not to rub nor run," Hurston depicts Victor Anderson's understanding of race as a "deep symbol," deeply sedimented in U.S. culture. In other words, Hurston understood the virtual impossibility of deconstructing the broad agreements that made race a reality. She knew Zora was no more.[22]

Racialization's permanence notwithstanding, Hurston did not share her compatriots' perpetual existential angst about it. She claimed that she was not "tragically colored. There is no great sorrow dammed up in my soul, nor lurking behind my eyes. I do not belong to the sobbing school of Negrohood who hold that nature somehow has giving them a lowdown dirty deal and whose feelings are all hurt about it."[23]

Eatonville had taught her differently. She watched her parents and others build an all-black township. Black people of all stripes worked together, governed themselves, and painstakingly built life for the community. She knew her father began as a sharecropper in southern Alabama, but greater ambitions possessed him and he rose to become a three-term mayor.[24] As the daughter of the town's highest elected official, she saw the day-to-day work of developing laws and governing a people after slavery. The knowledge that African Americans could, with collective effort, determine their destiny permanently resided with her.

In fact, Hurston locates herself with a tone of smug satisfaction. "I am colored but I offer nothing in the way of extenuating circumstances except the fact that I am the only Negro in the United States whose grandfather on the mother's side was *not* an Indian chief."[25] Unlike her colleagues, she brandished black life in the rural South unashamedly. It was her life and it shone in her works. She needed no Native American blood to mitigate her blackness because, for her, blackness in all of its modes of being lacked nothing.

Biblical Religion: Searching for a God of Action and a People Who Would Follow

Although Hurston was sanguine about race, religion—particularly black religion—confounded her. As with race, her position on religion, a staple cultural marker for many African Americans, further signified her as pillar of fire. Growing up, Hurston saw black religion's power Sunday after Sunday when she experienced her father's popular and poetic sermons:

> Both at home and from the pulpit, I heard my father, known to thousands as 'Reveren Jno' explain all about God's habits, His heaven, His ways and mean. Everything was known and settled. From the pews I heard a ready acceptance of all that Papa said. Feet beneath the pews beat out a rhythm as he pictured the scenery of heaven. Heads nodded with conviction in time to Papa's words. Tense snatches of tune broke out and some shouted until they fell into a trance at the recognition of what they heard from the pulpit.[26]

In the Black Church, her community found catharsis, hope, and faith to meet the onslaught from the world around them. Nonetheless, Hurston could not understand why the power of those religious experiences did not transform the social world she inhabited. She wanted more than a religion that made status quo life more bearable. The congregants who were moved by her father's preaching but not empowered to change their world frustrated her:

> Come love feast some of the congregation told of getting close enough to peep into God's sitting-room windows. Some went further. They had been inside the place and looked all around. They spoke of sights and scenes around God's throne ... They should have looked and acted differently from other people after experiences like that. But these people looked and acted like everybody else—or so it seemed to me. They plowed, chopped wood, went possum-hunting, washed clothes, raked up back yards and cooked collard greens like anybody else. No more ornaments and nothing. It mystified me. There were so many things they neglected to look after while they were right up there in the presence of All-Power.[27]

She wondered how people came into the presence of the "All-Powerful" sacred on Sunday morning and returned to the mundane without critique? That congregants testified to encounters with the divine and yet remained mired in deprivation did not make sense to her. Hurston developed serious suspicions about religion's persistence despite little evidence of divine activity in the course of people's day-to-day lives. In anthropology, she found some answers, but not all. Rather, she followed her training and turned her focus on the transformative power of human agency. She had seen it in Eatonville. The town's success was not a product of the supernatural, but of abiding struggle and cooperation among those who resided there. Religion, thoughtfully constructed, could catalyze the ordinary folk of her world to extraordinary action, but ultimately, people themselves must create the world they desire.

Hurston found such a model in the Hebrew Bible. Long before she claimed her place in the New Negro Movement, the Hebrew Bible fascinated young Zora. Ironically, she encountered the "Book of Salvation" when her mother punished her for some infraction. Typically, Zora was locked in her parents' room where the Bible was the only reading material available. Instead of penance and redemption, Zora found wonder inside the stories of the Hebrew Bible. She marveled at David's penchant for smiting people without much deliberation over "sin and things."[28] For Hurston, David was a man of action after her own heart. She also saw the biblical God who created David as a deity of action. It was no wonder Hurston described biblical Israel's God as she did. "The Jews had a God who laid about Him when they needed Him. I could see no use waiting till Judgment Day to see a man who was just crying for a good killing, to be told to go and roast. My idea was give him a good killing first, and then if he got roasted later on, so much the better."[29] Unlike the New Testament, whose narrative culminated in a yet unrealized Parousia, Hurston saw the Hebrew Bible as a powerful document because its narratives gave her both climax and dénouement.

At the center of the Hebrew Bible, Hurston saw exodus as a story about the limits of religion, the construction of identity, and the quest for freedom and fulfillment in nation-building. All were questions that she believed faced African Americans in the post–World War I era. She drew broad parallels between African Americans and biblical Israel. Both experienced slavery. Both knew exile in a foreign land, although

African Americans experienced slavery and exile in the same event, namely, the Trans-Atlantic Slave Trade. Both had been liberated from slavery and both negotiated (albeit differently) the meaning of their respective freedom. Both had to resolve what it meant to construct an identity in relationship to other ethnic groups, and to their God.

Perhaps her mother's teaching sparked these concerns. Hurston had encountered the Bible at the hand of her mother's discipline, but she commended its message to her readers in the spirit of her mother's defiant hope. Her mother, Lucy Ann Potts-Hurston, although diminutive in stature, was ambitious, self-assured, and, according to Hurston, smarter than her father.[30] She taught her daughter to "jump at de sun," that is, to push the limits of human potential. As Hurston explains, her mother meant that "[w]e might not land on the sun, but at least we would get off the ground."[31] Hurston's father was less appreciative of his wife's robust encouragement. He feared the type of violence his daughter, and any black girl "with too much spirit," faced in the Deep South. But he was no match for Hurston's mother, who maintained, "Zora is my young'un . . . I'll be bound mine will come out more than conquer."[32] So Hurston grew up with a deep appreciation for the complex and even contradictory models of life that constituted her parents and populated the black world that formed her. She wanted to teach each of them and, by extension, all of those who struggled for the meaning of fulfillment in the wake of slavery, exactly what her mother had taught her—to "jump at de sun." In *Moses, Man of the Mountain*, the first novel-length treatment of the book of Exodus, Hurston shows her people how.

Moses, Man of the Mountain: Toward a Humanist Critique

Hurston's *Moses, Man of the Mountain* narrates a complex world shaped by religions and their attendant cultures. In exodus, Hurston explores questions about the limits of religion and religious imagination that perplexed the young Zora of Eatonville. She offers a strident critique to many in the Black Church and a people who have accepted the religion of their enslavers, a cautionary tale about the limits of any singular mosaic hero, and message of hope about the power of the collective's religious imagination. Hurston's exodus contravenes mainstream exodus narratives of the Black Church but signifies her own pillar of fire stance.

From the beginning of the novel Hurston configures the forces of religion, law, and economy to match those in her own world; they contort bodies to conform to their regimes. The painful opening scene illustrates the connection:

> "Have mercy! Lord, have mercy on my poor soul!" Women gave birth and whispered cries like this in caves and out-of-the-way places that humans didn't usually use for birthplaces. Moses hadn't come yet, and these were the years when Israel first made tears. Pharaoh had entered the bedrooms of Israel. The birthing beds of Hebrews were matters of state. The Hebrew womb had fallen under the heel of Pharaoh.[33]

The speaker, a Hebrew woman in labor, directs her cry for mercy to the "Lord," which usually refers to the Hebrew deity, Yahweh. Hurston takes the ambiguity of the woman's language to expose a similar ambiguity in the connection between a religion and the political, social, and cultural interests it serves. Although the women in Hurston's novel cry out to the Lord, in the book of Exodus, the name of the God of the Israelites has not even been revealed to Moses, let alone the Hebrews.[34] If she is calling to the only deity present, Pharaoh, then her cry has no hope of eliciting a favorable response. The imperial system does not show mercy to the conquered. However, if she intends to summon another divine presence, one both powerful enough to relieve her agony and sympathetic enough to will her release, then Hurston introduces transcendence. It is key to an oppressed people's religious imagination. The woman's hope arises from her ability to envision a reality that is not present. But as Hurston directs the plot, the woman's petition goes unanswered. Rather, the presence of an Egyptian deity, Pharaoh, fills the birthing chamber not with mercy, but with crushing imperial power. Both the agony in the woman's cry and the imperial response recall similar unanswered petitions from innumerable women in slave quarters throughout the South as they brought life into the world. Despite the unanswered petition, the power of humans to imagine life as other than it is continues to drive Hurston's plot.

In a parallel scene between Amram and Caleb, two Hebrew men, and an unnamed Egyptian foreman, Hurston shows how cultural interests and religious interests are coterminous. Amram appears fitted with the conscience of the New Negro, but articulated through southern speech and rural wisdom. His strident critique conveys sobering truths borne out by Hurston's anthropological training. The scene opens with a doxology from the Egyptian, "Ah, Horus, golden god! Lord of both horizons. The weaver of the beginning of things."[35] While he celebrates the sun, a symbol of fertility and prosperity for the ruling class, Hurston directs her readers to Amram and Caleb, who are held in slavery. Amram looks up from his labor long enough to comment to Caleb, "Horus may be all those good things to the Egyptians, brother, but that sun-god is just something to fry our backs."[36] As the scene progresses, Amram and Caleb take account of the effect of the law that alienated them from their religious practice. Caleb begins, "And look what he done done! Passed a law we can't go in the temples no more. He says their gods ain't our gods."[37] Hurston plays with the irony of a human usurping a people's deity. It is both an absurdity and a harsh reality. Acts of religious devotion in part keep a deity "alive" in the culture of a people. Without access to the temples, these deities can no longer participate in Hebrew religious life. At first, Caleb reacts with surprise, "Like what other gods do we know anything about. It gives a real empty feeling not to have no gods anymore." Perhaps he is even incredulous about the possibility of discovering another God. But at least he gives voice to the possibility. Nonetheless, the possibility that Caleb raises is one that African Americans foreclosed on long ago.

In the next sentence, Caleb quickly reverses course. His short-lived thought experiment gives way to despair, "a real empty feeling," when he considers life without any God. "If we can't go to the temple in Thebes and Memphis and Luxor, we could build us one in Goshen and sacrifice, Amram. Maybe if we do that they might help us get our rights back again."[38] Even devotion to the God of his oppressors is more palatable than wandering through life absent any divine presence. Caleb refuses to hold the religion of his oppressors accountable for colluding in his people's oppression. Rather, he faults what he believes are the insufficient devotional acts of the oppressed. In Caleb's response, Hurston obliquely invokes the images of countless black churches erected across the United States. They also petition the God given to them by their oppressors in hopes of securing basic rights and human freedoms. When Caleb wants to invest in the Gods of Egypt, Amram's sobering reply is damning: "Caleb, those temples were built by Egyptians and those gods were made by Egyptians. Gods always love the people who make 'em. We can't put no faith in them."[39] For Hurston, a religion's gods do not hover autonomously over the cultures they serve. Rather, religion's power serves the culture out of which it emerged.

Certainly, Hurston intended the apparent parallels for African American life. The Christian deity introduced to African Americans under the slave regime still lived in the sermons of many black preachers. That deity, much like Pharaoh, extended repressive power into the churches, laws, homes, and every other dimension of the life world of black people. However, Caleb continues to press his angst, "Don't say that, Amram. That don't leave me no way to turn at all. Makes me feel like my insides been ripped out."[40] But Hurston cannot give Caleb the last word. Amram's point is too important to be lost, so he refuses to relent to Caleb's despair. For any devotee of another culture's religious constructions, Amram offers a hard truth. Whether it is Marduk over Babylon, Khemosh over Moab, Pharaoh over Egypt, or Yahweh over the ancient Israelites, for Hurston, gods are as neutral and as interested as the cultures that construct them. So Amram is unrelenting: "Well, Caleb, I'm giving it out just like I figured it out. We just ain't got no out that I can see. Anybody depending on somebody else's gods is depending on a fox not to eat chickens."[41] Hurston leaves the Hebrews in Egypt in a position similar to African Americans in the United States; both live in their oppressor's land without their own God.

Hurston's most incisive critique of religion appears in her portrayal of Moses. She dislodges Moses from his miraculous beginnings and makes him a product(ion) of the people of Goshen. The lessons from Eatonville, the skepticisms from her childhood, and her challenge to her people come to bear on her protagonist. As early as Harriet Tubman, black people celebrated the work of those whom they interpreted as Moses figures. They vigilantly awaited the next as each one receded from the public scene. They claimed that God particularly endowed each for such a time in history. In Moses, Hurston asks her people, "What if this were not so? Might a people exercise a will to self-empowerment as she had seen in her community in Eatonville?"

In the book of Exodus, Moses' story begins with a narrative of an extraordinary birth. It is a literary form that the writers of the Hebrew

Bible use to signal an important male hero's arrival. Whether the obstacle is a mother who is a "barren woman" such as Sarah who gives birth to Isaac, Rebekah who gives birth to Esau and Jacob, Rachel who gives birth to Joseph, or Hannah who gives birth to Samuel, these male characters overcome great odds to come to birth. Moses overcomes two obstacles: the edict to kill male Hebrew infants and the dangers of the Nile. In her presentation, Hurston places the narrative in doubt. She wonders what would happen if Miriam had not been able to verify that her brother had indeed been rescued during the princess's morning bath. A little girl, fearful of the consequences of having fallen asleep and disappointing her mother, Miriam first admits to her negligence but then recants and quickly reports to her mother that the princess found the basket and had taken it to the palace. A frantic and angry Jochabed demands Miriam's assurance that she is telling the truth, but what child would admit to such a grave mistake given the circumstances and the gravity of the consequences? When Miriam affirms her story of a royal rescue, Jochabed is left with a choice to accept the unthinkable—that her baby had drowned or had fallen prey to the crocodiles—or to believe that perhaps her son, out of all the boy babies hidden in the Nile that night, was rescued. In Hurston's story Miriam chooses the latter and so does her family. And eventually, despite evidence to the contrary, the people of Goshen accept the story of Moses' extraordinary birth, rescue, and rise to the palace. With this innovation in the plot, Hurston, a trained folklorist, begins to explore the power and limits of folk tradition among oppressed people.

The power of a story that claims that one of their own resides among Pharaoh's court both amuses and empowers the people in Goshen. The story itself possessed power that acted even beyond evidence to the contrary. When Jochabed inquires at the palace if she might be a nursemaid for the princess's new baby, the court officials deny any knowledge of a new baby. "Still and all, Goshen never gave up their belief in the Hebrew in the palace. It was something for men to dream about. Jochabed became a figure of importance—the mother of our Prince in the palace. Miriam told her story again and again to more believing ears. It grew with being handled until it was a history of the Hebrew in the palace, no less."[42] For Hurston, the tradition resonated with the multitudes of stories of African Americans who passed into white circles, existed even in prominent families, and even held high office undetected by the most vehement racists.

By the end of the episode, it is clear that the significance of Moses' life and activity is among his people. His life in the palace is their doing, rather than the Egyptians. In effect, Hurston relocates divine intention and activity from a transcendent place and re-places it among the people themselves. Her narrative move turns the story's focus to the Hebrews' agency. Moses is powerful because they have created him. Likewise, when the Hebrews' God appears later in the story, the reader knows that Yahweh will affirm them because Yahweh is the *Hebrew's* construction and not the Egyptian's.

For Hurston, Moses and Yahweh become an exploration and a critique of the potency of an oppressed community's religious imagination. Such an imagination has the power to create and deify leaders and to develop theologies that ultimately lead to freedom. In the biblical story, Moses embodies both divine power and human frailty. Hurston exaggerates both to test the limits of the New Negro as a mosaic hero. Hurston's Moses gradually transitions from human to deity and then to human again. Throughout the story, each transition reflects the people's expectations. In effect, their beliefs transform Moses to meet their needs as they journey from bondage to autonomy. Moses' power is no more than any priest steeped in Egyptian wisdom.

> Moses had lifted his right hand in Midian and the people feared it. The first few times that he made the gesture before a miracle nobody noticed it particularly. But when it kept on happening, that right hand became a symbol of terror and wonders. Then it quit being a sign of power to the people; it became to them power in itself. He lifted it and they experienced the miracle of water turned to blood. It had been done in a small way by the Cushite priests for a long time. But Moses lifted his hand and extended it imperiously and the rivulets and springs and wells and streams ran blood all that day. Moses lifted his hand and a malicious gossip was struck with leprosy. It was Moses who learned the secret power to command the power of flame. It was Moses who could bring on or drive off the cattle disease.[43]

Although Moses' powers only match that of religious figures of the day, it possesses a double signification that increases Moses' stature. Because

Moses' religious power comes in the form of a singular person without the benefit of state apparatuses, the Egyptians marvel at him. They are amazed that he has no temple, no army, no patronage from any ruler, yet his displays are evidence of one who has had the privilege of years of study uninterrupted by the demands of subsistence. The opposite is true for the Hebrews who lived in Goshen. They immediately recognize Moses' abilities and identify them with the immense power of the Egyptian state. Ironically, it is this association with the symbols of imperial power that legitimates Moses.

For Hurston, there is a short slippage from hero to deity as she describes it in the life of Moses.

> It was Moses, too, who saw in the little puff of white smoke that rose from the incense on the altar the symbol of the Presence behind the clouds on the crest of the holy mountain and he developed the smoke into a thick white mass that hung stationary and huge above the altar for as long as the ceremony lasted. It rested there in volume and mystery like the Presence it symbolized. It made the voice of the unseen Moses speaking behind the altar seem like the voice of God. It seemed to the people that Moses but lifted his right hand and the cloud from Mount Horeb appeared upon the altar. From so many signs and wonders that they had witnessed when Moses extended that right hand before him, they came to believe that the hand of Moses held all of the powers of the supernatural in its grasp. It had a separate existence from the rest of his body. So when Moses lifted his hand the smoke of the incense ceased to be smoke. It became the Presence. If it was not the actual Presence, then it enclosed and clothed the Presence. Finally, the smoke itself was deified. It was not understood so it became divine.[44]

While Hurston leaves the two identities in tension, it is clear that the people make Moses a god. Hurston revisits the tension at key junctures in the narrative, such as the deliverance at the Red Sea, the wars in Canaan, and in the deaths of Miriam and Aaron. At each, the people emphasize Moses' divinity while Hurston has Moses struggle with his own humanity. Hurston's Moses is absolutely conflicted throughout. He is both selfish and altruistic. He willingly abdicates his royal privilege to lead the Hebrews in their struggle for freedom, but his leadership is as parochial as any *man's*.

Hurston takes up the tension in Moses' identity to explore the third theme: the limits of any singular, mosaic hero. Sexism, classism, and hubris become the focus. She highlights the limits of Moses' leadership in the interplay between Moses, Aaron, and Miriam. She begins by interpreting the Priestly writer's insertion of Aaron's deeds and speeches throughout exodus as Aaron's attempts to maintain his own stature in the face of Moses' new and dynamic leadership. The biblical story presents Aaron as a Levite, a priest, and an authority figure in his own right. Hurston complicates family roles by portraying Miriam as a prophetess with her own following in Goshen. Both served their people long before Moses arrived. But Hurston wonders what happens when old structures of authority, such as those that supported Miriam and Aaron, come into conflict with new social orders as a people journey toward freedom.

Hurston casts Moses' relationship with Miriam as a critique of contemporaneous leadership struggles among African Americans. The relationship between the siblings is contentious throughout. In Miriam's final scene Hurston illustrates the absurdity of deifying *men* as messianic figures. While the reader is aware that the people constructed Moses' legendary origins, Miriam is not privy to Moses' origins even though she played a seminal role in Moses of long ago as a child. By the end of her life she also comes to believe that Moses was a demigod, and that his power extended even over life and death. So when the journey to Canaan becomes unbearable for her, and she wants to die, she believes that she can do so only if Moses grants her leave.

> "Moses, I come here this evening to ask you to let me die." "Why, Miss Miriam!" "I ask you kindly, please, Moses, to let me die." "What makes you think you got to get my consent to die?" "Cause I know I can't die without it. That right hand of yours—it's got light in front of it and darkness behind. Moses, I come in the humblest way I know how to let you know I done quit straining against you. I done quit putting my poor little strength up against yours. I'm just a beat old woman and I want to die." "But, Miss Miriam, you ain't had time to enjoy your freedom yet. You ought to want to live to enjoy it and to see Israel a nation."[45]

The scene becomes one of several in which Hurston levels a complex critique of sexism in the public sphere. Miriam in particular complicates

Moses' work because he is unable to accept authority embodied as a woman or a style of leadership that is not militaristic.

Before Moses arrived in Goshen, Miriam possessed wonderful gifts with which she served the people. Moses had no room for her role among the people, nor did he understand Miriam's work in his vision for Israel, so he marginalized her from the beginning. In the end, Miriam takes her leave from life and from the journey to Canaan. Miriam's struggle resonates with countless stories of women who lived in frustration because men in power ignored their gifts for the public sphere. It reflected the experiences of black women who worked in black struggles from the antebellum period onward. In another scene Moses and Jethro dismiss Zipporah and her struggles for stability and fulfillment as a distraction. Throughout, Hurston portrays both women through the gaze of men who relate to them. Hurston herself experienced similar treatment by some of the male Renaissance artists.

As the Israelites' journey neared the Promised Land, Moses plans for their national life without him. As with Miriam, he and Aaron never found common ground. Moses could not understand why Aaron and Miriam refused to sacrifice what he saw as minor goods, namely status and creature comforts, for the broader advancement of the people. Reciprocally, Miriam and Aaron could not understand why Moses expected them to do so. Moses' expectations arose from his class privilege. Abundance and comfort shaped his life. He chose to sacrifice for the Hebrew people, but Miriam and Aaron did not have the privilege of making such a choice. They had spent their entire lives in a space of deprivation. If anything, freedom for them meant at least some modicum of fulfillment, however meager.

As the story concludes, Hurston turns to hubris. In the end, Moses determines that Aaron's leadership is too great a liability to leave behind. The scenes are worthy of lengthy quotation:

"You got your power and your brains, Moses, but you ain't never made the people happy like you said." "I never said I'd make them happy people. I promised to make them great. Anyway, happiness is not something you can catch and lock up in a vault like wealth. Happiness is nothing but everyday living seen through a veil." "Well, I can give 'em what they want better than you ever did, and I'll show you when we get over there. You can't scare people away from what they want over there. We won't need you any more. My time is coming just like I always knowed it would." He gave Moses a look full of triumph and old hatred. "Take off those robes, Aaron," Moses said shortly. Aaron acted as if he didn't hear Moses right away. Then he gave Moses a scornful look. Then he chuckled slightly and crossed his legs and smoothed the skirts of his priestly robe. "Aaron, take off those robes." God put these robes on me and He'll have to be the one to take 'em off. I know you been begrudging 'em to me for a powerful long time. I just wouldn't step down for you." "God didn't put no robes on you, Aaron. I put 'em on you and I'm taking them off, because they don't fit you." "You mean God never called me down there in Egypt at all?" "No, Aaron." "You told me He did." "Yes, I did, Aaron. I thought I needed you for the big job I had to do because you were of the Hebrews. I did need you too, but you didn't do the job I picked out for you." "You always held me back. You—" "No, you got the wrong idea altogether. You held yourself back. You didn't think about service half as much as you did about getting served, Aaron. Your tiny horizon never did get no bigger, so you mistook a spotlight for the sun."[46]

A charismatic leader, Moses relied upon his own counsel. He brought with him the modes of state organization that he knew, which were hierarchical. He never understood the value of the systems of authority or modes of relationality that were in place before he began to lead. When styles of leadership conflict in the story, Moses ultimately deposes Aaron as punishment for what he sees as Aaron's shortcomings. However, even after removing Aaron, Moses does not believe he cannot leave Aaron among the Israelites if the nation is to survive once it reaches Canaan. So he intends to sacrifice Aaron for the sake of the people.

"Moses, spare me, if you please." Moses looked way off across the plain where the tents of Israel stretched for miles and held his eyes for a long pause. Then he said, "I haven't spared myself, Aaron. I had to quit being a person a long time ago, and I had to become a thing, a tool, an instrument for a cause. I wasn't spared, Aaron. No." "No, and you didn't spare my two sons at Sinai—just for dancing and making a little ceremony before a god of Egypt which we had always known. My poor boys—you killed them!" "I didn't kill your boys at Sinai, Aaron, though I know that you have always accused me of it, and hated me. But you know just as well as I do why they died. What they signified had to die if Israel was to be great." "Let me be high priest over there, Moses, in the big new tabernacle with—" "No, Aaron." Aaron crawled to the knees of Moses and clasped them. "Moses, looks like pity and mercy would—" "Aaron, the future of Israel is higher than pity and mercy. And why should I spare you? I did not spare the first-born. I did not spare Pharaoh. I did not spare myself. I did not spare my wife and my friend. Jethro is dead and I might have spent several more happy years with him instead of out in the wilderness leading a people and being reviled for doing what was best instead of what was popular. No, Aaron, nothing and nobody has been spared to make this nation great." [47]

Although Moses kills Aaron, he does not commit the act without remorse and deep reflection. He believes that Aaron's selfish ambition will infect the priesthood and destroy everything he worked to build. Moses arrogates for himself the divine prerogative of taking human life. With knife raised, Hurston's Moses wonders what this journey has done to him. He no longer knows whether he is God or human. But in that moment, he gives himself to hubris and reveals that he is fully human.

Hurston's Moses is as flawed and as heroic as anyone. His leadership is as noble and as parochial as Hurston understood that the best of male leadership could achieve. In both episodes, Hurston turns to extremes to make clear that she is uncomfortable with the idea of a community enduring repression as they wait for the salvific work of a singular messianic figure. By emphasizing Moses' fallibility coupled with his unchecked power, Hurston warns against charismatic leadership and commends instead a radical democracy where authority and its legitimation are broadly distributed.

Ultimately, the limits of religion and religious leadership confound both Hurston's Moses and the Israel he led. Along the gritty and complex road to freedom, Hurston's Moses realizes that both his leadership, which he trusted unfailingly early on, and his deification, which the people trusted, were too dangerous to sustain. By the end of the journey, he is unsure of the decisions that he made and ways that he had deployed unchecked power. As he had sacrificed so many others for Israel's advancement, he realizes that he also must leave the people and allow them to develop their own structures of authority and accountability. For Hurston, Moses' leadership, as any charismatic mode of leadership, reaches a point where it does more harm than good and stunts the collective's growth toward self-actualization.

For Hurston, exodus's redeeming value lay in its cautionary quality. She believed in that way, the story offered an insightful critique for a black community spying out its Promised Land only seventy-four years after enslavement. In *Man of the Mountain*, Hurston offers her people a way forward. She locates the power of God in both its utility and danger among the people. She believed a people's vision and governance were the property of the collective. One person could not be entrusted to do the work of all. Ironically, inasmuch as her work offers a strident and, at times, an acerbic critique of contemporaneous black ecclesial communities and their authority structures, Hurston displayed a deeper faith than those whom she criticized. She refused to wait for any God to send some man (or woman) to interpret freedom or lead her people toward fulfillment. No, her faith resided in the people themselves. As she portrayed it, their religion's power did not reside in the hope of any supernatural intervention. The power of religion lay in its ability to lead a people to transcendence. That is, to envision a world of freedom and fulfillment that is beyond the present condition and to construct that world together. That kind of power could not belong to any one person, but to everyone. When they knew that, they all could "jump at de sun" together.

4

Exodus in the Civil Rights Era: Returning the Struggle to the Black Church

Now, may the Constitution of the United States go with you, the Declaration of Independence stand by you, the Bill of Rights protect you. And may your own dreams be your only boundaries henceforth now and forever.
From *Purlie Victorious* by Ossie Davis

By the end of the Harlem Renaissance, the small cadre who were its nucleus had performed no less than a miracle. They constructed a New Negro who had broken free from the manacles of slavery. His cultural productions, including biblical interpretations, showed the world a new consciousness. But song and poetry could not ensure the right to vote. Paintings could not grant equal access to public accommodations. Despite the power of expressive culture, this New Negro still had little voice in the public sphere. The architects who had created a Renaissance could not take the New Negro to the civic arena. Rather, Black Churches and their grassroots communities rose to the task. They summoned the exodus narrative to interpret an elusive hope—freedom for a people yet second-class.

Over generations, their learned and dynamic pulpiteers preached its themes and idiom into well-established motifs in the African American religious imagination. Their sermons refracted the narrative's symbols of bondage, freedom, and struggle over a collective history of resistance as their people faced slavery, lynching, and now Jim Crow. From the pulpit, they signified upon Moses with Harriet Tubman. They gave the Jordan River, the Israelites' last boundary to emancipation, real-world analogues in the Ohio River, the Mason-Dixon Line, and the border between Canada and the United States. With the exodus story, they led their congregations to hermeneutical understanding where the horizon of the Israelites' struggle met their own.

Powell (1908-1972)

From this tradition emerged two of the more prescient voices of the time, namely, Adam Clayton Powell, Jr., the congressman from New York and pastor of the largest Protestant congregation in the United States, and Martin Luther King, Jr., the Civil Rights Movement's leading figure. Both men were the sons of prominent clergy families. Both grew up in their fathers' churches and were raised ensconced in the privilege of the black middle class. Both were educated at some of the best schools in the nation. The senior Powell sent his son to Colgate University, where he earned his bachelor's degree in biblical literature.[1] Martin Luther King, Sr., affectionately known as "Daddy King," sent the young Martin to the exclusive Morehouse College, where he earned his bachelor's degree in sociology. Powell later completed a master's degree in education at Columbia University.[2] King completed his education at Crozier Theological Seminary, and Boston University, where he earned a master of divinity and PhD in theology, respectively.[3]

Perhaps the biographical parallels in their lives destined these two men to be princes of the black Baptist church and leaders in the African American community. Their differences, however, as stark as cloud and fire, illumine their politics. Powell grew up in Harlem, New York at the center of the Jazz Age and the Harlem Renaissance—and his pillar of fire politics "showed it off." Harlem's black population enjoyed life relatively unfettered by the type of Jim Crow culture and brutality that shaped the South. Powell styled himself in sharp contrast to his father's religious piety and political conservatism. Flamboyant and brash, he called himself "the first bad nigger in Congress." He was fond of saying, "I do not do any more than any other member of Congress, and by the grace of God, I'll not do any less."[4] Powell meant that his race required no more and no less of him than any of his white counterparts.

Powell - Flamboyant and brash, "show off" pillar of fire

King, however, saw the matter differently. Born just ten months before the Great Depression, he grew up in Atlanta among its socially conservative southern, black middle class. He had seen southern racism's repression first-hand. His pillar of cloud politics accepted the burden of demonstrating black moral worthiness for full inclusion. Writing, "We feel that we are the conscience of America—we are its troubled soul—and we will continue to insist that *right* be done because both God's will and the heritage of our nation speak through our echoing demands," King believed that African Americans should be moral exemplars for the nation.[5] As different as they were, both men devoted their lives to lift their people still forsaken by a nation that yet refused them equality, and both men would reinterpret the exodus narrative in the new era toward a common emancipatory end.

Civil Rights: Responding to Narratives of Ascent and Containment

On July 2, 1964, two days before the nation celebrated its one hundred eighty-eighth birthday, Adam Clayton Powell, Jr., and Martin Luther King, Jr., shared a major victory. That evening, President Lyndon Baines Johnson signed a new Civil Rights Act. In the document, the nation affirmed its commitment to the equal protection of all of its citizens. For the congressman, the new legislation finally vindicated his controversial "Powell Amendment." For more than a decade Powell had taken pride in stoking the ire of southern Democrats by attaching the codicil to every piece of federally funded legislation. He often said, "If they want segregation, let them pay for it."[6] The amendment barred federal funding for any racially segregated institution. When the amendment's effect held up funding for school systems in the segregated South, meaning that some black schools were denied funding, even black leaders criticized him. Nonetheless, Powell remained resolute. He believed firmly that funds raised from the entire people should not be used to benefit only a segment of the people. In the new Civil Rights Act, Powell's amendment became the law of the land.

For King and others who had led a generation to march in the streets, to pray in public squares, and to sing the songs of Zion in southern jails, it meant that the work begun in Montgomery had not been in vain. In those carefully staged public confrontations, King practiced his pillar of cloud politics by casting blacks as moral exemplars. He used television media to juxtapose images of unarmed African Americans against violent and depraved southern segregationists. He had led them into streets throughout the South to face down police dogs, fire hoses, nightsticks, and burning crosses. Although the past decade brought a barrage of criticism for his tactics, King remained steadfastly wed to nonviolent social action. He firmly believed the marchers had risked their lives because ultimately they knew their cause was just. In each confrontation, they had placed their bodies on the frontlines to face white supremacy because they were convicted that their own suffering would redeem not only the segregationist's humanity, but also the soul of a nation damned by its hate. Now, in this legislation, the struggles and the sacrifice had proven worthwhile.

The legislation, Powell's towering congressional stature, King's rise to national prominence, and the decade of strikes, boycotts, and other increasingly more visible expressions of black protest signaled a new racial dynamic. Black life had fundamentally changed—not precipitously, but slowly, in halting increments. Beginning as soon the U.S. Army closed the last plantation, African Americans slowly molded their newfound freedom into a better life. Thus began a national narrative of oppositional social forces working simultaneously: African American struggles for social ascent through migration, commerce, and education, which were met at every turn by the nation's efforts at surveillance and containment. The changes were almost imperceptible by themselves. But together they formed a whelming tide that transformed the nation's political economy.

First, blacks migrated. In 1877, when the forty-fifth U.S. Congress abandoned Reconstruction, it recalled federal troops, leaving African Americans unprotected in the former Confederacy. Vulnerable to violent reprisals, African Americans fled the South in droves. By migrating, the nation's daughters and sons of slavery abandoned *their place* and seized the privilege to locate themselves geographically and sociopolitically for the first time. Without the slave regime to restrict mobility, migration diminished the work that race could perform. Both the slave and sharecropping economies had depended upon the racial system to ensure that African Americans remained geographically *in their place* and thus retained them as an always-available source of labor. To be black no longer meant being identified with a slave owner or plantation. Responses to routine questions such as, "Who are you," or "Where are you from," no longer required a slaveholder's surname or the plantation that held one in bondage. Migrating blacks no longer had to refer to themselves as "Mr. Charlie's boy," or from "Mr. Charlie's plantation." Each move slowly changed the meaning of race. Blacks fled to northern cities such as New York, Philadelphia, Boston, and Washington, a Promised Land that had once been accessible only by the Underground

Railroad. Between 1870 and 1950, New York City's black population mushroomed from 52,081 to 918,191 and Harlem's black population rose to 341,000.[7] By the 1920s the population increase made Harlem ripe to form the Sr. Powell's Abyssinian Baptist Church, at that time the largest Protestant congregation in the nation. Moreover, by 1940, Harlem's growth warranted a new congressional seat, which Adam Clayton Powell, Jr., filled.

Many African Americans who remained in the South left sparsely populated rural areas to congregate in the safety of larger black communities in cities such as Atlanta, Birmingham, Charleston, Memphis, and New Orleans. In Montgomery, where Martin Luther King, Jr., Rosa Parks, and E. D. Nixon led the Montgomery Bus Boycott, the black population increased from 5,183 in 1870 to 42,538 by 1950.[8] And, by the start of the boycott in 1955, Montgomery's black population held formidable economic power.

As African Americans migrated, they entered the working class seeking higher education, and then entered the professional classes. No longer slaves, they forged a new economic relationship with the nation. They now possessed the value of their own labor and deployed it for whatever wages they could, however meager, forcing employers to compete. Blacks did not earn more than their urban or northern counterparts. However, for the first time in the nation's history, it was not uncommon for blacks in the industrial North and the urban South to earn more than white agricultural laborers. Many of those who remained in agriculture purchased farmland rather than work for others. By 1875, black farmers owned between 80,000 and 100,000 acres of land in Virginia and 400,000 acres in Georgia, with similar rates of land acquisition throughout the South. Across the nation black farmers owned an estimated 3 million acres. By 1900 the number had increased to 12 million.[9]

At the same time, black commercial endeavors soared. Between 1900 and 1929, the number of black-owned businesses grew from 20,000 to 70,000.[10] Between 1900 and 1914, forty-seven black-owned banks opened.[11] Commercial endeavor, however, could not remove the boundary that literacy maintained. The slave regime had enforced illiteracy to make African Americans fit only for agricultural labor. When access to education no longer meant risking life and limb, African Americans

[handwritten margin note, top: MORREHOUSE College –]

[handwritten margin note, left: Produced First Post-slavery generation of Teachers, Doctors, Dentists]

pursued it virtually en masse. By the end of Reconstruction, the Freedman's Bureau had educated almost 250,000 students in more than 4,000 schools.[12] Between 1890 and 1940, black illiteracy decreased from 79.9 percent to 10.2 percent. In the North, schools such as Harvard, Yale, Columbia, and Boston University, along with Powell's alma maters, Colgate and Columbia, had long admitted African Americans in small numbers. During the same period, a robust network of institutions formed the basis of higher education in the South. King's alma mater, Morehouse College, which was founded in 1867, among several others, produced the first post-slavery generations of teachers, doctors, dentists, clergy, attorneys, and other professionals.[13]

Each move from chattel to proprietor and from slave laborer to working class blurred economic distinctions between black and white people, along with the racialist categories that gave these distinctions meaning. The new relationship between race and education ensured the most enduring change for African Americans. Degrees, once granted, could not be rescinded; knowledge, once obtained, could not be taken away. In all, African Americans had made significant progress toward transforming contemporaneous meanings race. Together, these two groups, working and professional urbanites in the North and the South, formed the middle-class communities to which Powell and King belonged.

Had black political and economic advances proceeded unchecked, there might have been no need for the rise of an Adam Clayton Powell, Jr., or a Martin Luther King, Jr. But the racial system did not concede its strategies of surveillance and containment to black progress. As African Americans composed a compelling narrative of social ascent, the nation's political economy simultaneously employed strategies of suppression. Each hard-won advance was accompanied by heartbreaking setbacks. Despite slavery's absence, race reinscribed its meaning upon the political economy. It deployed the legislature, the judiciary, and, most often, targeted violence to maintain the political and economic boundaries that distinguished black from white. Black populations soon found that neither education nor wealth removed the racial system's repressive veil.

[handwritten margin note, left: Yet neither followed nor wealth removed the racial systems repressive veil]

Enfranchisement and segregation simply replaced the old markers of slavery and literacy. Southern states quickly moved to strip the right to vote from African Americans. By 1910, constitutional provisions effectively disenfranchised blacks across the South from Virginia to Okla-

BY 1910 BLACKS HAD AGAIN LOST THE VOTE

homa.[14] Losing the vote only marked the beginning of the retrenchment of racialization. Tennessee enacted the first "Jim Crow" law in 1875. The remainder of the South followed suit, effectively barring African Americans from participating in every aspect of civic and commercial life. By 1883, the Supreme Court declared the Civil Rights Act of 1875 unconstitutional.[15] The most devastating shift came in 1896, when the Court upheld "separate but equal" in the landmark *Plessy v. Ferguson*. *Plessy*'s consequences were far reaching. The decision reinscribed race upon the U.S. political economy in its most pervasive form since the plantation system. Soon, every aspect of public life was separate, including schools, parks, zoos, buses, restaurants, clubs, and taxis. Without the plantation system to govern black mobility, *Plessy* empowered cities in the North and the South to enact ordinances to restrict blacks to "Negro blocks."[16] The laws forced blacks, irrespective of their financial ability, to live in substandard housing often owned by white landlords. Many cities made it illegal for blacks to walk through "white neighborhoods" unless employed by a resident. Without laws to ensure black illiteracy, *Plessy* restricted blacks to substandard schools with inadequate funding. Without the slave system to prevent competition between black and white workers and their commercial endeavors, state legislatures invoked *Plessy* to restrict the arenas where blacks could compete and the clientele that black businesses could serve.[17]

LEGAL SEGREGATION

While these laws frustrated black communities' aspirations, blacks no doubt saw the relative ease with which other groups achieved upward mobility. During the same era, Poles, Germans, Irish, Italians, and other Europeans, eager to achieve the American dream, immigrated in unprecedented numbers. Unlike many Latino and Asian immigrants, European immigrants replaced markers of their respective ethnic origins with those of Anglo-Saxon ethnicity. As a reward, they transcended painful and repressive processes of ethnicization and became simply "white." They found ethnicity to be a far more permeable boundary than race. African Americans, Asian Americans, Latinos, and Native Americans, however, could not count on full inclusion. Even when their achievements outpaced segregation and its impediments, they could not break free of the racialized system.

Where legal segregation failed to maintain racial differences, violence in the form of lynching or the seizure of property served as the judiciary's able partner.[18] The violent spectacles reminded blacks that irrespective of their advances, emancipation had not yet come. Frustrated by these repeated strategies of surveillance and containment, by the 1950s, African Americans in the North and South leveraged their economic and political gains to protect their progress. They wanted far more than social ascent; less than a generation after the Harlem Renaissance, the New Negro demanded civil rights!

Adam Clayton Powell, Jr.: Offspring of the Harlem Renaissance

Before Adam Clayton Powell, Jr., was three months of age, his family moved to Harlem, New York, where his father accepted the pastorate at Abyssinian Baptist Church. In the 1920s, Harlem was the capital of black America. It was a black world unto itself. Until he left for college, it was also Adam Clayton Powell, Jr.'s world. Its four square miles shone as a pillar of fire against a nightscape of black degradation that marked much of the national geography. Between 96th and 155th streets, black life flourished. On Sunday mornings, Harlem's high-steepled and storefront churches nurtured black religion. During the week, black attorneys and doctors built thriving practices within Harlem's professional and working classes. At night, Harlem's cabarets came alive with music, dance, liquor, and a social freedom unlike any in the world. As a teenager, Adam satiated himself with Harlem's flamboyant social life. He moved to its rhythms; he loved its women, and by the time he reached adulthood, he grew to relish its blackness.

Amid the vibrant intellectual and social environment, young Adam grew up in the shadow of the Harlem Renaissance. At times during Adam's childhood, Harlem counted Langston Hughes, W.E.B. Du Bois, Zora Neale Hurston, and James Weldon Johnson among its residents. The Harlem that they created in literature and other cultural expressions was the world that formed Adam. Years later as a congressman, a mature and brazen Adam Clayton Powell, Jr., would translate the Renaissance thinkers' New Negro aesthetic to the political sphere.

But as a child, Adam was lost in Harlem's black world. He struggled early on to find his place within the ambiguities of the nation's racially structured society. A black child born with blonde hair and hazel eyes, and a child of privilege in the midst of the Great Depression, Adam was *out of place* among his own in Harlem's black paradise. Against the backdrop of a racially polarized society, Adam's own presence conveyed the ambiguities that constituted his person. It was both blessing and burden. His appearance gave him privileges that were denied his darker sisters and brothers. White skin afforded him "passage" into some of the advantages of "whiteness," but the black blood flowing through his veins rendered him dangerously *out of place* among whites as well.

Over time, Powell learned to negotiate his life between these two identities. For him, whiteness meant the privilege of a life free of the burden of race. It enabled one "to do no more or less than anyone else"— neither to be forced to compensate for nor to be advantaged by the color of one's skin. He had experienced episodes of such white privilege at times in his youth and he refused to relinquish it. Throughout his career, Powell worked to extend such privilege to all. As the young Adam developed his racial consciousness, each new encounter forced him to choose an identity and his *place* on either side of the nation's racial divide— black or white.

But while his appearance afforded him the privilege of choosing, knowing how to negotiate racial politics was entirely another matter. From childhood through college, painful trial and error marked his experience. He recalled three incidents from his childhood as he awakened to racial conscientiousness:

The first night that my father sent me out to buy the evening paper in our new neighborhood, on 136th street, a gang of Negro boys grabbed me and asked, "What are you, white or colored?" I had never thought of color. I looked at my skin and said, "White!" whereupon I was promptly and thoroughly beaten. The very next night I had to go to Eighth Avenue to get something from the store for Mother and a gang of white boys grabbed me and demanded, "What are you?" Remembering my answer, and my beating of the previous night, I answered, "Colored!" whereupon I again was bloodied. On the third night, another group of colored boys grabbed me on Seventh Avenue and asked the same question, "What are you?" Remembering once more my previous experiences, I said, "Mixed!" One of the boys yelled out, "Oh, he's a Mick!" And I was sent home crying for a third time.[19]

Powell's responses are telling. In the first encounter, he claims not to have thought of "color." Indeed, Powell is apparently oblivious to the ways that racial identity transcends color. After assessing his skin's hue and the choices offered him, "white or colored," he responds at the level of apperception. Mistaking color for the significance of race, he gives the wrong answer, "White!" In the second and third encounters, Powell repeats the same mistake. In each instance, the query calls for Adam to choose both an identity and a side of the racial divide. In other words, Adam's appearance confounded the work of racialization to *place* him. At every turn, his social world demanded of Adam to articulate his *place*.

By the time he entered college, Adam had learned that he could deploy his somatic qualities to *choose* his *place*. At Colgate, Adam entered as a white student and even attempted to join a white fraternity.[20] During his first semester he developed a close friendship with his white roommate. However, a semester later, racism shattered that relationship. That spring, the senior Powell spoke in chapel and advocated for "Negro concerns." While Adam, Jr., described his father's presentation as well received by most of the student body, his roommate abruptly ended their friendship and had Adam moved to a different dormitory. Adam recalled: "It came as a tremendous shock to me. Patterson and I had been such good friends . . . buddies. And just because my father, logically and factually, presented the cause of the Negro people, he refused to have me stay in our room any longer . . . and the University Dean had agreed to put me out."[21]

On one hand, he learned that blacks faced severe consequences for transgressing white racial boundaries. Incarceration and even death were not unusual. Fortunately for him, the dean only removed him from the room. On the other hand, he saw, heard, and experienced what his darker skinned brothers and sisters would never know. By the spring semester, a maturing Adam Clayton Powell, Jr., had become more sophisticated about racial politics. He used his appearance to deploy race. Where his complexion afforded him advantages, he would extend those to other blacks. Unbeknownst to his professors, he identified for his black classmates those professors he believed were racist.[22] Where his appearance confounded racial categories, he mocked race to show its absurdity. For example, during the summer Powell worked at an exclusive resort in Vermont where Abraham Lincoln's son, Robert Todd Lincoln, dined nightly. Of the former president's son Powell recalled:

> He hated Negroes and whenever a Negro put his hand on the car door to open it, Mr. Lincoln took his cane and cracked across his knuckles. The manager asked me if, at a special increase in salary, I would take care of Mr. Lincoln's car each night when it arrived. So promptly every day, when Robert Todd Lincoln's chauffeured car rolled up with the son of the former President of the United States, I, whose father had been raised by a branded slave, would open his door. And Mr. Lincoln, looking at my white hand, was satisfied.[23]

Powell grew to understand that among whites he was an imposter, and always subject to being returned to *his place*. Blacks, however, valorized him because he had "renounced" white privilege and chosen to identify with them. From Colgate onward, Powell determined his own place amid the racialized political economy and refused its strategies to *place* him.

When Powell returned from school he continued to deploy his privilege for more than personal advantage. Powell began to practice in the public square the fearless style of pillar of fire politics that marked his character and career. By 1935, the Great Depression had ravaged Harlem, the city Powell loved. The conditions had become so unbearable that average citizens began to revolt. After Mayor Fiorello LaGuardia failed to address the discrimination, Powell seized a citywide platform and penned a series of articles in the *New York Post* denouncing the mayor. He explained that Harlem had not rioted, but had staged "an open, unorganized protest against empty stomachs, overcrowded tenements, filthy sanitation, rotten foodstuffs, chiseling landlords and merchants, discrimination on relief, disenfranchisement, and a disinterested administration."[24]

In the meantime, Powell stepped up his use of demonstrations. The protests crippled local business that discriminated against black consumers and forced others to change unfair hiring practices. When he encouraged the community, "Don't buy where you can't work," they rallied. In 1938, when the Consolidated Edison Light and Gas Company refused to hire African Americans, Powell led picketers to the streets in mass protest, and directed blacks in Harlem to turn off lights in the evening and to disrupt the business by paying their bills in pennies.[25] In 1941, Powell took on the New York City Omnibus and Fifth Avenue Coach, the bus companies that provided transportation throughout the city. Both refused to hire black drivers or mechanics. Two decades before Rosa Parks refused to relinquish her seat on a Montgomery bus, Powell organized the nation's first successful bus boycott and got jobs for black drivers. Later, he and the Abyssinian congregation would give a young Martin Luther King, Jr., advice and funds for the boycott in Montgomery.

Powell's style was as significant as his public successes. In each protest, he solidified his brand of brash political engagement. While others such as Roy Wilkins or A. Philip Randolph pursued black uplift with a more conciliatory tone, Powell was intentionally confrontational. He intended its effect. As he characterized his work in an interview, "All my life, an irritant. My father before me. It's my heritage. Whenever a person keeps prodding, keeps them squirming . . . it serves a purpose. It may not in contemporary history look good. But as the times roll on, future historians will say, they served a purpose."[26] Even Bayard Rustin, the master organizer who worked with King, admired the "magnificent way he thumbed his nose at the white establishment," and celebrated the way that Powell was "not afraid to give white folks hell."[27]

By the time he took over the pulpit at Abyssinian, Adam was practiced in the type of pillar of fire politics that leveraged color, class, and education to black people's political advantage. But Powell believed that lasting change would come only when African Americans fully participated in governing the republic. In 1941, he saw his opportunity and won a seat on the New York City Council. By 1944, Powell bypassed A. Philip Randolph to become the second African American elected to Congress.

Exodus as a Call for Civil Rights and a Mandate for Civil Responsibility

The first Sunday of advent in 1953 must have puzzled many attending the Abyssinian worship service that morning. To be sure, they were accustomed to the many ways their pastor did not *fit*. His politics became a badge of honor for the congregation. Powell flaunted his unorthodox theological views. He denied much of the historicity of the biblical narratives and held that only the words of Jesus were significant for his faith.[28] Where most pastors warned their congregants of the perils of Harlem's robust nightlife, Powell was as comfortable in a speakeasy as he was speaking from the pulpit. Abyssinian congregants appreciated their pastor-congressman regaling them weekly with his experiences in Washington. They were proud that he brought news from the nation's capital first-hand and refracted through a perspective that served their people's interests. Powell enjoyed the position as well. On Sunday mornings, he preached an aspirational gospel and during the week he legislated to bring life and aspiration closer to one another. His sermons always exposed the American dilemma, the gap between the nation's founding creeds and its current practices.[29] Powell reveled in exposing sites where America's practices were wanting, especially with regard to people of color. This Sunday, however, was different. Powell challenged African Americans to see their own culpability in the nation's moral shortcomings and called them to take responsibility for participating in the nation's reform. As he ascended the Abyssinian pulpit that Sunday, he summoned the exodus narrative to preach, "Stop Blaming Everybody Else."[30] The sermon challenged African Americans to reach beyond the horizon of traditional "Negro concerns" and to see that they had as much of an interest in the growing McCarthyism as white citizens.

It was an unusual subject for a black preacher. McCarthyism was a secular political concern that, for many African Americans, was out of place in the church. For most African Americans, the capitalism versus communism culture war, in every dimension, spoke only to white political concerns. Such matters were *not their place*.

Publicly, the black activist community concurred. When Walter White assumed the presidency of the NAACP and shifted the organization sharply to the right, he discouraged its members from engaging McCarthyism. Many other black activist groups followed suit. They simply eschewed communism and effectively admonished rank-and-file members that debate on the matter was not the business of black people. Powell's sermon charged his congregation and, by extension, black America to accept greater responsibility for the Republic, even in arenas that were not *their place*.

For Powell, any issue that impacted the Republic's orientation toward freedom was absolutely the business of blacks as well as whites. As such, Powell called African Americans to his pillar of fire politics. If blacks demanded the rights of full inclusion, then they must accept the attendant responsibilities that accompanied such rights. Powell fought for both. He believed he could empower African Americans to shape the Republic with the same legitimacy and accountability as their white counterparts.

Powell's vision stretched beyond the racially turbulent political reality to commend the radical equity that comprised his core commitments. Those same commitments also led Powell briefly to support the American Communist Party (ACP) and made him a target of the McCarthy machine. But for Powell, this was precisely where black political interests lie. Prior to World War II, the ACP had played a robust role in the nation's political landscape. It had participated in organizing American institutions such as the AFL-CIO and had brought black and white workers together to see their common interests. For African Americans, the ACP had funded the defense of the Scottsboro Nine and been the most ardent supporter of anti-segregationist legislation. But by 1947, the nation's business community had effectively tied the ACP to the Cold War with the Soviet Union in order to roll back President Franklin D. Roosevelt's New Deal progressivism. Many viewed anti-segregationist agitation as a Soviet ploy to undermine the nation. Worse for African Americans, as McCarthyism went unchallenged, it grew into a cancer that slowly rotted the infrastructure of black political activism.

Zealous McCarthyites at various levels of government blacklisted prominent figures such as Paul Robeson, Canada Lee, and Powell's own wife, renowned pianist Hazel Scott, or confiscated their passports so that they could not get work domestically or abroad. When McCarthyites working with Congress's House Un-American Activities Committee (HUAC) targeted progressive black faculty with unsubstantiated suspicions, such as Giovanni Rossi Lomanitz and Lee Lorch at Fisk University, black institutions buckled under the pressure and summarily dismissed dedicated educators.[31] Across the country, HUAC used black informants to help prosecute black activists such as Henry Winston and Benjamin J. Davis, a New York City councilman.[32] By 1951, the paranoia had so risen that when HUAC's surrogates arrested W.E.B. Du Bois for allegedly serving "as an agent of a foreign principal," a leading black newspaper, the *Chicago Defender*, declared, "it is a supreme tragedy that he should have become embroiled in activities that have been exposed as subversive in the twilight of his years."[33]

By that Sunday morning in 1953, Powell had had enough. Righteous indignation drove him to Exodus 32 and he opened the sermon by holding African Americans responsible for their quiet assent to the "Big Lie" and its havoc on the black community.[34] In the sermon, Powell beckoned African Americans to join him in moving beyond *their place* (as in what Negroes *should be* concerned about) to claim a place of their own determination, circumscribed by their own interests, and discerned from their own deliberations. Mimetically, the journey followed the African American migrations from the rural South. However, this *new place* had no geographical component, so its Promised Land challenged Powell to reinterpret the exodus narrative and to imagine emancipation as both the privilege and the responsibility of full inclusion.

As he preached, Powell stood where he was most comfortable—squarely between the civic and the ecclesial. He would not be reduced to either. He began with his text, only three verses in Exodus 32:

> And Moses said unto Aaron, "What did this people unto thee, that thou hast brought to great a sin upon them?" And Aaron said, "Let not the anger of my lord wax hot: Thou knowest the people, that they are set on mischief. For they said unto me, 'Make us gods, which shall go before us: for as for this Moses, the man that brought us up out of the land of Egypt, we wot not what is become of him.'"[35]

The passage finds biblical Israel at a crucial juncture. They have arrived at Sinai. They are no longer slaves to Pharaoh, so there is no returning to the familiarity of Egypt. They are also not yet constituted as a people; they have no land and have not fully realized their covenant with the deity who brought them up from bondage. The way forward is foreboding and their leader, Moses, has seemingly deserted them to commune with this unfamiliar God, Yahweh.

The text fits within the ambiguities of Powell's life. He had just completed his ninth year as the representative from Harlem. While Powell had broken barriers within the halls of Congress, he knew that he had little more than symbolic progress to offer African Americans who were looking for tangible gains toward equality. In the process, he had rebelled against black leadership by supporting then Republican presidential candidate Dwight D. Eisenhower over Adlai Stephenson and found himself alienated from many in the civil rights community. Worse, it appeared that his gamble on Eisenhower might not pay off. Eisenhower had not pursued a civil rights agenda as vigorously as Powell had hoped. The president believed the nation's racial dilemma could be solved through education and goodwill rather than legislation. Even more disappointing for Powell, by the end of the year it was clear that Eisenhower would not confront McCarthyism, so its machine would proceed unchecked. The way forward for Powell appeared as murky as the path of Israelites from Sinai to the Promised Land. Nonetheless, Powell forged ahead under the banner of his core belief, a civil religion deeply enmeshed in his Christian faith.

With no introduction, he began his sermon abruptly:

We are living, today, in the midst of the Big Lie. The leader of this new cult of deceit is Senator Joseph McCarthy. He has perjured himself countless times. The greatest perjury was this past week on television, when he said that President Truman's definition of McCarthyism was "word for word, line for line, comma for comma, taken from the *Daily Worker*." Reporters, when questioning his aide about this statement, asked him, "What edition and what page of the *Daily Worker*?" McCarthy's aide stated that the Senator did not quite tell the truth, there was no edition or page of the *Daily Worker* that printed the definition that President Truman used. McCarthy has never admitted any of the lies that he has stated. Despite all of this perjury, he has set himself up as the one single standard upon which the future of the United States of America must depend. An even greater tragedy is the full and unequivocal stamp of approval placed upon McCarthy by his church in Amsterdam, The Netherlands, when just a couple of weeks ago Cardinal Spellman unequivocally praised the Senator. McCarthyism, the Big Lie, is our responsibility because it is our fault. It is a reflection of the moral irresponsibility of the church, which condones him, the press, which praises him, and the large numbers of American people who follow him. The hour has arrived for the vast majority of American people who believe in the Protestant heritage of freedom and truth to, first, admit that McCarthyism is our fault and, second, atone for this national disgrace by purging McCarthyism from our national life.[36]

With the phrase "cult of deceit," Powell takes the nation's struggle against communism, a subject ostensibly unrelated to black church life, and places it squarely in the purview of religion. For Powell, McCarthyism was religion. It possessed its own doctrines and categorical truths: communism was evil and dialectically opposed to the so-called American way of life. It claimed zealous adherents such as Senator McCarthy, J. Edgar Hoover, the American Legion, and thousands of devotees across the nation. Powell proceeds to frame McCarthyism not simply as religion, but false religion. It was, in his words, "the Big Lie" that undergirded the "cult of deceit." That is, McCarthyism was leading the nation away from "true" patriotism just as the golden calf turned ancient Israel from the "true" worship of Yahweh.[37]

Powell's sharp judgment of McCarthyism emerged from his own background. Trained at Colgate with a deep grounding in the Protestant faith, Powell saw the "American experiment" itself as ordained by God and any ideology that contravened the Republic's forward movement toward freedom was not simply unpatriotic, it was apostasy.

After raging through his diatribe on "the Big Lie," Powell finally observes proper homiletic form and pauses to announce his subject: "One of the more prevalent sins of people, including religious people, from the beginning of time has been the habit of blaming everybody else for their personal, group or national sins. So I come today to preach from the subject 'Stop Blaming Everybody Else.'"[38] Immediately, he takes a more traditional course, an examination of biblical characters, namely, Aaron, the narrative's anti-hero. After consenting to the Israelites' request to forge an image of God, Aaron organized the congregation's contributions for the task. When an angry Moses descended the mountain to discover what had transpired, a pointed discourse between the two ensues: "What did this people do to you that you have brought so great a sin upon them?" Aaron refused to take responsibility for participating in constructing the golden calf (Ex. 32:21). Instead, he deflected the accusation implicit in Moses' question and retorted, "You know the people, that they are bent on evil. They said to me, 'Make us gods, who shall go before us; as for this Moses, the man who brought us up out of the land of Egypt, we do not know what has become of him' " (Ex. 32:22–23). Aaron's response implied that Moses should have known how these people, who are "bent on evil," would behave in his absence. His retort played on the Hebrew word *yada'*, "to know." It is an intimate knowing that suggests both a "belonging to" as in being a part of the Israelite people and as a "possession of" as in "they belong to Moses and he is responsible for their behavior." Earlier in 32:7, God had done exactly the same and handed the people over to Moses: "The Lord said to Moses, 'Go down at once! Your people, whom you brought up out of the land of Egypt, have acted perversely.'" In the same manner, Aaron now washed his hands of the matter and claimed the people belong to Moses.

By Exodus 32, Moses was well acquainted with this God whose audience required journeys to the mountain's summit. He had received the Covenant Code, which began with the Ten Commandments. The laws called the Children of Israel to subordinate their differing allegiances and varying subjectivities under nationhood. They became the covenanted people of God. However, while Moses was away receiving the law, the people had no experience in operationalizing the covenant; it was still new. God had called them to the base of the mountain only to consent to the covenant. They did not have the benefit of Moses' experience. They did not meet God at the burning bush nor did they commune with God upon the mountain for long intervals as had Moses. For the people, obedience rather than a voluntary response to a call characterized their relationship with God.

The story presents the difference with stark contrast. Moses enjoyed harmonious communion with Yahweh, but the Children of Israel struggled to understand who they had become upon crossing the Red Sea. The sermon's text presents a crucial point in their striving. The din from the valley abruptly interrupted Moses' tranquil audience with God. So disruptive are the people's strivings that it foreclosed any peaceful transition to realize the covenant. So Moses returns to indict Aaron and subsequently the people for violating the covenant to which they consented but had no experience upholding. Moses envisioned what the others could not—the creation of people who would be autonomous, whole, and holy to Yahweh. He believed the qualitative good of the covenant far outweighed the tragic violence that resulted from its enforcement.

Powell's subject position was not unlike that of Moses. He had committed himself to a civil religion that affirmed the American Republic as God's creation. Its "heritage of freedom," as Powell phrased it, was the nation's sacred orientation toward liberty and the telos of its divine intentionality. However, similar to the Israelites, African Americans had little experience with the covenant of civil religion that had been a hallmark of Powell's training at Colgate. Indeed, Powell's grand vision did not reflect the embedded theologies held by average Americans, black or white. For most citizens, the nation's current capacities for producing equity in opportunity rather than its ideal potentialities determined their allegiance. African Americans in particular had little reason to accept responsibility for citizenship in a nation where they had been treated as second class. Thus, Powell's fidelity to the republican ideal stood in contradistinction to the mainstream. He believed that citizenship was a categorical commitment; common nationhood supplanted racialized difference. From this fundamental position Powell challenged African Americans to the responsibility of rejecting McCarthyism.

Having pressed both his challenge and admonition, Powell concludes the sermon by finding a merger of horizons between the text and his congregation. With an appeal to responsibility ethics, Powell exhorts the congregation to embrace four virtues that he conceived of as indispensible to full participation in the American project: "*first*, that each one of us accounts for his own deeds. No one can excuse himself because 'everybody is doing it.'"[39] The widespread acquiescence to McCarthyism's terror cannot excuse African Americans from raising their voices of critique. Such criticism was in their self-interest and in the interest of the nation. Powell's commitment to a radical equality finds it particularly unacceptable for blacks to look to whites for cues on the right demonstration of patriotism. Blacks must deliberate upon their own interests and take the responsibility to act for themselves. "*Second*, what you get out of life depends largely on what you put into it. For example, Aaron put into the fire golden earrings and brought out a golden calf. *Third* stop evading your responsibilities!"[40] For Powell, the American Republic was an experiment that reached its highest ideals only as citizens rose to accountability for its character. If African Americans demanded full inclusion, then they must rise to shape the nation's political economy toward a more radical vision of justice. "*Fourth*, a confession of guilt is much more to one's credit than insincere excuses."[41] Powell calls the community to an act of piety and recommitment. Implicit in the admission of guilt is an acknowledgment of agency. In this last admonition, Powell empowers the black community with more than an awareness of the evil of McCarthyism; he awakens them to their own power to act and to take ownership within discourses that have been "none of their business."

Powell casts the sermon's final section within the Black Church's homiletical tradition by affirming the providence of God. He turns from Aaron's negligence and commends Moses' patriotism as worthy of emulation. To his congregation and by extension to his constituents across black America, he poses an interrogative "What can happen when you play your part?"[42] The question implies that all African Americans have a role in the "American project." Such a role operates simultaneously as both a religious and a political obligation. Powell explains in the first part of his celebration:

> Moses played his part: "Oh, this people have sinned a great sin, and have made them gods of gold. Yet now, if thou wilt forgive their sins—and if not, blot me, I pray thee, out of thy book which thou has written." But God refused to forgive them; He flatly refused to go with them anymore: "... I will send an angel before thee ... for I will not go up in the midst of thee; for thou art a stiffnecked people ..." Moses stood his ground and pleaded for the people. They talked together "face to face, as a man speaketh unto his friend." And Moses beseeched, "... if I have found grace in thy sight, shew me now thy way, that I may know thee ... and consider that this nation is thy people." And God relented. "I will do this thing also that thou has spoke: for thou has found grace in my sight, and I know thee by name."[43]

Moses' intercession on behalf of the Israelites changed his people's fate. It was both an act of love for his people, the Israelites, and a seminal act of patriotism that anticipated what would become the Israelite nation. As a result, God relented on the intent to destroy them.

By 1953, McCarthyism's ravages appeared as destructive to national life as the golden calf had been for the Children of Israel. The crisis demanded that African Americans accept the responsibility inspired by

Powell's civil religion. In a heightened and celebratory tone, Powell offered assurance to the congregation as he enumerated what God did as Moses "played his part." His confidence lay in his belief that "the Protestant heritage of freedom" was ultimately right and that the God who ordained the Republic would be faithful to its fruition.

Powell begins the second portion of his celebration with a question. It signals a break between this and the previous section. He offers four corresponding consequences to the four admonitions.

> What were the results? *First*, new tablets for the testimony of God. *Second*, a new concept of God: "The Lord, the Lord God, merciful and gracious, long-suffering, and abundant in goodness and truth, Keeping mercy for thousands, forgiving iniquity and transgression and sins". . . . *Third*, a new convenant. "Behold, I make a convenant: before all thy people I will do marvels, such as have not been done in all the earth, more in any nation: and all the people among which thou art shall see the work of the Lord: for it is a terrible that I will do with thee." *Fourth*, a new Moses. "It came to pass, when Moses came down from Mount Sinai . . . the skin of his face shone while he talked."[44]

The "New Tablets" and new concept of God signify a new law now for a people who, because of Moses' pleadings, found grace in God's sight. For those who heard the sermon that morning, the "new law" held the promise that if they did their part, a legislative justice would supplant the old laws of Jim Crow under which they suffered. The "new covenant" recalled God's covenant with ancient Israel in Genesis 12 and God's covenant with Moses at Sinai. Powell imagined that as the nation repented and reclaimed a trajectory of radical equality and freedom, God promised a marvelous new reality with privileges and concomitant responsibilities. Equity distributed across the political economy required accountability. As biblical Israel could not have envisioned the Promised Land from Sinai, so the American Republic could not envision its glorious telos from the present site of McCarthyism's terror.

Finally, Powell's celebration points to transcendence. As God's emissary, Moses was transfigured. By "playing his part," Moses not only saved his people, but he has done God's will. In this last exhortation, Powell connects civic participation with religious duty and signifies McCarthyism with apostasy. As he closes, he does not leave God's reward for faithfulness in the realm of the spiritual; he concludes the sermon by returning to more pragmatic consequences of Moses' epiphany. "And when Aaron and all the children of Israel saw Moses, behold, the skin of his face shone; and they were afraid to come nigh him."[45] With these words, Powell promised more than participatory agency, but power. For those hearing Powell's sermon, the promise of power to match the forces of surveillance and containment was sufficient assurance of the worthiness of their struggle.

King: The Politics of Public Piety as Pillar of Cloud Performance

Powell emphasized black people's responsibility to uphold the law, but King wanted to show that black people were worthy to be granted equality under the law. In the nascent stages of the Civil Rights Movement, King turned to the exodus story as the textual basis for two important sermons, "Death of Evil upon the Seashore" and "Birth of a New Nation." Although delivered only two years apart, the sermons' starkly disparate politics bear witness to King's keen attentiveness to the evolving historical circumstance and his ability to adapt his interpretive activity to it. King preached "The Death of Evil Upon the Seashore" on July 24, 1955, less than three months after he defended his dissertation.[46] The sermon emphasized personal piety and traditional Christology with only tentative gestures toward the contemporaneous local struggles for emancipation that would soon coalesce to become the Civil Rights Movement.

The text for King's sermon was but one verse, Exodus 14:30, "And Israel saw the Egyptians dead upon the seashore." Israel's struggle was seemingly over. They were free from bondage, their enemy was defeated, and their deliverer, Yahweh, had proven faithful. But this juncture only marked the beginning of their perilous journey to the Promised Land. King's choice of texts collapses the exodus into a single, but, for King, seminal event—the defeat of the Egyptians. Encapsulated in the title, King conveyes the image of Egyptian bodies strewn across the shore of the Red Sea with powerful representational force. The spectacle of an oppressor brought to dramatic destruction stood mimetically for the hopes of black people's centuries-long struggle against repression. Symbolically, the transfers were almost self-evident. Death signified finality. Evil simultaneously referred to biblical Egypt and the Jim Crow regime. Its death could only be brought about by a supernatural act of God. Analogous to biblical Egypt, Jim Crow's repressive structures proved beyond the power of human efforts to subdue. Accordingly, King minimizes human agency, but insists that God ultimately destroys evil.

King's position befitted his politics. While many have dubbed King's politics as prophetically radical by highlighting his public demands for black civil rights, his posture nonetheless was of the reformist tradition, which conformed to valences of legitimate civil agency.[47] King had good reason to choose a moderate course at the beginning of his ministry. Similar to Harper, King's politics were characterized by the markers of middle-class respectability, particularly personal piety. It was a staple of his Baptist heritage. Both King's upbringing and the class status his family had enjoyed for two generations naturally gave him cause to be invested in the privileges that civil society bestowed upon its elite, even those who were black.

Born in January 1929, just ten months before the Great Depression, King grew up among Atlanta's black middle class. Their fiscal and theological conservatism reflected both economic necessity and the racial hierarchies to which they were always vulnerable. King's mother, Alberta Christine Williams King, taught in the Atlanta school system, while his father served as pastor of the prominent Ebenezer Baptist Church. Both were college-trained professionals.[48] King was aware of his privilege: "My mother, as the daughter of a successful minister, had grown up in comparative comfort. She had been sent to the best available school and college and had, in general, been protected from the worst blights of discrimination."[49] Although the senior King, who grew up as a sharecropper's son, faced segregation's "brutalities at first hand," he achieved a class status that perhaps buffered him from some of the South's worst brutality by the time he became Ebenezer's pastor.[50] Of his father, King wrote,

> From before I was born, my father had refused to ride the city buses, after witnessing a brutal attack on a load of Negro passengers. He had led the fight in Atlanta to equalize teachers' salaries, and had been instrumental in the elimination of Jim-Crow elevators in the courthouse. As pastor of

the Ebenezer Baptist Church, where he still presides over a congregation of four thousand, he had wielded a great influence in the Negro community, and had perhaps won the grudging respect of the whites. At any rate, they had never attacked him physically, a fact that filled my brother and sister and me with wonder as we grew up in this tension-packed atmosphere.[51]

King admired his father's seeming invincibility, but the senior King's stature arose from a far more confrontational politics than his son would ever deploy. King recounts two episodes where he witnessed his father's politics. On these occasions, the Sr. King showed his son how to leverage their class status as a response to injustice:

> I remember a trip to a downtown shoe store with Father when I was still small. We had sat down in the first empty seats at the front of the store. A young white clerk came up and murmured politely: "I'll be happy to wait on you if you'll just move to those seats in the rear."
>
> Dad immediately retorted, "There's nothing wrong with these seats. We're quite comfortable here."
>
> "Sorry," said the clerk, "but you'll have to move."
>
> "We'll either buy shoes sitting here," my father retorted, "or we won't buy shoes at all." Whereupon he took me by the hand and walked out of the store.[52]

The elder King and his son were not concerned with affording shoes, but rather with being granted the respect deserved by any *paying* customer. At one fell swoop, Daddy King taught his son that having the means to purchase also meant having the power to choose. In this case such power meant the right to request service or the ability to purchase elsewhere. On another occasion, the elder King resisted a police officer:

> I remember riding with him another day when he accidentally drove past a stop sign. A policeman pulled up to the car and said:
>
> "All right, boy, pull over and let me see your license."
>
> My father instantly retorted: "Let me make it clear to you that you aren't talking to a boy. If you persist in referring to me as boy, I will be forced to act as if I don't hear a word you are saying."

The policeman was so shocked in hearing a Negro talk to him so forthrightly that he didn't quite know how to respond. He nervously wrote the ticket and left the scene as quickly as possible.[53]

King watched his father, a well-spoken and prominent African American minister in the city of Atlanta, assert himself and trump even a white, working-class police officer. Since such occurrences were not the norm, the story only reinforces King's sense of "wonder" at the stature and power his father possessed. Perhaps this dilemma marks the limits of King's reformist politics.

King shared his father's frustration with segregation, even if reflections on his early life betrayed his class-consciousness.

> There was a pretty strict system of segregation in Atlanta. For a long, long time I could not go swimming, until there was a Negro YMCA. A Negro child in Atlanta could not go to any public park. I could not go to the so-called white schools. In many of the stores downtown, I couldn't go to a lunch counter to buy a hamburger or a cup of coffee. I could not attend any of the theaters. There were one or two Negro theaters, but they didn't get any of the main pictures. If they did get them, they got them two or three years later.
>
> As a teenager I had never been able to accept the fact of having to go to the back of a bus or sit in the segregated section of a train. The first time I had been seated behind a curtain in a dining car, I felt as if the curtain had been dropped on my selfhood. Having the usual growing boy's pleasure in movies, I had yet gone to a downtown theater in Atlanta only once. The experience of having to enter a rear door and sit in a filthy peanut gallery was so obnoxious that I could not enjoy the picture.[54]

These childhood memories revealed both King's investment in the fundamental arrangements of civil society and his frustration with the manner in which racial hierarchies trumped his class privilege. In other words, he was prevented from enjoying the benefit that his socioeconomic status (and disposable income) should have afforded him.

Nonetheless, King's politics were not his father's. His reflections show a different response to white repression. King deploys personal piety and projects it into public performance. In the face of immanent violence and sure bodily harm from white segregationists, he called black demonstrators to kneel before them, to pray publically, to sing the songs of Zion whose lyrics ran deep in black cultural history. They appeared vulnerable as they performed the highest of moral virtue, but they were not. All the while, news cameras broadcasted disturbing images of rabid segregationists unleashing vicious brutality upon the innocent and, most important, upon the pious. They sang their way into jails and prayed their way out, but they did not strike back. Piety became King's mask and the hallmark of his pillar of cloud performance. It both offered protection and claimed a moral high ground. It had served him well since he was a boy.

> When I was about eight years old, I was in one of the downtown stores of Atlanta and all of a sudden someone slapped me, and the only thing I heard was somebody saying, "You are that nigger that stepped on my foot." And it turned out to be a white lady. Of course I didn't retaliate at any point; I wouldn't dare retaliate when a white person was involved. I think some of it was part of my native structure—that is, that I have never been one to hit back. I finally told my mother what had happened, and she was very upset about it. But the lady who slapped me had gone, and my mother and I left the store almost immediately.[55]

Retaliation, tantamount to vengeance, would have provoked sure and swift consequence. King knew better. No doubt motivated by fear and prudence, his response nonetheless performed the Christ-like piety of Matthew 5:44. Wrongfully accused, judged, and convicted by the woman, King, like Christ, stood in silence.

Reflecting upon the attack even years later, King's writing does not show the same disgust toward the woman that he expressed about the movie theater's balcony or being forced to sit in the back of the bus. It is important to note that King's writings themselves were also performative. To a degree, King crafted this recollection for a white audience to evoke their sympathies for the Civil Rights Movement. King was aware of his audience, its moral and social sensibilities, and appetites. He foregrounds passivity as a boy who did not respond when the woman attacked him and, more particularly, he emphasizes the same in his reflection on the episode years later as an adult, "Of course I didn't retaliate at any point; I wouldn't dare retaliate when a white person was involved. I think some of it was part of my native structure." As a southerner, King knew, as did most black boys, the dangerous racialized and sexualized connotation of any encounter with a white woman, even for a little boy. In 1955, the year King completed his doctoral studies, a fourteen-year-old Emmitt Till was murdered for being *im*-pious rather than deferential in his random encounter with a white woman. Till had come from Chicago and was not privy to ways that black southerners deployed piety as a tactic for protection. But King knew its value well and made it the core of his strategy of nonviolent resistance.

Perhaps this was his first experience with nonviolent resistance. As King's political conscience developed, he took on the burden of moral exemplariness and commended the same politics to those quarters of the Civil Rights Movement under his leadership. Upon being arrested in Montgomery on a false loitering charge, King affirmed that the practice of such a politics was a divine calling as he stood before Judge Eugene Loe:

> Your honor, you have found me guilty. My wife and I have talked and prayed over the course of action in the event this should happen. If I am fined, I must tell you that I cannot in good conscience pay a fine for an act I did not commit and for brutal treatment I did not deserve. I am inwardly compelled to take this stand. We are commanded to resist evil by the God that created us all.[56]

Early in his career, King was not interested in a radical racial politics. He believed African Americans could transform the nation by seizing the moral high ground of nonviolent resistance to evil. Doing so, they would demonstrate the great potential of the nation's ideal. In each episode of resistance, he availed himself of the modes of action (nonviolent protests such as mass marches, boycotts, political lobbying, and grassroots organizing) that were legitimately available to him and those in the movement as citizens of the Republic.

King: Exodus, the Death of Evil, and the Witness of Human Agency

In 1954 King moved to Montgomery, Alabama, to begin a career in ministry as pastor of the prestigious Dexter Avenue Baptist Church. Ironically, King succeeded Vernon Johns—the towering intellectual and nationally renowned social gospel preacher—who shared King's passion for social justice but did not have the patience for King's pillar of cloud politics. Johns gained a reputation both for his blistering condemnation of the white racism that structured Montgomery and his relentless criticism of the Dexter Avenue congregation for "their obsession with status and prestige."[57] For most of his five-year tenure, Johns and the congregation remained at loggerheads. Johns's zealous activism discomfited Dexter Avenue, while the congregation's apparent complacency and elitism provoked Johns to repeated moral admonishment from the pulpit. Ultimately, the perpetual conflict led to Johns's resignation. When King arrived, he found Dexter Avenue populated by middle-class professionals where both social and theological conservatism characterized the ecclesial culture.[58] Their class values and social commitments mirrored those of King's own upbringing. In Montgomery, Alabama, they understood that any agitation only exposed them to reprisals for which they had little defense. So in 1955, when King preached "Death of Evil" resonant with themes that affirmed personal piety more than social justice, the sermon found a welcome reception.

In April 1957, King again turned to the exodus story in the Dexter Avenue pulpit. Instead of soft-pedaling his social gospel message, King preached "Birth of a New Nation." He laid bare the evils of colonialism and imagined a coalition of the African and Asian nations struggling toward emancipation together. The title, a reference to the D. W. Griffith movie, showed King's keen sense of irony.[59] The sermon celebrated the birth of the nation of Ghana, which had risen in triumph over British colonial repression. King was aware that the intervening period between 1955 and 1957 brought about a transformation in political and social circumstances. The Civil Rights Movement (CRM) had progressed. It had taken its first faltering steps when the Montgomery Improvement Association confronted segregation in the municipal public transportation system. But 378 days later it had beaten the Montgomery City Commission and won a victory for justice. The experience had tested King's leadership.[60] Professionally, King was no longer a recent graduate student; he had come into his own as pastor of the renowned Dexter Avenue congregation. Success in Montgomery raised his stature nationally and internationally. Theologically, the Montgomery Bus Boycott evidenced for King the efficacy of human agency in the struggle to resist repression. The sermons' differing treatments of the exodus narrative reveal a transformation in King's thought. Four distinctions are clear in the two sermons: They differ in emphases on personal piety and traditional Christology. They differ in attentiveness to the exposition of the exodus story itself. They take up opposing portrayals of Egypt. Most striking, they differ in their appraisals of human agency.

While both "Death of Evil" and "Birth of a New Nation" present what King understood as a worldwide struggle to overcome colonialism, "Death of Evil" repeatedly emphasizes themes absent in the later "Birth of a New Nation." In "Death of Evil," King offered a cautious critique of colonialism and focused on personal piety and traditionally fundamentalist themes such as the providence of God in human suffering. "Death of Evil" begins with a long meandering discourse on evil as an abstract concept:

> Is there hardly anything more obvious than the fact that evil is present in the universe? Its nagging, prehensile tentacles project into every level of human existence. We may debate over the origin of evil, but only the person victimized with a superficial optimism will debate over its reality. Evil is stark, grim, and colossally real. Affirming the reality of evil in unmistakable terms, the Bible symbolically pictures the conniving work of a serpent which injects discord into the beautiful, harmonious symphony of life in a garden.[61]

He takes care to conclude the first section with a reference to a Christological vision of evil, and a minor celebration at the end of the introduction, "Evil is ultimately doomed by the powerful, inexorable forces of good. Good Friday must give way to the triumphant music of Easter."[62] Throughout the introduction, King makes repeated references to the Bible's portrayal of evil and its defeat by the work of Christ. The first example of such evil is "tragic lust and inordinate selfishness."[63]

King refers briefly to social evil, namely, "imperialistic nations crushing other people with the battering rams of social injustice," but closes the section only after a firm exhortation of a classical Christological cosmology, "Caesar occupied a palace and Christ a cross, but the same Christ so split history into A.D. and B.C. that even the reign of Caesar was subsequently dated by his name."[64] King leaves evil virtually uncontextualized; it is a matter for the transcendent work of Christ.

Second, "Death of Evil" engages a full exposition of the exodus, but King gives no such attention to the exodus story in "Birth of a New Nation," even though it is the textual basis of both sermons. In the second section of "Death of Evil," King recounts the exodus story, repeatedly amplifying the concept of evil at successive junctures. Each description presents evil with increasing clarity. He introduces the story by identifying biblical Egypt as an "evil in the form of humiliating oppression, ungodly exploitation, and crushing domination and the Israelites symbolized goodness in the form of devotion and dedication to the God of Abraham, Isaac, and Jacob."[65] In dramatic oratory, King imagines the two nations in an irreconcilable conflict. Biblical Egypt's struggle to "maintain her oppressive yoke was locked with Israel's struggle to gain freedom." Finally, he concludes, "evil is recalcitrant and determined, and never voluntarily relinquishes its hold short of a persistent, almost fanatical resistance."[66] Even after the Israelites cross the Red Sea, ostensibly escaping oppression, evil pursues and is destroyed only when God draws the waters across the sea bed and drowns the Egyptian army.

In "Birth of a Nation," no such exposition exists. King passes through the biblical exodus with two sentences, merely a nodding glance, pausing only to comment, "It is the story of the exodus, the story of the flight of the Hebrew people from the bondage of Egypt, through the wilderness, and finally to the Promised Land. It's a beautiful story."[67] This time, King introduces Cecil B. DeMille's epic film as the text for the exodus story.

I had the privilege the other night of seeing the story in movie terms in New York City, entitled "The Ten Commandments," and I came to see it in all of its beauty—the struggle of Moses, the struggle of his devoted followers as they sought to get out of Egypt. And they finally moved on to the wilderness and toward the Promised Land.[68]

The film had been released only six months earlier, but its images by sheer cinematic force had by then shaped the nation's religious imagination. King appeals to the film's images as a shorthand exposition of the exodus text. Charleton Heston's and Yul Brynner's portrayals, the embodiments of good and evil, offer King an opportunity to universalize the story's dramatis personae. "This is something of the story of every people struggling for freedom. It is the first story of man's explicit quest for freedom. And it demonstrates the stages that seem to inevitably follow the quest for freedom."[69] In effect, he takes the film up as a simulacrum where Heston's and Brynner's performances, which personified good and evil respectively, concretize their moral positions in faces, flesh, and blood.

Two years earlier, when King preached "Death of Evil," he understood this struggle as a cosmic battle ultimately to free humanity from sin. He attributed the struggle and consequent victory to the work of Christ. However, in the sermonic narration of "Birth of a New Nation," King changes codes and reads the exodus through contemporaneous geopolitical events. No Christological references appear in "Birth of a New Nation's" exposition of evil. Slavery in exodus, the quintessential symbol for oppression, holds in tension both *corvée labor* of the ancient world and Western colonialism's repression. King replaces the abstract evil represented by his descriptions of Egypt in "Death of Evil" with the "real" evil of colonialism now embodied in the names of active nation states.

> And there was a big scramble for power in Africa. With the growth of the slave trade, there came into Africa, into the Gold Coast in particular, not only the Portuguese but also the Swedes and the Danes and the Dutch and the British. And all of these nations competed with each other to win the power of the Gold Coast so that they could exploit these people for commercial reasons and sell them into slavery.[70]

Evil's presentation is neither cosmic nor abstract. Rather, it is immanent and identified in contemporaneous real-world relationships between colonial powers and subject peoples.

Inevitably, Egypt becomes a contested sign as King structures this moral geography. Biblical Egypt symbolizes oppression, while the Egypt of 1956 struggled for emancipation in the wake of the British occupation.

Early in the sermon, King sets up a tension between the two referents of the same linguistic sign, Egypt, but leaves both significations intact. On one hand, he presents biblical Egypt, in the manner of the black preaching tradition, as a symbol of universal oppression:

> There is something in the soul that cries out for freedom. There is something deep down within the very soul of man that reaches out for Canaan. Men cannot be satisfied with Egypt. They tried to adjust to it for a while. Many men have vested interests in Egypt, and they are slow to leave. Egypt makes it profitable to them; some people profit by Egypt. The vast majority, the masses of people never profit by Egypt, and they are never content with it. And eventually they rise up and begin to cry out for Canaan's land.[71]

On the other hand, King situates Egypt in the contemporaneous geopolitical frame of African nations resisting colonial powers.

> Egypt is in Africa . . . You also know that for years and for centuries, Africa has been one of the most exploited continents in the history of the world. It's been the "Dark Continent." It's been the continent that has suffered all of the pain and the affliction that could be mustered up by other nations. And it is that continent which has experienced slavery, which has experienced all of the lowest standards that we can think about, and it's been brought into being by the exploitation inflicted upon it by other nations.[72]

As the sermon progresses, King returns to the Egypt of biblical tradition but only as an increasingly de-historicized symbol. He makes no declarative statements about Egypt, but each time, he uses Egypt in the objective form.

As he narrates Ghana's story of independence, he compares Ghana's journey to freedom to that of the ancient Israelites. "This was the birth of a new nation. This nation was now out of Egypt and had crossed the Red Sea. Now it will confront its wilderness. Like any breaking aloose from Egypt, there is a wilderness ahead."[73] King gives Egypt the same presentation as he offers his congregation lessons from the Ghanaian struggle:

Ghana reminds us that whenever you break out of Egypt, you better get ready for stiff backs. You better get ready for some homes to be bombed. You better get ready for some churches to be bombed. You better get ready for a lot of nasty things to be said about you, because you're getting out of Egypt, and, whenever you break aloose from Egypt, the initial response of the Egyptian is bitterness.

In each reference, King loosens the symbol from the system of signs that refer to it as a historical nation of people who enslaved the Israelites. "Egypt" begins to appear in the sermon as "out of Egypt" and "from Egypt" not as a biblical nation, but a state of bondage. King allows the biblical Egypt to recede and finally connects Egypt's struggle to the rising tide of anti-colonial resistance. Similar to David Walker, King turns to a positive moral presentation of Egypt.[74] Referring to the 1956 Suez Crisis, King writes:

Egypt, a little country; Egypt, a country with no military power. They could have easily defeated Egypt, but they did not realize that they were fighting more than Egypt. There were attacking world opinion; they were fighting the whole Asian-African bloc, which is the block that now thinks and moves and determines the course of the history of the world.[75]

With this, the sermon's final representation of Egypt, King's language returns to declarative statements. He does not recover the biblical symbol of Egypt to contrast it with Canaan—representing the deep mythic symbols of bondage and freedom respectively. Rather, King rewrites the African American cultural myth and re-signifies Egypt as a symbol of resistance to evil rather than a symbol of oppression. By carefully manipulating presences, absences, and emphases, his representation of Egypt turns the biblical portrayal on its head. Egypt itself comes to "birth" as a part of King's "new nation," which not only refers to Ghana, but to what he calls the whole "Asian-African bloc" struggling for freedom. The direction King takes reveals his emerging international consciousness in conflict with his biblical theology. He resolves the two by contextualizing the historical Egypt as an African nation, which dislodges the symbol's signification with biblical Egypt.

The fourth difference in the sermons' presentations is their view of human agency. Reinhold Neibuhr's Christian realism clearly influences "Death of Evil."[76] As King presented the exodus story, evil's formidable and persistent forms surpass human ability to defeat it utterly, and only an act of God in the form of the sweeping waters of the Red Sea could destroy it. In the sermon's introduction, King claims such activity to be properly the work of Christ, a cosmic struggle between "God and Satan."[77] The third section of "Death of Evil" reinforces this position explicitly, "God may not break in and smash the evil schemes of wicked men."[78] King concludes that human efforts to resist evil are not ultimately determinate but rather, "evil dies on the seashore, not merely because of man's endless struggle against it, but because of God's power to defeat it."[79] Such a tentative appraisal of the efficaciousness of human struggle against oppression befitted a young, well-educated, but untested Boston-trained theologian. King had only recently begun his tenure leading a conservative congregation that was more conscientious about its social status than social justice. It also befitted a pastor and a congregation formed in the milieu of southern racism.

More striking, however, King attributes progress in the African American struggle for emancipation to external actors, rather than to the struggle's internal impulses and initiatives. "Death of Evil," resembles Absalom Jones's celebrated "Thanksgiving Sermon," which located God's work only in an act of Congress, and not also among Africans resisting repression.[80] King names Thomas Jefferson's conscience to represent the "numerous abolitionists [who] were tortured in their hearts by the question of slavery."[81] Rather than recalling the litany of slave revolts or resistance efforts on the part of Africans held in slavery to fight for their own freedom, King turns to the Emancipation Proclamation and the days when "Abraham Lincoln faced squarely this matter of slavery" as the next critical juncture in the African American struggle for freedom.[82] Ultimately, King describes "a world shaking decree by the nine justices of the United States Supreme Court," not a Moses who emerges from among the oppressed that would "open the Red Sea."[83] Unlike the exodus story, which empowers the Hebrews through Moses, who challenges and defeats pharaoh in successive contests, King's depictions of Moses are quiescent and impotent in the face of contemporary pharaohs. He laments, "Despite the patient cry of many a Moses," these pharaohs "refused to let the Negro people go."[84]

However, in "Birth of a New Nation," King's interpretive work shows a different view of human agency. Paralleling evil's portrayal as real colonial repression, King also finds a real-world Moses in Kwame Nkrumah. In the sermon, King deftly brings the Joseph and Moses stories together as he composes a sermonic iconography for the Ghanaian president. Reminiscent of the biblical narratives heralding a male hero, King narrates the story using the convention's epic literary form, "About 1909, a young man was born on the twelfth of September. History didn't know what the young man had in his mind."[85] As Moses was educated as a member of the Egyptian royal house, so King emphasizes Nkrumah's analogous experience among Anglo-American powers, noting how Nkrumah "went down to Pennsylvania, to Lincoln University. He started studying there, and he started reading the great insights of the philosophers . . . And went over to the University of Pennsylvania and took up a master's there in philosophy and sociology . . . He got a ship and went to London and stopped for a while by the London School of Economy and picked up another degree there."[86] Although they were members of the royal house, neither Moses nor Joseph abandoned their Hebrew identities. Their ethnic consciousness led them to respond to their people's suffering. Similarly, King dramatizes Nkrumah's sense of place and nationalist loyalty, quoting the leader as declaring, "I want to go back home. I want to go back to West Africa, the land of my people, my native land. There is some work to be done there."[87]

The cosmic battle between good and evil, or God and Satan, recedes into the background in "Birth of a New Nation." Instead, human efforts, both good *and* evil, come to the fore. Progress for Nkrumah comes because "he worked hard, and he started getting a following."[88] Ultimately, the death of evil comes not as a result of some supernatural act, but because of the

> struggling that had been going on for years. It was now coming to the point that this little nation was moving toward its independence. Then came the continual agitation, the continual resistance, so that the British Empire saw that it could no longer rule the Gold Coast. And they agreed

that on the sixth of March 1957, they would release this nation. This nation would no longer be a colony of the British Empire, that this nation would be a sovereign nation within the British Commonwealth.[89]

King underscores his position, declaring, "All of this was because of the persistent protest, the continual agitation on the part of Prime Minister Kwame Nkrumah and the other leaders who worked along with him and the masses of people who were willing to follow."[90]

In contrast to his historical frame in "Death of Evil," which left African Americans at the banks of a "Red Sea opened," King turns to a narrative of Ghanaian national history to frame the struggle for emancipation in "Birth of a New Nation." He had just returned from the inauguration of Ghana's first prime minister. Ghana's struggle for emancipation offered him an example of successful resistance to colonialism that fit both his nonviolent philosophy and his belief in the ultimate triumph of justice over evil. He attributes emancipatory progress to human efforts in their struggle. Before mapping a narrative of African American struggle upon the exodus story as he did in "Death of Evil," King maps his narrative of Ghanaian national history onto the exodus story. This time King's appraisal is more optimistic; it extends to the border of the wilderness rather than stalled at "the Red Sea opened." Kwame Nkrumah's inaugural ceremony as prime minister signaled that "[t]his nation was now out of Egypt and has crossed the Red Sea."[91]

King understood well the economic, political, and social challenges that would confront the new sovereign state as it repaired the damage of colonial rule. He believed these challenges would constitute Ghana's wilderness. The triumphant story of Ghanaian independence leads King once again to plot African American progress toward emancipation along the exodus schema. This time King is far more confident in the progress of the African American struggle; he parallels African American progress with that of the Ghanaians, writing "we ourselves find ourselves breaking loose from an evil Egypt, trying to move through the wilderness toward the promised land of cultural integration."[92]

Finally, King is also more confident about the agency of African Americans acting for themselves. He replaces the tentative appraisals that characterize human activity in "Death of Evil" with strong affirmations pleading for vigilant resistance:

So don't go out this morning with any illusions. Don't go back to into your homes and around Montgomery thinking that the Montgomery City Commission and that all the forces in the leadership of the South will eventually work this thing out for Negroes. It's going to work out; it's going to roll in on the wheels of inevitability. If we wait for it to work itself out, it will never be worked out. Freedom only comes through persistent revolt, through persistent agitation, through persistent rising up against the system of evil.[93]

The new confidence reflects both the triumph in Ghana and the victory in Montgomery. In Ghana, King witnessed an example of African people throwing off the yoke of British colonialism and establishing a stable government with just societal arrangements. In Alabama, he and the African American community had defeated the Montgomery City Commission. In the yearlong struggle, he had experienced the power of collective human agency among African Americans, and he had been transformed. To be sure, evil had died on the seashore, but in Montgomery and in Accra, the people along with God killed it together.

Exodus at the Intersection of the Black Power Movement and the Black Church

But if you listen attentively to his voice and do all that I say,
then I will be an enemy to your enemies and a foe to your foes.
—Exodus 23:22

By the end of 1965, Jim Crow was pronounced legally dead. If the *Plessy* decision signed de jure segregation's birth certificate, then the Civil Rights Act of 1964 and the Voting Rights Act of 1965 together signed its death certificate. From *Plessy* onward, Jim Crow had ably performed the express will of the Supreme Court of the United States. Its laws devastated black lives from one end of the nation to another. Jim Crow was the slave regime's worthy successor. It was more effective than localized Black Codes or even the southern plantation economy because it made legalized segregation the national standard and maintained racialized hierarchies without the plantation system. By the time it was outlawed, almost a century later, Jim Crow had indelibly shaped American culture.

Legalized segregation's death thus meant that 1965 held the promise of new civil liberties. The law of the land, although often weakly enforced, had finally shifted from maintaining racialization in public life to mitigating it. Black people greeted Jim Crow's passing as they had done with the slave regime's demise; they composed yet another narrative of ascendance. They were eager to make up the generations of losses since the end of Reconstruction. But the Deep South, in particular, resisted the new era. Its fragile social psyche and political economy were still too dependent upon black subjugation to survive an abrupt shift toward legal equality. (The same was true regarding Latinos in the Southwest and Asians in the West.) Once again, southern intransigence forced the federal government to deploy its agents to the American South to ensure civil liberty, just as it had for the few years during Reconstruction. Under the watchful eyes of federal examiners, African Americans seized the opportunity and registered to vote at rates the nation had not seen since the 1870s. Between 1964 and 1969, black voter registration rates in four former confederate states skyrocketed. In Georgia, rates rose from 27.4 percent to 60.4 percent; in Alabama they rose from 19.3 percent to 61.3 percent; in Louisiana, they rose from 31.6 percent to 60.8 percent; and in Mississippi, they rose from 6.7 percent to 66.5 percent.[1] Newly enfranchised black voters took their ballots and transformed the landscape of elected representation. In 1966, they had only ninety-seven black elected state legislators, and only six black members of Congress. But by 1973, they had elected more than two hundred black representatives to state legislatures and sent sixteen members to the U.S. Congress.[2]

Black consumers took similar optimism to the commercial sphere. They had long been constrained by their race, and now they wanted to be considered by their financial wherewithal. For the first time black people could shop in any department store and try on clothing, eat in restaurants of their choice, and competitively ply their businesses and trades—at least legally. They spent their hard-earned dollars with new enthusiasm, sometimes with ill-advised abandon, but always with the dignity that demanded equal treatment.

As with earlier iterations of the narrative of black ascent, this one also took place amid simultaneous strategies of containment and surveillance. Jim Crow may have been dead, but it had lived long enough for the political economy to revive old, horrific methods of suppression, and to devise new ways of maintaining racialized hierarchies that no longer required explicit legal enforcement. In those same former confederate states where black enfranchisement rose, vigilante violence also increased to alarming levels. Soon, the same backlash infected national and state politics. Angry conservatives made President Johnson the face of white racial sovereignty's betrayal. In the 1964 primary season, staggering numbers of white Democrats supported the rabid segregationist governor of Alabama, George Wallace, over Johnson. Although Johnson won the general election, Barry Goldwater, the anti–civil rights Republican, took a majority of the popular vote in the Deep South. It was the first time that a Republican had received all of the electoral votes in Georgia, Alabama, Mississippi, South Carolina, and Louisiana. The South was "solid" again. This time it was solidly Republican. It remained so for another ten years until the election of President Jimmy Carter in 1976.

White reaction to black progress did not stop at the voting booth. Concerted backlash across various arenas including employment, housing, education, and commerce demoralized African Americans despite their hard-won gains. The laws that forced white-owned establishments to open their doors, dining rooms, and even restrooms to black, Latino, Asian, and other customers could not force proprietors to extend the same quality of service. Often they gave these patrons the worst rooms at hotels, offered substandard service and poor quality food at restaurants, charged higher prices for lesser service, and otherwise made them know that they were despised. Many white-owned restaurants and other public establishments became private clubs for members only. Where they could afford to do so, wealthier white families developed private or "Christian" schools whose charters recreated de facto segregated education. Unfortunately, these new manifestations of segregation were often legal under the existing laws.

Full equality still had not come, but not because the laws had failed. The great measures of civil reform had done their work, but they were never intended to complete the Republic's unfinished project of freedom. Rather, they were meant to be tools to work toward fulfilling the U.S. Constitution's lofty promises for all of its citizens. Where African Americans expected more progress than the legislation could bear, and where whites found legal ways to circumvent the laws' intentions, its limits became evident.

The litany of litigated and legislative victories, including *Brown vs. Board of Education* in 1954, the Civil Rights Act of 1964, and the Voting Rights Act of 1965, brought these limits to light. They resulted in few material gains in the real lives of African Americans. In fact, by many measures, black life declined. Between 1964 and 1971, black unemployment rose from 9.6 percent to 9.9 percent, while the white unemployment rate rose from 4.6 percent to 5.4 percent during the same period. In 1969, the median black income was $4,472 for a family of four with an eighth grade education, while the median income for a white family of four with the same education was $7,018.[3] Sure enough, the laws had given black people rights. But black people wanted more than the *right* not to be discriminated against in public life. Rather, they wanted what white citizens took for granted, namely the *power* to build satisfying lives, and to protect their families, homes, property, and persons, and to educate themselves and their children.

The backdrop of the successes and the limits of civil rights legislation raised black progress toward the Promised Land to greater relief. Young activists built on impressive gains of their CRM forebears. They focused on challenges to black life at the limits of the legislation's effectiveness and articulated a clearer vision of what freedom meant. Organizations such as the Student Nonviolent Coordinating Committee (SNCC) and the Black Panther Party for Self Defense (BPP) redoubled their grass-roots work toward fulfilling the long withheld promise of the "blessings of liberty." For these and similarly oriented organizations, "blessings" meant autonomy in black communities, full employment, freedom from police brutality, and equal access to housing and education, among others.[4] As SNCC moved further left and as the BPP rose to prominence, they extended visions of freedom from the Civil Rights Movement, but articulated these new meanings of milk and honey with a more radical politics.

Young black activists spoke, and black America listened. By 1966, attitudes had changed. Disillusioned by what appeared to be the limits of reform, black people saw possibility in these new meanings of a Promised Land. Many began to lose patience after years of public policy that fettered black life in the North, and decades of Jim Crow and state-sanctioned violence that targeted black life in the South. For others, patience had long run out. For too long, black optimism had believed in white integrity only to be disappointed when even white liberals simply malingered for more time to reform. Year after year, black hope relied on white structural power "to make real the promises of democracy," but no more. Two centuries after the American Revolution, a Black Power generation assumed their place as heirs to earlier patriots who believed that the blessings of liberty are not "conferred," but must be "secured" by those who would enjoy them. Righteous anger had already combusted in Watts, Newark, and other cities across the nation. This new generation presented the nation with a choice: join them in the urgent battle to form "a more perfect union" or stand by and watch them burn it down. Either way, African Americans determined that they would cross the Jordan by the power of their own people. This time, they would rely on Black Power!

Albert B. Cleage, Jr., Nation Time!: Black Church, Black Nationalism, and Black Power

When Albert Buford Cleage, Jr., was born in Indianapolis in 1911, Black Power was in no way a political ideology, let alone a movement, but Ethiopianism, in movements such as the Honorable Marcus Mosiah Garvey's Universal Negro Improvement Association, had already planted its seeds. Young Albert's parents, Albert, Sr., and Pearl Cleage, ensured that those seeds took root in their son's imagination. [5] However, those seeds bore nationalist rather than reformist fruit. So even though Powell's, King's, and Cleage's paths occasionally intersected within the Civil Rights Movement's leadership circles, their ideologies did not. Cleage rejected the reformist traditions and social gospel preaching embraced by the two giants of the Civil Rights era. In fact, Cleage rejected much of the ideology associated with the Civil Rights Movement. He saw Powell's and King's theologies as no more than concessions to the nation's racialist system. In turn, Powell saw Cleage's Black Christian Nationalism as a threat to the cultural fabric of the American Republic, and Cleage's theology as heretical to even Powell's own heterodoxy. Likewise, King believed that a Black Christian Nationalist theology mimicked the hatred that he had fought to defuse since Montgomery. Despite Cleage's opposition to the goals of the mainstream Civil Rights Movement, he rose to the national scene in the latter portion of the twentieth century as Powell had done decades earlier. He emerged as a pillar of fire who refused to *fit* within the nightscape of black clergy committed to the Civil Rights Movement's reformist tradition.

Cleage's politics were fundamentally Black Nationalist. So it made sense that he interpreted the exodus narrative as a story of the struggle of a people who escaped slavery and came together to build a nation. He took the story's plot as a sacred blueprint for Black Nationalist Christianity and grounded his work in both Black Nationalist philosophies and a new Black Theology.[6] When he did so, he stood alone among major African American Christian clergy. Black Theology, he imagined, would guide the Black Church's transition from the reformist emphases of the Civil Rights Movement to the radical political philosophy of the Black Power Movement. By 1967, Cleage institutionalized his philosophy by establishing the Shrines of the Black Madonna, later the Pan-African

Orthodox Christian Church. At the "Shrines," as they were called, black people found a God who could hear their cries from the Egypt of a post–Civil Rights Movement malaise, and they flocked to the new church. Soon the Pan-African Orthodox Christian Church expanded with congregations across the nation.

Akin to Powell's and King's stories, Cleage's journey to national prominence was fraught with the lessons of racial politics. Similar to Powell, color and class rendered Cleage out of place from his beginning. His father's professional career elevated the Cleages to elite status, and, by appearance, his family could pass for white. Either by choice or circumstance, both markers could have alienated them from much of the black community. But early in life, Pearl and Albert, Sr., modeled ways to deploy both color and class in service of black uplift. Albert, Jr., learned the lesson well. Where many light-complexioned black families passed to escape the cruder manifestations of racial repression, Albert, Jr., saw his parents do just the opposite. In an interview, his sister, Barbara (Cleage) Martin, affirmed, "We never passed. We never even tried to pass."[7] Likewise, some black families saw their class privilege as an opportunity to escape the ways that race deprived the quality of black life. They took advantage of their status with little or no concern for the masses of black people, but not Albert Cleage, Sr. The only black physician in Indianapolis, the Sr. Cleage could have built a thriving practice that served both black and white patients. Rather than vie for clinical privileges at one of the white facilities, he moved his family to Detroit and helped to establish the city's first black hospital.[8] Nonetheless, both social forces, color and class, privileged Albert, Jr., and his siblings within the black community. Like the Powells, they experienced early on the esteem that black communities offered to its lighter-complexioned members of the professional class who chose not to pass.

The same political and social ambiguity that constituted Albert, Jr., configured his social world. On one hand, he recalls accompanying his father on house calls into Polish, Irish, and other ethnic districts in Detroit where residents "would call out and hold up their babies which he had brought into the world and say, 'See how much they like you.'"[9] On the other hand, at school, he was no longer the son of a well-respected physician, but simply another black child in a segregated educational system. He painfully recalled one occasion where his elementary school refused to allow him to join the newspaper staff and forced black children to sit in the back row while all the other children sat in alphabetical order.[10] Later, in his Shrines of the Black Madonna, Cleage dealt with both markers of his identity as his family had taught him: he subordinated them to nationalist ideals of racial esteem and racial advancement. He became, as Angela Dillard describes, "an enigma: a Christian minister who contended that almost everything about traditional Christianity was false; a Black nationalist who by outward appearances could 'pass' for white; and a self-styled champion of the poor, the marginal, and the dispossessed with impeccable middle-class credentials."[11]

If Cleage's upbringing was complex, he charted a similarly circuitous vocational path; perhaps it was a mimetic representation of the ambiguities he embodied. Again, Cleage's choices set him apart from his peers among black activist clergy. Unlike Powell and King, who grew up as heirs apparent to prominent black Baptist church pulpits, Cleage mapped his own theological formation. He forsook denominational allegiance for another organizing marker, namely social activism. As a young adult, he associated himself with Father Malcolm Dade at St. Cyprian Episcopal, Reverend Horace White at Plymouth Congregational Church, and Reverend Clarence Hill at Hartford Memorial Baptist Church, the three leading activist black pastors in Detroit.[12] Each advocated the social gospel, which Cleage early on embraced.

Of these, Reverend White's ministerial model, which integrated psychosocial, political, and spiritual dimensions of black life, struck Cleage as far more comprehensive than the others. While he pastored Plymouth Congregational, White served the black community in Detroit as a state legislator and worked as a psychiatric social worker at the University of Michigan.[13] Cleage pursued a similar model and engaged black life at the nexus of religion and the social sciences.[14] At one point, Cleage believed that White's policy work in the legislature, along with his training as a social worker, equipped him well for service within the black community without the pastoral ministry. In fact, Cleage's early professional training did not include religion. While he studied at Wayne State University, Cleage majored in psychology, and in 1936, he became a social worker in Detroit.[15] Later, for close to a year, Cleage went on to train with the renowned sociologist, Charles S. Johnson, at Fisk University.[16] But by 1938, he realized that his studies in the social sciences alone were inadequate to respond to the challenges facing black life. A call to ministry and the study of religion filled the lacuna. That year, Cleage enrolled at Oberlin Divinity School to earn the master of divinity.[17] As a trained minister, Cleage believed that he could more adequately address the complexities of black life than as a professional in the social sciences alone.

At Oberlin, he found the work of another Detroit minister, Reinhold Neibuhr, compelling: "I read Niebuhr for a time, especially as an antidote to the social gospel. Horace White [pastor at the Plymouth Congregational Church who influenced Cleage] was essentially social gospel, which had little connection with reality. It was too utopian, full of action, but not much realism."[18] The two met on several occasions.[19] Neibuhr was convinced of humanity's deeply flawed nature and inability to create a society with just arrangements. Cleage found Neibuhr's Christian realism to be a sobering but pragmatic corrective to the social gospel that his mentors preached.[20] Niebuhr's perspective persuaded Cleage as a more adequate account of the systemic racism that infected national life, and he moved further from his mentors. The evolving position only clarified his pillar of fire posture from civil rights tradition.

Cleage's perspective was evident early, as his difficult tenure at the Church for the Fellowship of All Peoples shows. Upon the recommendation of his former professor, Charles S. Johnson, who by then had become the first black president of Fisk University, Cleage served as interim co-pastor until Howard Thurman could assume the position. With one black pastor and one white pastor, the church's leadership and its congregation promised to be a grand model in integration, and a model of the best of interracial cooperation. Perhaps more important for Cleage, the experience was one last test of the validity of the social gospel. During his tenure, Cleage complained that his counterpart, Albert G. Fisk, a white Presbyterian pastor and philosophy professor at San Francisco State College, was "well-meaning," but preached an optimistic social gospel. Cleage was particularly disturbed that Fisk's preaching avoided crises such as the Japanese interment and the treatment of black soldiers.[21] Fisk's glaring silence on such important issues of faith and life disillusioned Cleage. If even this grand experiment could fall short of its hope, then it confirmed white Christianity's utter inability to address systemic moral evil. Cleage departed upon Thurman's arrival, but he remained deeply affected by his tenure at the church.

Cleage never returned to the social gospel. Perhaps convinced more than before by his Niebuhrian position, he evolved steadily toward the firm belief that black and white theological interests were fundamentally oppositional. As he did with Fisk's preaching, Cleage focused on the limits of the social gospel. He attended to the looming sources of racial repression that social gospel preaching could not address, namely the cumulative psychic damage wrought by slavery, Jim Crow, and the multiple manifestations of white supremacy. These he termed collectively the "declaration of Black Inferiority." He traced its roots from the existence of black life in the American Republic to the deprivation that lived around him. "In the slave ship, on the slave block, on the plantation, fleeing from the lynch mob, fleeing north into slum ghettoes . . . everything possible was done to make that 'declaration' a statement of fact." From his vantage point of the wreckage after the urban rebellions of the late 1960s, Cleage believed the "declaration" was "basic to all American life."

The "declaration's" most apparent work manifested in disparities between whites and others in employment, access to healthcare, housing, education, and other social markers, but Cleage was more concerned about the psychic harm to black people themselves. The "declaration," as he understood it, drove black people to believe its pronouncements.

> Not only does the Black man then hate himself, in terms of this overall declaration of Black inferiority, but he hates all other Black people, on the simple theory that if it were not for all those obnoxious Black people, white people would not dislike him. The Black man then begins to hate everything about his community, everything about his culture, everything about his imitation institutions which he has patterned after white institutions, believing that all of these things are inferior because he is inferior.[22]

Black people who believed that whites were categorically more human, more trustworthy, more intelligent, more industrious, and, by extension, superior to themselves anguished Cleage. Their strivings toward the whiteness they could never attain meant that the "declaration" had done its most pernicious work. Cleage determined that he would show that white projections of black humanity were not "facts" but only social knowledge. He knew "the Black man could accept this declaration of inferiority or he could reject it."[23]

Unlike King and Powell, Cleage rejected the idea that civil society would produce just arrangements for African Americans. The "declaration" could not be "reformed" by their strategy and so the Civil Rights Movement's hope of full integration was unachievable:

> This is a kind of realism necessary for a revolutionary struggle. We've got to make sure the definitions of human nature and society are both sound. If they are not sound, then your whole revolution gets off the track. This was the problem of Dr. King. He was not realistic. You can hope for change, but it must be predicated on reality, not what we dream of. It must be based on people—and their nature—rather than dreams.[24]

Cleage's criticism merges Niebuhrian realism with his attraction to another thinker, Jean-Paul Sartre and his existentialist philosophy. Cleage was particularly impressed with the Sartrean position dramatized in the play, *No Exit*. The play, an allegory for the absurdity of the human condition, emphasizes humanity's propensity for "creating hell for each other."[25] Cleage remarked that as in the play, there is no God to come and relieve the human condition. "In fact, nobody is really outside to straighten out the situation if people themselves do not do something."[26] Sartre and Niebuhr's influence led Cleage to recognize with a sense of urgency that black people's freedom must come from black people themselves, not from some transcendent deity, and certainly not from white America.

Cleage's opposition to the social gospel, his emphasis on human agency, and his recognition of white supremacy's durability led him to take three radical stances. Each was fundamentally at odds with the mainstream Civil Right Movement. First, he claimed that integration, the movement's Promised Land, only led black people into deeper repression. Second, he challenged black people to trust in their collective power to ensure their quality of life rather than the authority of the U.S. Constitution. Third, he summoned the Black Church to be more than a portal to some afterworld, but to be the hub of a Black Nation. Any one of his positions alone was heresy for mainstream black Christian clergy. Together, these positions constituted Cleage as a pillar of fire who blazed a brilliant path toward Canaan amid a nightscape of despair in the aftermath of the Civil Rights era.

Cleage took up the first position against integration head on. By the mid-1960s, black sentiment by and large had been converted to believe that integration was their best hope for equality. They saw the victories in Little Rock in 1954 and in Montgomery in 1955 as proof positive. Cleage believed otherwise. He had no use for aspirational integrationist rhetoric because he doubted its power to effect material change. He turned his most strident critique on the movement's liberal dream and on its most visible standard bearer, King:

> "Integration Now" was the heroic battle cry of Dr. Martin Luther King. "We Shall Overcome" our separation was the anguished cry of the Black man's faith that escape from Blackness was possible. The dream of integration is the Black man's acceptance of the white man's declaration of his inferiority and is a mechanism that perpetuates his enslavement.
>
> This is not easy for white people to understand. For the white oppressor who has declared Black people inferior to say, "I believe in integration," is one thing. But for a Black man, after all the suffering, oppression, brutality, and inhumanity which he has suffered at the hands of white people to say, "I believe in the possibility of integration," or "I dream of integration," "I work for integration," "I would accept integration" is obviously a sign of insanity.[27]

It is no accident that Cleage terms King's "dream" an instance of "insanity." His early training in psychology influenced the ways that he saw black struggles for resistance and shaped his analysis of both white supremacy and his Black Christian Nation. He believed that such a "dream" in the face of contrary evidence defied reality, so logically Cleage saw it as irrational.

Cleage's focus on the "declaration" itself differentiated him from Powell and King. He believed that the "declaration," not the systems that its ideology supported, was the root cause of white supremacy. Powell and King had led black people to transform an unjust system, but Cleage was convinced that their cause was hopeless. At worst, their naïveté was unintentionally destructive to black life. At most, Cleage believed that

Powell's and King's reformist activity could *fit* black people into a system with unjust social arrangements, and Cleage would not have that.

Nonetheless, Cleage admired the way King's catalyzing work emboldened black protest. When he and other Detroit activists collaborated with King during the Walk to Freedom on June 23, 1963, Cleage came alive as he beheld the power of mass spectacle:

> During the Detroit Freedom March in 1963, approximately two hundred thousand Black people walked down Woodward Avenue with Dr. Martin Luther King, and I will never forget the pathetic sight of police officers assigned to keep order and the policemen on motorcycles who were expected to keep the marchers in an orderly procession. Their frightened faces as they try to stay out of the way revealed their knowledge that a crowd of two hundred thousand Black people could have walked them into the asphalt of the street without even striking a blow. The preponderance of sheer people power reduced to absurdity the thought that a few thousand police officers could keep order. And so I say that the authority of the state cannot be maintained by police power. The citizens of the state must be programmed to believe that the authority of the state ought to be accepted because it is right and that the power of the state is invincible, even though it is not. So actually the power of the state is a myth. The state can exist only so long as the people permitted it to exist.[28]

In 1963, King did not agree with Cleage's interpretation of black Detroiters' response to his inspirational address.[29] Only two months after the Walk to Freedom, King would stand on the National Mall and give the fullest articulation of that dream in one of the most historic addresses in the nation's history. When he spoke in Detroit, King was developing his "Dream," with an early version of the landmark speech, but Cleage saw a different reality. When Cleage looked across the throng of Detroiters, he saw Black Power, not imagined, but in action.[30]

The 1963 march was not the only time Cleage found King's work useful. On the Sunday after King was assassinated, Cleage seized the opportunity to shape King's legacy. He began by confessing, "I was not a follower of Dr. Martin Luther King. I respected him, but very early in his ministry, I differed with him in his approach to the problems of black people."[31] Then Cleage makes an important distinction: "I never agreed with most of the things he said, but I have loved everything he did because the things he did had no relationship to the things he said."[32] In that dissonance between the intentionality of King's rhetoric and its social effects, Cleage found a place of solidarity with the civil rights icon. To the wider national and international publics, King's rhetoric presented African Americans as moral exemplars unjustly denied full inclusion. But in the black community, Cleage saw a different effect altogether. He claimed that black people were not learning what King called redemptive suffering—that is, to willingly suffer unjustly with the aim of vindication and social change.[33] In the sermon, Cleage celebrates King even as he unmasks the civil rights leader's pillar of cloud performance. "Black people marching every day felt more and more that they were a people. . . . Dr. King was saying one thing and they were learning another. He set up the situation, he set up the confrontation, and black folks, as they stood up against white people, saw that these people were not invincible."[34] Ironically, King's work performed exactly Cleage's response to the existential dilemma; it was an exercise in the human will to self-empowerment. In fact, by the end of King's life, his rhetoric was closer to Cleage's positions than Cleage would publicly admit.[35]

Cleage's second position brightened the flame of his pillar of fire and distanced him further from the mainstream activist community. Most civil rights activists hoped that mass protests could demonstrate black people's earnest petition to take their rightful place as responsible members of civil society. After full integration, black collective consciousness would be unnecessary. African Americans could transcend racialization just as Poles, Germans, and Irish had transcended ethnicization and *fit* in as Americans. However, for Cleage, collective consciousness was not a mediate good, but an ongoing virtue. In the collective struggle, Cleage saw black people fighting alongside one another, sacrificing for one another, and facing their enemies in Jim Crow together. Black people emerged from the mass demonstrations knowing that they were safer, that their efforts were more effective, and that they wielded more power when they acted together rather than individually. The protests were organized, programmatic events that taught black people to resist white repression, and equally as important, to resist their own impulses toward an individualism that fulfilled self-interest at the expense of group solidarity and collective progress. Cleage believed that such impulses had dangerous consequences: "The Black man's fantasy is to believe that the white man will accept him as an *individual* of superior merit, even if he won't accept other Black people. This means that Black people in the final analysis are reduced to an individualistic struggle against one another."[36]

Perpetually nurtured collective consciousness offered the only sure and perpetual protection from the "declaration." So Cleage valorized those behaviors such as collective resistance that located individual interests within those of the group. Each protest nurtured black people's group consciousness. Each victory emboldened African American collective confidence that together they could achieve freedom.

Collective consciousness and collective resistance were as far as Cleage could travel peaceably with the mainstream Civil Rights Movement. Cleage's third position forsook the civil rights reformers' ultimate hope and the Republic's fundamental aim, namely, to be "one nation, indivisible." In city after city, the Civil Rights Movement "marched" toward a telos that he could not share. Why undertake the hard work of building collective consciousness only to disperse it by integrating it?[37] For Cleage, the hopes, dreams, and real fulfillment of the black collective could only be realized in a "Black Nation." A black collective consciousness was but a penultimate goal. As often as he could, he reminded the collective to exercise their energies in service of nationhood. The "Black Nation," as Cleage conceived it, was an agreement that affirmed black life similar to the way that the state, as it was configured, was a compact that subjugated it:

> In defining our program it is necessary to state clearly what Black Christian Nationalism means by a "Black Nation." We're not seeking five states in the south for black people, or seven states, nor are we advocating a "back-to-Africa" movement, although we have no objection to any of these ... We seek to create a *Nation within a Nation*, uniting Black people in such a way that we have the basic benefits of nation.[38]

With his "nation within a nation," Cleage called black people to a consciousness that transcends geographic separation. "The Black people of Harlem will feel a kinship with the Black people of Alabama, Louisiana, and Mississippi, and Black people in Chicago will feel a kinship with Black people in Los Angeles, Philadelphia and Detroit—a kinship which is more than an emotional feeling, because it has the tangible attributes of Nationhood."[39]

This "nation" was more than shared identity. By structuring economic relationships among African Americans, nationhood would materially benefit black life. Cleage challenged black people to control institutions within their communities such as schools, housing, employment, and the like that directly affected the quality of black life.

To ground his Black Nation, Cleage turned to the Black Church. From the hush harbors of the eighteenth and nineteenth centuries, the Black Church arose as the Invisible Institution[40] and created a religion of freedom out of the slavers' Christianity; Cleage called it to do so again. Reimagining it theologically and institutionally is Cleage's most radical performance. He envisions a Black Church that no longer preoccupies itself with shadowing the white church or being its conscience. As he believed about political reform, Cleage saw no merit in a Black Church that devoted its energies to challenging white churches to do justice. Years earlier in San Francisco, he concluded that reforming white Christianity was futile. Rather, Cleage takes another pillar of fire position and conceives of a Black Church that will attend to the souls and bodies of people looking for God while living under oppression.

He set about the ambitious task of rethinking just such a theology. First, Cleage emphasizes Moses' leadership as the hermeneutical key for black Christian faith rather than as the center of human history. Cleage even presents Jesus' life as a continuation of Moses' struggle for freedom. In fact, Cleage begins biblical Israel's faith with Moses' leadership, not with Abraham's faith, as in most genealogies of the Christian tradition.

The religion of Israel began with Moses, who was an African. Having killed an Egyptian and fearing the anger of Pharaoh in whose palace he had been reared, Moses fled, leaving his people in bondage. He settled among the Black people of Midian, who thought him an Egyptian, and married the daughter of Jethro, the Midianite high priest. He sat at the feet of Jethro and was taught the religion and culture of Black Africa. Watching his father-in-law's flock, he pondered the oppression of Israel and, almost against his will, committed his life to a liberation struggle which he must create and to which he must call the Nation Israel.[41]

Second, Cleage returns to a historical interpretation of Jesus' life in line with first-century Judaism rather than a triumphalist Christianity. For Cleage: "Jesus was a revolutionary Black religious leader fighting for the liberation of Israel. We can understand Jesus more fully by looking at Moses and the Maccabees than by looking at the Apostle Paul with pagan concept of blood redemption."[42] Post-bellum black Christianity interpreted the gospels through the Pauline and Deutero-Pauline letters, but Cleage argued that Roman citizenship compromised Paul. Paul was more loyal to the empire than to the marginalized Jewish community under Roman occupation.

Cleage knew that his people did not need a black messiah to assure them some far off and otherworldly salvation. A Christianity that had become preoccupied with sending people to heaven one by one rather than freeing them here on earth was for Cleage an irrelevant religion. It led black people to believe that individually they could resist interconnected and overarching systems of repression. So Cleage replaced blood atonement for individual sin, a central "truth" of orthodox Christianity, with commitment to one's people as the criterion for salvation. He claimed that "[t]he first task of the Black church is to liberate the Black man's mind. It must be willing to deal with truth and stop telling fairy tales to men and women. . . . It must help Black people begin to think realistically about everyday problems."[43] Only from relentless clear-eyed realism, not speculative theological idealism, could black people give meaning to the absurdity of life under daily repression.

Cleage formulated his understanding of the Holy Spirit along similar lines.[44] He deemphasized the typical "fruits" of the spirit as Paul outlined them in Galatians, namely, love, joy, peace, forbearance, kindness, goodness, faithfulness, gentleness, and self-control. As an aggregate, they encouraged behaviors that preserved status quo life. Cleage preferred a more active role for the Spirit. He claimed that the Holy Spirit had activated black people's consciousness just as God had done in the moment when the Israelites decided to resist. Through the church, the Holy Spirit will drive the nation to freedom:

It [the Holy Spirit] is rage, anger, hatred, commitment. It is divine dis-
content. It is the mystery of a magic moment when we are touched by a
power which we cannot understand.

Only a people can feel the Holy Spirit. God does not speak to individuals. Ordinary Black men and women came together in Montgomery,
Alabama and decided that they could no longer sit in the back of the
bus. We wonder what at that moment made the back of the bus more
irksome than it was a week before or a decade before. Why did Black
people suddenly decide to walk? What happened? The most reasonable
explanation is the simple one. In this time and in this place, these Black
people were touched by the Holy Spirit. The conviction that God had
created them equal gave them a new sense of dignity. They were no
longer able to ride in the back of the bus. They had been touched by the
Holy Spirit. They were forced to walk, and so they walked for more than
a year. How can we say what touched a Black mother, whose child had
been going to an inferior segregated school, who suddenly decided that
she would take her child to an integrated school where the child could
get a decent education? Where did she get the courage to face a mob? It
was the Holy Spirit.[45]

Even the robust role he ascribes to the Holy Spirit is consistent with
his long-held theological positions. Cleage can remain deeply suspicious
of the idea of a transcendent God who directs human affairs, because
his high theological anthropology emphasized God's power as embodied in each human and manifested in community.[46] He interprets the
Holy Spirit's work beginning with a very human moment, an arbitrary
instance of repression whose cumulative weight was too great a burden.
That instance provoked an openness to the Holy Spirit that ever calls
humanity to freedom and fulfillment. In that moment, black people in
Montgomery responded. When they did, the world saw African Americans expanding the reach of constitutional liberty, but again Cleage saw
something more. He saw the power of the Black Church animate the
inchoate strivings of a black nation and drive its members to stand up as
the human beings that God created them to be.

With a reformulated theology, Cleage hoped that the Black Church
could reclaim its role as its people's primary liberating institution as it
had been during the slave regime. But in its new incarnation, Cleage

demanded that the Black Church extend its institutional life to the Black Nation: " 'Black Nation' is the concept of an emerging Black church that considers itself related to Black people as the Temple in Jerusalem was related to Israel. It considers all Black people a part of the Nation to which it ministers. It ministers not to a congregation but to the Pan-African Black community, the Black Nation."[47] He describes the Black Church as an all-encompassing institution, synonymous with his Black Nation. Furthermore, Cleage determined the Shrine would set the new paradigm: "Instead of selling 'deliverance,' the Black Church must become a center for education, organization, and the involvement of black people in meaningful struggle and conflict. The Black Church must become more than a place where black people perform magic dances in an attempt to induce God to perform miracles."[48]

In the Shrine, worship services did exactly that. Cleage preached sermons to direct black congregants toward attitudes and activities that affirmed black empowerment. Throughout the week, members engaged in spiritual disciplines such as study in history and theology, and participation in community uplift activities that were designed to break the "declaration's" psychological hold. In both, Cleage challenged black Christians to discover the cosmic power that he believed constituted each person as a gift of God's creative encounter and to direct such power toward their people's highest good.

Cleage was as intentional about shunning individualism in the Shrine as he was in black public life. He wanted to avoid building a cult of personality. He reflects the same value in another interpretation of Moses' work where he deemphasizes Moses as a charismatic leader and focuses on biblical Israel instead:

> [Moses] took more than two million disorganized Black people out of Africa, kept them together for more than forty years in the wilderness, and finally brought them to the Promised Land. The king of Moab looked down in fear at the Nation Israel and said, "A people has come out of Egypt." No greater feat of sheer organization has been achieved anywhere in the annals of human history.[49]

With the same intentionality Cleage emphasizes that it was a people who escaped Egyptian bondage. He believed that by organizing itself as a nation, biblical Israel ensured that it would endure beyond any single personality. As Cleage saw it, this was King's and Powell's oversight:

> Powell never organized Harlem. That would have been power. Black people would go out and vote for him because he was a Black Messiah. Black people never controlled an election in New York City or New York State. He never organized them. He never made a serious effort to organize the Negroes all over America. Black people are no closer to power today than when Powell first came on the stage 23 years ago.[50]

> The day of national black leaders is over. King, as long as he lived, maintained a certain position, but he was not a national black leader because he had no way of giving a program on a national scale to black people.[51]

Cleage was determined not to be a Black Messiah—that is, one who based his leadership on the cult of personality, so he worked arduously to cultivate power among ordinary black people by organizing them. He encouraged their allegiance to one another rather than to himself. His stature paid the price for his concept of leadership. Cleage never enjoyed the adoration that Powell received or the power that the Harlem congressman wielded single-handedly. Neither would he achieve the acclaim that accrued to King. But Cleage accomplished what they did not. In the Pan-African Orthodox Christian Church, he succeeded where even the U.S. Constitution failed. Cleage organized a Black Christian Nation that offered protection, dignity, purpose, and humanity to all of its "citizens."

Exodus as Black Nationalist Manifesto

During 1967 and 1968, a decade after King delivered "Birth of a New Nation," Cleage preached a prophetic and explicitly nationalist interpretation of the book of Exodus in four sermons, "But God Hardened Pharaoh's Heart," "The Promised Land," "Coming in Out of the Wilderness," and "What Can We Give Our Youth."[52] On those Sundays, as he stood in the pulpit of Detroit's Shrine of the Black Madonna, the promise of civil reform for black life that had inspired Powell and King must have felt a world away. Indeed, only a few months earlier, on July 23, 1967, the same neighborhood where the Shrine stood, where black children played, and where black families lived, worked, and worshipped was transformed into a war zone. Fifteen hundred state troopers and National Guard personnel along with tanks and other artillery filled the streets.[53] The nation's machinery of war that had devastated Vietnam now invaded their neighborhoods. The bloody racial violence ravaged Detroit's 12th Street community. But for four consecutive days, the people resisted. At the height of the rebellion, Governor George Romney gazed down from his helicopter upon black neighborhoods and commented that Detroit looked "like a city that had been bombed." While Romney surveilled the wreckage, Detroit's black residents watched in horror, but the suburbanites of Dearborn and Ann Arbor felt a bit safer.

For Cleage, the rebellion signaled the collapse of civil reform's promise. It had carried black people as far as it could. The revolts across the nation's urban landscape meant that both King's and President Johnson's power and sway were in full decline. Cleage took the opportunity to show a new route to Canaan. Each Sunday, he seized the sermonic moment to craft a pillar of fire performance of the positions that constituted him and the hopes that he commended to his people. While he preached to the Shrine's congregation, he crafted his messages for African Americans across the nation. As a body of interpretation, Cleage's sermons, like Powell's, challenged black people to commit to a civil religion. Unlike Powell, the center of Cleage's civil religion was not the American Republic, but the Black Nation.

In the sermons, Cleage exhorted his congregation along three lines: waiting for American society to accept them was a futile proposition; neither individual acquiescence nor individual resistance was fruitful; black people's salvation resided in the Black Nation. Each time Cleage stood in his pulpit, he pointed the people from Detroit to a Promised Land of fair housing, equal education, full employment, and freedom from police brutality. But to get there, he told them they must cross the Jordan as a "Black Nation."

Integration Is Futile: Resistance Is Not

Cleage took for granted that integration was a lost cause, but most other African Americans, including members of the Shrine, were not necessarily convinced. Like many of Cleage's counterparts, they were persuaded by the CRM's victories that progress was rolling in and that their arrival in the Promised Land was imminent. It was only a matter of distance, not strategy. More reform would eventually get them there, but Cleage wanted them to see that white America had long rejected this possibility. He reminded his congregants how much African Americans and others had hoped, worked, suffered, believed, and died for equality, but it had not yet come. No matter how much they prayed, watched, waited, and believed, black people were never going to politely integrate into the land of milk and honey.

In "But God Hardened Pharaoh's Heart," Cleage makes a passionate case for his brand of realism. His title, which quotes Exodus 9:12, is itself an exercise in such realism. It foregrounds theological problems that most black preaching avoided.[54]

Unlike those in the mainstream CRM, Cleage had no use for any theology that obscured the hard reality of white supremacy. In the biblical writer's claim, Cleage saw a description of two entrenched powers, Pharaoh, and Yahweh, that represented oppositional interests, biblical Egypt, and biblical Israel, respectively. So, he frames black and white America fatefully locked in oppositional struggles just as the biblical writer placed Egypt and Israel. Early in the sermon, Cleage argues that the mind of white supremacy cannot change. Just as in exodus, Pharaoh could not relent and veer from the disastrous course by changing his mind and releasing the Hebrews.[55] "Let me tell you, anybody who has power and is faced with the necessity of giving up any part of that power has his heart hardened time after time. God doesn't have to do it. This was a black Jewish historian writing and he wanted it to sound a certain way ... Year after year these white folks harden their hearts."[56] The biblical writer sees God's will behind Pharaoh's intransigence, and Cleage sees a similar unseen force in structural power and racialized privilege. Both privilege and power colluded and led white Americans to believe that the "declaration's" claims were natural facts, not social knowledge. Together, they made it virtually impossible for white Americans to do justice.

Having set out his proposition, Cleage makes his case in grand black preaching style with three carefully framed anecdotes that relate events after the rebellion. Each builds upon the other to paint a picture of black frustration. In each, he brings his congregation to a merger of horizons with biblical Israel to show that black America faced Pharaoh's hardened heart as well. In the first, he recalls a meeting with the New Detroit Committee, a task force charged with repairing relationships within the city.

> Recently, I talked with a member of the new Detroit committee. A couple of attorneys were there. We tried to outline a number of basic things that should be done if the committee he heads is to be meaningful. We tried to point out that it had to be the kind of committee on which black people had some equality of representation so that it could speak on the committee and the committee could then use its power to do the things which the black community demanded. He was very pleasant, very nice, very friendly, but he didn't do any of the things we suggested, and this is very typical of the white Establishment. They talk to you, act friendly, suggest all kinds of concessions which are about to be made, and then they go right along doing everything just like they always have.[57]

Lest his congregation conclude that the problem is peculiar to the local municipal government, Cleage next recounts a meeting with Justice Department officials along with Cyrus Vance, who was then Deputy Secretary of Defense:

> The Justice Department people took copious notes just as they did all over the South when black people were being whipped to death. The next day they came back and brought Cyrus Vance with them. Vance took up another afternoon, and he, too, took copious notes. Everybody wanted to know, "what should we do?" And then they nodded and wrote it all down. But nobody has indicated any intention of actually doing what the black community wants done.[58]

In the examples, Cleage exposes entrenched power. Its force acts unseen as the biblical writer claimed that God acted upon Pharaoh's heart. In the same way it is impervious even to individuals, such as Vance, or groups, such as the New Detroit Committee, charged with bringing about even minor change. In Cleage's description, both scenes recall the existential absurdity in "No Exit." Detroit's black residents and empowered committee members agree upon change, and perhaps even desire the new social and economic configurations that they conceived. Nonetheless, despite their best efforts, there is no escape from the deadlock between white supremacy and black humanity.

In the third example, Cleage shows why structural power remained impervious to black resistance: it insulates those whom it privileges and unleashes on others the gruesome violence necessary to protect that privilege. In other words, redemption was impossible, not because God desired it to be, but because the social forces that affirmed white supremacy protected those whom it advantaged. In the story, a white minister sees, for perhaps the first time, the nasty work that preserves his privilege.

> A white minister told me that he went to the precinct police station when they were bringing prisoners in. The ones who hadn't been bayoneted in the streets were bayoneted off the back of a truck at the station house. This is just a part of the procedure. A pregnant black woman was trying to climb down off of a truck and they told her to jump. She said, "I'm pregnant." They said, "Jump." She jumped and had a miscarriage in the street. They dragged her into the police station and threw her into a cell with all the other black prisoners. She screamed and yelled and cried, and they just didn't hear her. The white minister said he went out into the street and threw up.[59]

Cleage's story describes violence that is disembodied and impersonal. It does not notice the woman nor does it care about her pregnancy. It is simply a mechanism of a far larger structure. The personal story of a white police officer brutalizing a pregnant black woman gives way to the story of the enforcement arm of the state protecting the social order from change. Cleage's story hangs on the phrase, "they didn't hear her." Although the *minister* heard and saw the gross violation of humanity in the unfolding scene, the *police*, who represented forces that conserved the arrangements of the political economy, did not. In truth, for the police to "hear" the woman and to attend to her humanity and that of the others captured with her would require them to be derelict in performing their duty to the state.

Cleage's language is telling; he calls them "prisoners" to emphasize the fact that the state's structures of enforcement, such as the police, can only "apprehend" them as criminals. So the brutality appears just and the prevailing order is maintained while Black humanity is sacrificed. But when the minister sees the brutality in stark relief against the humanity of pregnancy and new life, he cannot reconcile the dissonance between the confidence he holds in his society and the work its legitimating structures performed to ensure his privilege. So strong is his revulsion that he responds biologically.

By the end of Cleage's third example, the congregation recognizes that their own struggle to affirm black humanity is inextricably deadlocked with those systems that protected white privilege. It is fundamentally oppositional just as the exodus story presents the relationship between the Hebrews and the Egyptians. Death for one (as in the horrific miscarriage) meant life for the other. As in the title of Sartre's play, Cleage temporarily leaves his congregation in a struggle with "No Exit."

Presenting full equality in integration as a hopeless goal only began Cleage's argument. All around him, he saw individual responses to the "declaration's" effects on their lives. They resisted by participating in the rebellion or they acquiesced by leveraging class to create some measure of comfort and the appearance of security, whichever made the most sense. Either way, they met with little success. Neither response led to the Promised Land. The former sacrificed black flesh to law enforcement's disciplining technologies. The latter slowly sacrificed black humanity to assimilation with the hope of achieving a cloud-like invisibility. As Cleage preached the story, exodus appeared divinely crafted to illustrate the perils of both types of individual responses to a world structured by white supremacy.

He begins with a fiery critique of the latter, and frames it as an individual narrative of ascent at the expense of the collective. It prefers comfort in bondage to self-determination as a collective. He interprets an analogous challenge for biblical Israel. Early in their journey, they reach a point where freedom in the wilderness required them to relinquish the familiar markers of status and value that they had known in Egypt. There, the newly freed community contemplates the unthinkable—a return to Egypt. With a tone of pastoral understanding, Cleage explains of both biblical Israel, and by extension, of African Americans, "they were afraid and divided. There were Jews who had more than others and were afraid that they might lose their position. . . . There were those who believed that the Egyptians were superior because they have superior power."[60] In the wilderness, biblical Israel's wealth and status, whose value inhered within the Egyptian political economy, soon became meaningless. To the degree that they had become invested in it, they were also invested in Egyptian life. Cleage claimed that biblical Israel's response arose from a sense of powerlessness, so they identified more with Egypt than with the possibility of nationhood. Leaving Egypt was both a material and psychological liability. To place their faith in their own potential for nationhood was too much to ask of a people recently out of bondage.

Next, Cleage takes the congregation to the place where their world intersects with biblical Israel's journey. Relying on the peculiar link between race and class in the U.S. political economy, Cleage turns the American virtue of individual ascendance into the vice of intra-racial stratification. He recounts a conversation with a reporter who opines insightfully (or so the reporter believed) about the recent Detroit rebellion and, with the story, performs a brilliant symbolic reversal. As Cleage presents the narrative, he shows that beyond a superficial luster, most individual black narratives of ascent only conform one to *fit*, while leaving those who strive toward them vulnerable to the "declaration."

Cleage prefaces the story by remarking that the reporter spoke for two hours about his "theory on the revolt," which he summarizes: "Black people revolted . . . because there is a golden door through which you can pass an escape from being a Negro—I mean black person. And the thing that made black people revolt was the fact that some were getting through the golden door before others. So the rest got irritated and frustrated."[61] The story conflicts with Cleage's commitments to both Christian realism and existentialism. Certainly, Cleage could not accept the "golden door," which according to the reporter's description was ostensibly a passage to whiteness. So, he presses the reporter to identify these black people who supposedly found "the exit." The reporter points to only one person, a man he calls "Jones," who is the special advisor for the police department. Then Cleage relates the reporter's "evidence" for the claim that Jones has "arrived," "[H]e has a nice home a nice car, and he doesn't have to fight for freedom." For his congregation, these goods held the same meanings as the Egyptian wealth held for biblical Israel. They represented the basic hopes of anyone living in substandard

housing, whose children attend second-class schools, and who face police brutality. In fact, Jones enjoys much of the freedom that the Black
Power generation articulates. It would have been apparent to the congregation that the higher one ascends in class the less one feels the effects
of being racialized. Absolute freedom meant the dignity of a life free
from struggle and a humanity that was not constantly under assault.
But Cleage's pillar of fire position stands in stark ideological contrast to
his peers. Other black churches perhaps counted at least one member
such as Jones on their roles, and celebrated them. Rather than commend
Jones's life, Cleage performs a daring symbolic reversal. He points to the
goods that seemingly lifted Jones above strife and claims:

> His very job is a flunkey job. He has neither dignity nor power. It doesn't
> matter which side of that mythical door you are on. In this country you
> are a Nigger wherever you are. There is no door that stops you from being
> a Nigger in the eyes of the white man, and anybody who thinks that there
> is some door through which he can escape will find that he is only going
> from where he is into Uncle Tom land. That is the only door there. He can
> stop identifying with black people and he can go through some door to
> where the white man is going to accept them as a good old Uncle Tom.
> There is no other door. There is no other escape.[62]

Again, Cleage's response echoes Sartre's "No Exit." There is no lasting or
durable freedom for individual black people in the United States who
are seeking to escape racialization's constraints. For Cleage, searching
for such a "door" distracted from the project of nation-building. These
"doors" led black folk to expend valuable energy to achieve goods that
they did not possess the structural power to control.

From his perspective, Cleage had good reason for alarm. He feared
the new modes of life opening for African Americans in the wake of
civil rights legislation and integration in the public sphere. Perhaps these
were the "doors" that concerned Cleage. For most of the Civil Rights
Movement's mainstream activists, these events signified the success
of their work. They were signs that the nation had begun to fulfill the
sacred but long forsaken promises inscribed in the nation's founding
documents. However, Cleage saw these developments as a Trojan horse;
they *promised* fundamental change, but ultimately robbed black people

of their most important resource—racial loyalty. The burgeoning plurality in black life in the post–civil rights moment was fast eclipsing former political and social unity. Without unity, Cleage doubted that black people in the United States could heal from the psychic damage of social repression and political inequality. Just as biblical Israel's sense of powerlessness led them to cling to familiar structures of Egypt, Cleage knew that black people's powerlessness might lead them to believe that these new "doors" were their only hope to escape the "declaration's" violence. They might take any path of ascendance to secure individual or familial welfare. Sadly, unless a Moses could convince them otherwise, they too would return to Egypt.

Jones's story, and narratives like his, threatened Cleage's hope for black life. In "What Can We Give Our Youth," he presents Joseph and Moses as correctives. He leverages their iconic authority to subvert the lure of individual ascendance and to turn the congregation toward the surer ground of collective consciousness. Joseph and Moses' ethnic identities determine their political loyalties even when they are faced with political and economic incentives to assimilate into Egyptian society. Although his brothers betray him, and the Egyptians befriend him, Joseph "maintained his sense of identity with the Nation Israel."[63] Similarly, Moses' status as the son of Pharaoh's daughter gave him access to "all of the people in power, yet he realized that he had kinship with the enslaved people of Israel."[64] In other words, neither Moses nor Joseph forgets his kinship to the Israelites. Their identities demanded a tenacious ethnic loyalty that even social ascendance could not violate. In fact, they self-consciously construct their identities in resistance to the social forces that shaped their world. Cleage wanted to instill the same in these would-be members of the Black Nation.

Cleage gives a more sympathetic critique of individual resistance, the second response to the "declaration," but remains firm that even its motivations are better actualized from within a group consciousness. In epic style, he takes Moses' character *pars pro toto* of Israel's progress toward a nationalist consciousness.

The story is told that [Moses] was walking one day and saw an Egyptian strike a Jew. He turned and killed the Egyptian, because the Jew was his brother, and the Egyptian was his enemy. Here is the inner sense of kinship and nation. There was not a moment's hesitation. Moses didn't have to think about it, to build philosophical arguments. His brother was being mistreated and he reacted spontaneously.[65]

Again, Cleage takes a biblical position oppositional to much of the black preaching tradition. Unlike most black preachers, Cleage reads Moses' murder of an Egyptian taskmaster as a moment of enlightenment rather than a cause for redemption. Cleage touts the episode as a publicly demonstrable sign of Moses' ethnic allegiance. In that act, Moses distinguished himself from the Egyptians and solidified his self-identification as a Hebrew. But the act itself was not enough to satisfy Cleage because it did not emanate from a mature nationalist consciousness. He tells the congregation that Moses' encounter with the Egyptian was an act of "emotionalism" without much regard for the nation. "But," as Cleage describes, Moses "sat and watched his father-in-law's flocks, he thought of the meaning of the situation in Egypt. He began to realize there was no possibility of freedom for people merely because individual Jews might strike individual Egyptians."[66] Cleage correlates Moses' activity with the unrest among black youth that his congregation saw every day. Alluding to the rebellions in the cities such as Los Angeles, Newark, and, of course, Detroit, Cleage recounts Moses' intellectual evolution toward nationalist leadership:

> Most young people strike out in anger, frustration, indignation, and emotionalism against the things that antagonize and oppress them. Moses had done just this. But as he grew older, it became clearer and clearer to him that . . . if the Jews were to stand against Egypt, then it must be a united people who stood against Egypt. A single Jew could not do it. He could kill one Egyptian or one hundred Egyptians, but the system of oppression would go on. If the children of Israel were to be free, they would have to develop the kind of unity, which would make it possible for a united people to stand against the system of oppression.[67]

Cleage concludes, "He [Moses] had come a long way from the impetuous anger of youth." But only a nation could harness the individual consciousness of resistance and direct it toward the liberation of the people.

In the end, Cleage oriented his sermons toward nationhood, the telos of his hope and the object of his civil religion. It was his greatest and most enduring gift. Ironically, it is under the strictures of nationhood that Cleage articulates his broadest vision of human relationship and civil liberty. When Moses marries an African woman, Zipporah, daughter of Jethro, a priest of Midian, Cleage does not struggle with the issue of ethnic difference. It is another instance where Cleage interprets differently from his counterparts. He allows the narrative's matter-of fact-presentation of the incident to speak to his point, "there he married a black woman. The Nation Israel was a Black Nation intermingled with all the black peoples of Africa. So there was nothing strange about Moses marrying a black woman. His father-in-law was a priest of Midian, and Moses tended his flocks."[68] Cleage's approach deploys race as a socially constructed phenomenon. Doing so allows him to accept the inter-ethnic union as long as a national ideology trumps the ethnic difference between the Midianites and the Hebrews. Both ethnic identities are subsumed under a new national identity— membership in what Cleage terms "the Nation Israel." They are free from forces of competing ethnic commitments because their loyalty lies with the nation. For Cleage, this marriage offers a model for African Americans to subordinate their social difference and divergent interests to their larger interest in the goods of nationhood. In the Nation, "we are all together—young and old, rich and poor, learned and unlearned."[69]

In nationhood, Cleage brings together black public struggle and black hope for transcendence into a seamless whole. Together, they culminate Cleage's civil religion. His pulpit exhortations slowly built to a powerful crescendo that celebrated salvation in nationhood. Under the Black Nation, Cleage takes vivid descriptions of hope and horror, and reorders the symbols that impinge upon black life. He replaces the existential absurdity with new meaning. In each of the sermons, Cleage takes familiar Christian symbols such as sin, repentance, Eucharist, salvation, love, and forgiveness and assigns them new significance. Each religious symbol possesses new moral significance within an ecology of patriotism. He exchanges their association within orthodox Christianity for everyday meaningfulness in the Black Nation. Each new association transfers meaning from a doctrine that acquiesced to white privilege to a vision where the collective work of the Nation might guarantee the quality of black life.

As he concludes "Coming Out of the Wilderness," Cleage signifies individualism with sin and collective repentance with atonement and reframes them with meaning for the nation.

> There is one story that is enough to make you cry. A white mob was chasing this very young black boy with nothing to do with the car. He ran to his father's house. And his father ordered him away. "Go away. I can't help you. If I do, they'll get me too." Can you think of anything more symbolic of individualism? His own son. "Get away from my house. Hide out there in the woods and swamps until the dogs find you. I don't want them to get me, too."[70]

> For every moment of cowardice when our grandfathers hid under their beds while black men died, there has to be a moment of courage before we can dare think about entering a Promised Land. . . . For every moment of individualism, there must be a moment of togetherness. We can't enter the Promised Land like this. There is too much blood on us.[71]

Cleage believed that the ritual power of collective repentance reminded individuals of a commitment to a meaningful life that is larger than themselves. For Cleage the "declaration's" effects would be difficult to overcome but not impossible.

Ultimately, in each of the exodus sermons, Cleage maintains his focus on "a people" rather than any singular instance of black racial genius. Only "a people" will come out of Egypt and only "a people" can build a Promised Land for themselves.

> We're building a Black Nation. And no matter what the white man does, it's my faith that we'll be here. We're going to survive because we're God's chosen people. A thousand years from today we'll be here, no matter what he does. We believe in the Nation that we're building—and we find in Christianity a new direction and a new truth. A Black Messiah and a Black Madonna. The Bible becomes something new when you understand that it is talking about a black people and a Black Messiah. This faith in our future we give our youth.[72]

From exodus, Cleage constructed a faith that would take black people across the Jordan. It required more than many were willing to give. He challenged them to become their own pillar of fire. As a pillar, he promised them collective strength enough to carry a nation. As fire, they would not blend quietly into the world around them, but they would shine brightly against a nightscape of despair and dispel false hopes of integration. They would blaze their own path and build their own Promised Land. As with biblical Israel, if they committed to the task, then their sacrifice would be their legacy. Their own work would lead to salvation. Their salvation would be their children's heritage.

Conclusion: Cloud, Fire, and Beyond

I'm here because somebody marched. I'm here because you all sacrificed for me. I stand on the shoulders of giants. I thank the Moses generation; but we've got to remember, now, that Joshua still had a job to do. As great as Moses was, despite all that he did, leading a people out of bondage, he didn't cross over the river to see the Promised Land. . . . There are still battles that need to be fought; some rivers that need to be crossed. Like Moses, the task was passed on to those who might not have been as deserving, might not have been as courageous, find themselves in front of the risks that their parents and grandparents and great grandparents had taken. That doesn't mean that they don't still have a burden to shoulder, that they don't have some responsibilities. The previous generation, the Moses generation, pointed the way. They took us 90% of the way there. We still got that 10% in order to cross over to the other side.
—2007 presidential campaign speech given by Senator
Barack Obama at the commemoration of the Selma Voting
Rights March

In March 1965, Dr. Martin Luther King, Jr., led the iconic march from Selma, Alabama to the state's capital in Montgomery to protest for voting rights. Thirty-two hundred people began the journey from Selma. Over the next several weeks, the state did its best to prevent the march from succeeding. It unleashed one strategy of containment after another. When legislative means failed to stop them, Governor George Wallace deployed violence at the hands of Alabama State Troopers. On March 7, in an incident that would be known as "Bloody Sunday," the troopers met the group of unarmed citizens at the Edmund Pettis Bridge and beat them mercilessly until they scattered. Still the marchers remained undaunted. They shared a singular goal of securing the guarantees of the U.S. Constitution for vast populations of African Americans throughout the former Confederacy who had been barred from exercising the franchise. They believed that their goal was worthy of the risks they faced together. So did the masses of black people along the route. By the time the marchers reached the capitol building in Montgomery, more than 25,000 people had joined the throng.

Five months later, in August, when Congress passed the Voting Rights Act of 1965, the movement had secured its goal. It would be one of the last times that the movement and its exodus rhetoric would capture the religious imagination and focus the energy of the masses of black people toward a singular vision of fulfillment in the Promised Land.

Forty-two years later, on March 4, 2007, then-senator Barack Obama made a campaign stop to address those gathered to commemorate the 1965 march. As he spoke, Obama invoked the legacy of the Selma march and the CRM. In the speech Obama claimed both his place as an heir of the movement and his right to interpret its continuing work.

Obama's Selma speech offers a prism for understanding a gradual shift in exodus interpretations beyond the eras of the Civil Rights and Black Power Movements. His speech deployed exodus at the intersection of two traditions. The first takes up exodus within the symbolic universe of the Black Church and follows what William D. Hart calls the Standard Narrative of Black Religion. Therein, Black Church and Black Religion are synonymous.[1] In that tradition, the signs and meanings that obtain within the Black Church are those that properly interpret exodus. Indeed, the Black Church has shaped the majority of African American biblical interpretation since the slave regime, including many of the interpreters in the preceding chapters, such as Jones, Walker, Harper, Jasper, Powell, King, and Cleage. When President Barack Obama who, during his first term, rarely spoke out on African American struggles for equality, deployed the idiom in 2007 at Brown Chapel AME church in Selma, Alabama, he participated in this tradition. By invoking exodus's language in that context, Obama confirmed his solidarity with the ongoing struggles of the nation's daughters and sons of slavery. The same continues in contemporary incarnation of "cloud" and "fire" forms, such as Bishop T. D. Jakes, who could scarcely criticize the Bush administration after Hurricane Katrina, but brokered funds for affected families and communities, or Dr. Jeremiah A. Wright, whose uncompromising jeremiad honors the tradition of the Hebrew prophets, Amos and Hosea.

But Obama's subject positionality complicates both components of Hart's standard narrative, namely, "Black" and "Church," and deviates from the tradition. This deviation signals a second tradition of interpretation that stands outside of the Black Church to offer critique or an interpretation impossible from within the rules of the Black Church's symbolic universe.[2] Zora Neale Hurston, discussed earlier, offers one such example. As Obama delivered his speech from a black church pulpit, the spectacle paid homage to those black clergy who led the Selma to Montgomery march, but Obama, although Christian, was neither clergy nor overtly religious. His primary entrée to activism was by way of his record as a deeply committed community organizer and a hard-working local politician. Moreover, unlike those who led the iconic march, Obama was neither the descendant of nor raised by a descendant of those who suffered under the slave regime, and so his subjectivity complicates "Black" as well. By troubling both components, Obama's speech moves exodus from the standard narrative to a second tradition. This second tradition, similar to the first, continues with varying political performances. For example, exodus appears repeatedly in the interpretive discourses of the Rastafarian movement and the Nation of Islam.

Obama also complicates exodus interpretation in a third way, with respect to ends. Black interpreters from Absalom Jones to Albert Cleage interpreted exodus through a religious imagination that culminated in a vision of black people en masse reaching Canaan, which was synonymous with fulfillment as political freedom. No matter the differing politics, they understood black people's interest to be singular and they believed black people's efforts to be uniformly focused toward achieving such a goal. However, Obama spoke as a presidential candidate, not as a black activist. Although his presence signified traditional black activism, Obama envisioned a coalition crossing the Jordan, not a singular people. Coalition politics, by nature, constructs a group whose interests are myriad. For Obama's electorate, black political freedom could only be one among a competing slate of goods.

A similar fracturing appears in the politics of new interpretations of the exodus story and the idea of a Promised Land for black hermeneuts who stand within and beyond the Black Church. Black political freedom as a primary goal recedes and becomes but one among many competing interests that mean fulfillment. Class, gender, sexuality, and theological commitments are among the many social forces that shape the vision of Canaan in the black religious imagination. Each competes with black political freedom as an end in interpreting the exodus story. The politics enacted to pursue each continue to arise in cloud and fire forms as best suited to achieve its ends.

Ultimately, Gronniosaw's Book remains silent, but African Americans and others continue to speak for it and to perform cloud and fire politics around it. Gronniosaw's declaration centuries ago upon his disappointing encounter with the silent Book, "when I found it would not speak, this thought immediately presented itself to me, that every body and every thing despis'd me because I was black," still resonates. The "everybody and everything," that Gronniosaw perceived in the West was a life-world that was hostile to him, represented by a political economy based on enslavement. In response, Gronniosaw spoke his own truth into the Book's silence and began a tradition of subject peoples trafficking in the Book's iconic power.

Like Gronniowsaw, African Americans centuries later encounter the same political economy that continues to meet narratives of black ascendance with old strategies of surveillance and containment. In one era after another it reconfigures itself using legislative, judicial, and other apparatuses such as targeted violence to reinscribe racialized hierarchies. The recent collusion between state legislatures that have enacted provisions to make voting more difficult and the U.S. Supreme Court, which struck down a key provision of the 1965 Voting Rights Act, evidence these shifts. At the same time police violence, in the form of the killings of Oscar Grant in Oakland, California, Rekia Boyd in Chicago, Illinois, John Crawford III in Beavercreek, Ohio, Eric Garner in Staten Island, New York, Tamir Rice in Cleveland, Ohio, Michael Brown in Furguson, Missouri, and the public beating of Marlene Pinnock in Los Angeles, California, among others, persists as the republic's most brutal and devastating tool.

As did Gronniosaw, these African Americans also encounter a silent Book. Its iconic power waits to be deployed by new generations who would speak for it. In each era, those who do so in the spirit of their pillar of cloud and fire forebears muster the political will and hermeneutical ingenuity to outmatch the forces that "despis'd" their people. So each interpretation becomes an exercise in transcendence, calling the people's religious imagination to conceive of a world of possibility beyond the horizon. Each one directs the Bible's iconic power toward freedom and leads a people one step closer to the Promised Land.

This project's work has been to recover two major strands of an interpretive tradition and its varying politics. Its fruits extend the work of biblical studies to a natural intersection with both cultural studies and cultural criticism, and it points toward new ways to analyze the rich but long ignored traditions therein.

NOTES

PREFACE

1 Culture Studies refers to a constellation of methodological impetuses that resists any singular definition. For our purposes here, I define culture as a set of shared meanings and values constructed through language and practice. However, as African American biblical interpretation has evolved, it has taken up cultural studies variously as different scholars deploy the method. Three basic approaches inform my understanding: sociological, anthropological, and political. For a sociological approach, see Raymond Williams, *Sociology of Culture* (Chicago: University of Chicago Press, 1995). For an anthropological approach, see Clifford Geertz, *The Interpretation of Cultures* (New York: Basic Books, 1973). Most recently, I have been influenced by the work of the Birmingham School of Cultural Studies. See Stuart Hall, ed., *Representation: Cultural Representations and Signifying Practices* (Thousand Oaks, CA: Sage Publications, 1997).

2 See, for example, Charles B. Copher, *Black Biblical Studies: An Anthology of Charles B. Copher* (Chicago: Black Light Fellowship, 1993); Randall C. Bailey, "Beyond Identification: The Use of Africans in Old Testatment Poetry and Narratives," in *Stony the Road We Trod: African American Biblical Interpretation*, ed. Cain Hope Felder (Minneapolis, MN: Fortress Press, 1991); Michael Joseph Brown, *Blackening of the Bible: The Aims of African American Biblical Interpretation* (Harrisburg, PA: Trinity Press International, 2004).

3 Fernando Segovia signaled this turn in biblical studies and identified it as a third methodological paradigm. Fernando F. Segovia, "And They Began to Speak in Other Tongues," in *Reading from this Place: Social Location and Biblical Interpretation in the United States*, ed. Fernando F. Segovia and Mary Ann Tolbert (Minneapolis, MN: Fortress Press, 1995).

4 Renita J. Weems, *Just a Sister Away: A Womanist Vision of Women's Relationships in the Bible* (San Diego: LuraMedia, 1988).

5 Cain Hope Felder, *Troubling Biblical Waters: Race, Class, and Family*, The Bishop Henry McNeal Turner Studies in North American Black Religion v. 3 (Maryknoll, NY: Orbis Books, 1989).

6 Cain Hope Felder, *Stony the Road We Trod: African American Biblical Interpretation* (Minneapolis, MN: Fortress Press, 1991). At the time of its publication in 1991, there were twenty African Americans with terminal degrees in biblical studies, eleven in New Testament and Christian origins, and nine in Old

Testament/Hebrew Bible. As a first exercise, the collaboration became the vehicle to address many urgent but unvoiced concerns. The volume was pressed into the service of the wide array of needs of black biblical scholars. Its initial articles focused on the theoretical foundations for African American biblical interpretation and made the case for legitimacy as a subfield. Other articles voiced the existential angst of being beholden to the questions of the guild while longing to pursue questions arising from African American communities. Still others expressed black scholars' struggles against racism and sexism in the academy and against sexism in the Black Church. A final section turned to the biblical text to demonstrate the application of these methods in the exegetical craft.

7 Vincent Wimbush, *The Bible and African Americans* (Minneapolis, MN: Fortress Press, 2003).

8 Randall C. Bailey, ed., *Yet With a Steady Beat: Contemporary U.S. Afrocentric Biblical Interpretation*, Semeia Studies (Atlanta: Society of Biblical Literature, 2003).

9 Randall C. Bailey, "Academic Biblical Interpretation among African Americans in the United States," in *African Americans and the Bible: Sacred Texts and Social Textures*, ed. Vincent Wimbush (New York: Continuum, 2000), 707.

10 Brown, *Blackening of the Bible*.

11 Brian K. Blount et al., *True to Our Native Land: An African American New Testament Commentary* (Minneapolis, MN: Fortress Press, 2007).

12 Hugh R. Page et al., eds., *The Africana Bible: Reading Israel's Scriptures from Africa and the African Diaspora* (Minneapolis, MN: Fortress Press, 2010).

13 For standard typologies of this type of work in African American biblical interpretation, see Bailey, "Academic Biblical Interpretation among African Americans in the United States." See also Brown, *Blackening of the Bible*. Beyond typology, Bailey's work continues to theorize this paradigm. Randall C. Bailey, "The Danger of Ignoring One's Own Cultural Bias," in *The Postcolonial Bible*, ed. R. S. Sugirtharajah (Sheffield: Sheffield Academic Press, 1998); Randall C. Bailey, "The Biblical Basis for a Political Theology of Liberation," in *Blow the Trumpet in Zion*, ed. Iva E. Carruthers, Frederick D. Haynes, and Jeremiah A. Wright, Jr. (Minneapolis, MN: Fortress Press, 2005). In addition to Bailey's work, Weems and Junior have theorized this paradigm. See Renita J. Weems, "Reading *Her Way* through the Struggle: African American Women and the Bible," in *Stony the Road We Trod: African American Biblical Interpretation*, ed. Cain Hope Felder (Minneapolis, MN: Fortress Press, 1991). See also Nyasha Junior, "Womanist Biblical Interpretation," in *An Introduction to Feminist Biblical Interpretation in Honor of Katharine Doob Sakenfeld*, ed. Linda Day and Carolyn Pressler (Louisville, KY: Westminster John Knox Press, 2006).

14 Stephanie Buckhanon Crowder, *Simon of Cyrene: A Case of Roman Conscription* (New York: Peter Lang, 2002).

15 Gay L. Byron, *Symbolic Blackness and Ethnic Difference in Early Christian Literature* (New York: Routledge, 2002).

16 Cheryl B. Anderson, *Women, Ideology, and Violence: Critical Theory and the Construction of Gender in the Book of the Covenant and the Deuteronomic Law* (New York: T&T Clark International, 2004); Cheryl B. Anderson, "Reflections in an Interethnic/Racial Era on Interethnic/Racial Marriage in Ezra," in *They Were All Together In One Place?: Toward Minority Biblical Criticism*, ed. Randall C. Bailey, Tat-siong Benny Liew, and Fernando F. Segovia (Atlanta: Society of Biblical Literature, 2009).

17 Brian K. Blount, *Cultural Interpretation: Reorienting New Testament Criticism* (Minneapolis, MN: Fortress Press, 1995); Brian K. Blount, *Can I Get a Witness?: Reading Revelation Through African American Culture*, 1st ed. (Louisville, KY: Westminster John Knox Press, 2005). Although *Can I Get a Witness* self-consciously takes up a method based in culture studies, the book focuses on interpreting Revelation.

18 Rodney Steven Sadler, *Can a Cushite Change His Skin?: An Examination of Race, Ethnicity, and Othering in the Hebrew Bible*, Journal for the Study of the Old Testament. Supplement series 425 (New York: T&T Clark, 2005).

19 Mignon R. Jacobs, *Gender, Power, and Persuasion: The Genesis Narratives and Contemporary Portraits* (Grand Rapids, MI: Baker Academic Press, 2007).

20 Wilda Gafney, *Daughters of Miriam: Women Prophets in Ancient Israel* (Minneapolis, MN: Fortress Press, 2008).

21 Love L. Sechrest, *A Former Jew: Paul and the Dialectics of Race*, Library of New Testament Studies (London; New York: T & T Clark, 2009).

22 Academic interpretation in general understands itself to be distinct from other forms of biblical inquiry because it has been shaped within the boundaries of method, a technical-reflective activity (generally historical-critical, literary, or one of the newer discursively constructed methods). As such, biblical interpretation as a formal academic project has enjoyed a "superior" status to the everyday ways that people discover the Bible. However, the majority of interpretive activity is this natural everyday discovery with the biblical text. Black biblical interpretation is no different in this regard. Black academic interpretation begins only as African Americans earned doctoral degrees in biblical studies (most after 1980), whereas the activity of black people's ordinary discovery of the Bible in myriad and complex ways has been an ongoing phenomenon long before their arrival in North America and continues to this day. I contend that both types of interpretive activity are enmeshed in culture. Both not only participate in the movement of history, but history's ebbs, flows, and trends influence both types of interpretive activity. Finally, both possess a politics that can be excavated.

23 Vincent Wimbush, "The Bible and African Americans: An Outline of an Interpretive History," in *Stony the Road We Trod : African American Biblical Interpretation*, ed. Cain Hope Felder (Minneapolis, MN: Fortress Press, 1991); Vincent Wimbush, "A Meeting of Worlds: African Americans and the Bible," in *Teaching the Bible: The Discourses and Politics of Biblical Pedagogy*, ed. Fernando F. Segovia and Mary Ann Tolbert (Maryknoll, NY: Orbis, 1998); Vincent

Wimbush, "Reading Darkness: Reading Scripture," in *African Americans and the Bible: Sacred Text and Social Textures*, ed. Vincent Wimbush (New York: Continuum, 2003); Vincent L. Wimbush, *The Bible and African Americans: A Brief History*, Facets (Minneapolis, MN: Fortress Press, 2003); Vincent L. Wimbush, *Theorizing Scriptures: New Critical Orientations to a Cultural Phenomenon*, Signifying (on) Scriptures (New Brunswick, NJ: Rutgers University Press, 2008).

24 Allen Dwight Callahan, *The Talking Book: African Americans and the Bible* (New Haven, CT: Yale University Press, 2006); Margaret Aymer, *First Pure, Then Peaceable: Frederick Douglass, Darkness and the Epistle of James* (New York: T&T Clark, 2008).

25 Wimbush, *Theorizing Scriptures: New Critical Orientations to a Cultural Phenomenon*, 5.

26 Bailey, "The Danger of Ignoring One's Own Cultural Bias."

27 Brown, *Blackening of the Bible*, 182.

28 Page et al., *The Africana Bible*, 5.

INTRODUCTION

1 James Albert Ukawsaw Gronniosaw, "A Narrative of the Most Remarkable Particular in the Life of James Albert Ukawsaw Gronniosaw, An African Prince, As Related by Himself," in *Unchained Voices: An Anthology of Black Authors in the English-Speaking World of the 18th Century*, ed. Vincent Carretta (Lexington: University of Kentucky Press, 1996), 38

2 First, I have in mind a hermeneutical distance. *Verstehen* or hermeneutical understanding is impossible without some basis for shared tradition. Even the possibility of "play" is limited. Hans-Geog Gadamer, *Truth and Method*, trans. Joel Weinsheimer and Donald G. Marshall, 2nd ed. (New York: Continuum, 1998), 39, 102. Second, I have in mind a phenomenological distance. The background meaning conditions for Gronniosaw and the captain were so different that there was no intersection between their life-worlds other than the moments they had shared on the ship. Even then, they grasped that event under vastly different structures of meaning.

3 In narrative form, his story inaugurated an African-English literary tradition. Gronniosaw was the first to use the talking book trope in his autobiography published in 1772. The trope reappears in the autobiographies of John Marrant (1782), Quobna Ottoba Cugoano (1787), Olaudah Equiano (1789), and John Jea (1815). Henry Louis Gates has shown that each successive writer revises the trope and signifies upon the previous work. Gates sees this body of work as the beginning of the African-English literary tradition. Henry Louis Gates, "The Trope of the Talking Book," in *The Signifying Monkey: A Theory of African-American Literary Criticism* (New York: Oxford, 1988).

4 They take up the "talking book" trope as a composite of the tradition of narratives from Gronniosaw (1772) to John Jea (1815). Two scholars, among many, who ably

mined this metaphor include Abraham Smith and Allen Dwight Callahan. Smith takes license from Gronniosaw's story to question the ethics of pre-reading, reading, and post-reading practices. See Abraham Smith, "'I Saw the Book Talk': A Cultural Studies Approach to the Ethics of an African American Biblical Hermeneutics," *Semeia* 77(1997): 115. Callahan, *The Talking Book*, 20.

5 Callahan, *The Talking Book,* 20.

6 Ibid.

7 I have in mind what phenomenologists term as "intending." Gronniosaw was already conscious of the book. He had experienced it as a participant in his enslavement and a source of the enslaver's power.

8 Charles H. Long, "Archaism and Hermeneutics," in *Significations: Signs, Symbols and Images in the Interpretation of Religion* (Minneapolis, MN: Fortress Press, 1986), 60.

9 Indeed, as Long states, "There is a history of the contact of those who were already at home when the conquerors came. There was, indeed a *new* world and an *other* world for them also. The great disadvantage for those who came into contact with the Europeans after 1493 was the simple fact that these natives of extra-European lands knew who they were. They had an identity and were secure within it." Charles H. Long, "Conquest and Cultural Contact in the New World," in *Significations: Signs, Symbols and Images in the Interpretation of Religion* (Minneapolis, MN: Fortress Press, 1986), 107.

10 Each of three early standard bearers of the modern era holds similar views of people of African descent. Immanuel Kant, *Observations on the Feeling of the Beautiful and the Sublime*, trans. John T. Goldthwait (Berkeley: University of California Press, 1991), 110–11; David Hume, *The Philosophical Works of David Hume*, 4 vols., vol. 3 (Boston: Little, Brown, and Company, 1854). 228; Georg Hegel, *The Philosophy of History*, trans. C. J. Freidrich (New York: Dover, 1956), 99.

11 Georg Hegel, *The Philosophy of History*, trans. C. J. Freidrich (New York: Dover, 1956), 99.

12 Ibid., 91–99.

13 Vincent Wimbush, "The Bible and African Americans, 86. Callahan, *The Talking Book*, 83; Mark A. Noll, "The Image of the United States as a Biblical Nation, 1776–1865," in *The Bible in America: Essays in Cultural History*, ed. Nathan O. Hatch and Mark A. Noll (New York: Oxford University Press, 1982), 43ff.; Albert J. Raboteau, *Slave Religion: The "Invisible Institution" in the Antebellum South* (New York: Oxford University Press, 2004). 304–05, 11–12. Eddie S. Glaude, Jr., *Exodus! Religion, Race, and Nation in Early Nineteenth-Century Black America* (Chicago: University of Chicago Press, 2000). Rhondda Robinson Thomas, *Claiming Exodus: A Cultural History of Afro-Atlantic Identity, 1774–1903* (Waco, TX: Baylor University Press, 2013).

14 By counter-history, I refer to Michel Foucault's notion of ways that the "conquered" weave counter-knowledge into a narrative that resists the legitimizing

impulses of the sovereign. Counter-history manifests as disruptive speech. It does not rely upon traditional legitimizing structures; it opposes them. Those who stand outside of the Western tradition attest, "We do not have any continuity behind us; we do not have behind us the great and glorious genealogy in which the law and power flaunt themselves in their power and glory. We came out of the shadows, we had no glory and we had no rights, and that is why we are beginning to speak and to tell of our history." Michel Foucault, *"Society Must Be Defended": Lectures at the Collège de France, 1975–1976,* trans. David Macy (New York: Picador, 2003), 70.

15 In classical political theory, the categories radical and conservative refer to ends with respect to the status quo rather than means. The classic use of these categories mischaracterizes the positions of both hermeneuts.

16 Kelly Miller, "Radicals and Conservatives," in *Radicals and Conservatives and Other Essays on the Negro in America* (New York: Schocken Books, 1968), 24.

17 Ibid., 25–26.

18 Joanne M. Braxton, ed., *The Collected Poetry of Paul Laurence Dunbar* (Charlottesville: University of Virginia Press, 1993), 71.

19 Indeed, "mastery" of one's self and the surrounding world was a defining early modern impulse in the United States. Thus, the Trans-Atlantic Slave Trade extended this impulse to master the "savage." African Americans participated mimetically. By cultural, intellectual, and moral attainment, African Americans demonstrated their humanity and rejected the slave regime's legitimacy. I have been influenced to a good degree by Houston Baker's discussion in Houston A. Baker, Jr., *Modernism and the Harlem Renaissance* (Chicago: University of Chicago Press, 1987), 81–83.

CHAPTER 1

1 Gary B. Nash, *Forging Freedom: The Formation of Philadelphia's Black Community, 1720–1840* (Cambridge, MA: Harvard University Press, 1988), 8.

2 Samuel M. Janney, *The Life of William Penn with Selections from His Correspondence and Autobiography* (Philadelphia: Hogan, Perkins & Co., 1852), 167.

3 Nash, *Forging Freedom,* 8.

4 Ibid., 137.

5 Ibid., 29–30.

6 Ibid., 40–42.

7 Ibid., 3–4.

8 W.E.B. Du Bois, *The Philadelphia Negro* (New York: Schocken Books, 1967), 411–18, appendix B.

9 Ibid.

10 See An Act for the Gradual Abolition of Slavery, March 11, 1780; http://www.portal.state.pa.us/portal/server.pt/community/empowerment/18325/quest_for_civil_rights/673923.

11 These virtues were rooted in the tradition of John Calvin, the sixteenth-century Protestant Reformer. Calvinist thought permeated the Episcopal, Presbyterian, and Methodist religious expressions in the Northeastern and Mid-Atlantic states.

12 Max Weber understood Calvinist strands of Protestantism as particularly congruent with the growth of capitalism. In Calvinism, Weber connected concepts of calling (*Beruf*) and predestination and identified them as ideals that encouraged capitalist formations among its practitioners. Max Weber, *The Protestant Ethic and the Spirit of Capitalism with Other Writings on the Rise of the West*, trans. Stephen Kalberg, 4th ed. (New York: Oxford University Press, 2009). 88. For Calvinists, call is a chosen vocation pursued with religious vigor and accountability. The labor required to pursue this vocation is not a means to an economic end, but a spiritual discipline and an end unto itself.

13 Nash, *Forging Freedom*, 67.

14 Ibid.

15 Ibid., 68. Jones continued to work for Wynkoop, who formerly held him in slavery, with the goal of freeing his wife, so that their children would be born free.

16 Ibid.

17 Ibid., 143.

18 Ibid., 137.

19 Ibid., 176.

20 Ibid., 177.

21 Absalom Jones, "Petition of Absalom Jones and Seventy-Three Others," in *Early Negro Writing 1760–1837*, ed. Dorothy Porter (Philadelphia: Black Classic Press, 1995), 330.

22 Albert J. Raboteau, *Slave Religion*, 133–36; Albert J. Raboteau, *A Fire in the Bones* (Boston: Beacon Press, 1995), 21–27. For Methodism among blacks in Philadelphia, see Nash, *Forging Freedom*, 110–17.

23 Nash, *Forging Freedom*, 118.

24 Richard Allen, "Life Experience and Gospel Labors," in *Afro-American Religious History: A Documentary History*, ed. Milton C. Sernett (Durham, NC: Duke University Press, 1985), 141. See also Richard Allen, *Life Experience and Gospel Labors* (Chapel Hill: University of North Carolina at Chapel Hill, 2000), 33ff. The society proved particularly instrumental in supporting black Philadelphians during the yellow fever epidemic of 1793.

25 Nash, *Forging Freedom*, 121–24.

26 Figural interpretations establish a connection between two events or persons so that the first signifies not only itself but also the second, while the second involves or fulfills the first. The two poles of a figure are separated in time, but both, being real events or persons, are within temporality. They are both contained in the flowing stream, which is historical life. See Eric Auerbach, *Mimesis: The Representation of Reality in Western Literature*, trans. Willard Ropes Trask (Princeton, NJ: Princeton University Press, 1968), 73. For Jones, the Exodus not

only recounted God's intervention in history to deliver the Children of Israel, but also signified for blacks enslaved in North America that their suffering would invoke God's intervention on their behalf.

27 Jones, "A Thanksgiving Sermon," 337.

28 Generally referred to as *corvée*, the seasonal conscription of laborers by the Crown from among the local citizenry for work on public projects such as temples, palaces, roads, aqueducts, and so forth was a common practice throughout the ancient world.

29 In terms of cultural contact as a disruptive force, see Long, *Significations*. See also Chinua Achebe, *Things Fall Apart* (New York: Alfred A. Knopf, 1992).

30 Jones, "A Thanksgiving Sermon," 336.

31 Bernice Johnson Reagon, *If You Don't Go, Don't Hinder Me: The African American Sacred Song Tradition* (Lincoln: University of Nebraska Press, 2001), 62–63.

32 Herbert Robinson Marbury, "Ezra-Nehemiah," in *The Africana Bible: Reading Israel's Scriptures from Africa and the African Diaspora*, ed. Hugh R. Page, et al. (Minneapolis, MN: Fortress Press, 2010), 281–82.

33 Jones, "A Thanksgiving Sermon," 336. Emphasis mine.

34 Ibid. Emphasis mine.

35 Ibid., 338.

36 "Work without rest in a vocational calling was recommended as the best possible means to acquire the self-confidence that one belonged among the elect. Work, and work alone, banishes religious doubt and gives certainty of one's status among the saved." Weber, *The Protestant Ethic*, 111.

37 Jones, "A Thanksgiving Sermon," 339–41.

38 A. Leon Higginbotham, Jr., *In the Matter of Color: Race and the American Legal Process: The Colonial Period* (New York: Oxford University Press, 1980), 62.

39 Cotton Mather, *The Negro Christianized. An Essay to Excite and Assist that Good Work, the Instruction of Negro-Servants in Christianity* (Boston: B. Green, 1706), 1.

40 Robin Blackburn, *The Making of New World Slavery: From the Baroque to the Modern, 1492–1800* (New York: Verso, 1998), 238.

41 K. G. Davies, *The Royal African Company*, 7 vols., vol. 7, The Emergence of International Business 1200–1800 (London: Routledge, 1999), 1–38.

42 Higginbotham, Jr., *In the Matter of Color*, 91–95.

43 Ibid., 91–97.

44 James Oliver Horton and Lois E. Horton, *Black Bostonians: Family Life and Community Struggle in the Antebellum North* (New York: Holmes and Meier, 1999), 5.

45 Peter P. Hinks, ed., *David Walker's Appeal to the Coloured Citizens of the World* (University Park: Pennsylvania State University Press, 2008), 6.

46 This date departs from the traditional birth date of 1785 determined by Garnet. In a recent biography, Peter Hinks discusses the problems in relying upon that date. Peter P. Hinks, *To Awaken My Afflicted Brethren: David Walker and the Problem of Antebellum* (University Park: Pennsylvania State University Press, 2000), 10–14.

47 Walker's father, however, would live his entire life under the burden of chattel slavery. Henry Highland Garnet, *Walker's Appeal and Garnet's Address to the Slaves of the United States* (Charleston, SC: BiblioBazaar, 2008), 11.

48 Ibid.

49 Hinks reports, "Ever since the establishment of the Lower Cape Fear's first colonies, whites had feared slave revolt. As early as 1721 an attempted insurrection had nearly resulted in the decimation of the southeastern coast's white population. Fear of revolt in 1745 led local magistrates to restrict black gatherings and, in 1747, ships filled with 'Mulattoes and Negroes' terrorized settlements along the Cape Fear River." Hinks, *To Awaken My Afflicted Brethren*, 40.

50 Both free blacks and those held in slavery had come together to constitute the congregation after successfully fending off or rebelling against attempts by both the South Carolina legislature and the Charleston city council to disband them. Ibid., 26–28.

51 The court possessed transcripts for only 71 of the 131 persons tried for the conspiracy. Of those whose transcripts were preserved, more than one-half of those tried were associated with the Charleston AME congregation. Ibid., 28.

52 Garnet, *Walker's Appeal and Garnet's Address to the Slaves*, 11–12.

53 Hinks, *To Awaken My Afflicted Brethren*, 69.

54 David Walker, *Walker's Appeal, in Four Articles; Together with a Preamble, to the Coloured Citizens of the World, but in Particular, and Very Expressly, to Those of the United States of America, Written in Boston, State of Massachusetts, September 28, 1829* (Boston: David Walker, 1830). See also Hinks, *David Walker's Appeal to the Coloured Citizens of the World*.

55 Vincent Harding, *There Is a River: The Black Struggle for Freedom in America* (New York: Vintage Books, 1983), 94.

56 Thomas Jefferson, *Notes on the State of Virginia* (Philadelphia: Pritchard and Hall, 1788).

57 Ibid., 267–68.

58 Walker was not the only person of African descent to challenge Jefferson's notions on race. In 1792, Benjamin Banneker wrote to then secretary of state Thomas Jefferson, in an attempt to persuade him to reconsider his position on the intellectual and moral inferiority of persons of African descent. See Benjamin Banneker, "Letter from Benjamin Banneker," in *Early Negro Writing 1760–1837*, ed. Dorothy Porter (Baltimore: Black Classic Press, 1995).

59 Walker's challenge participates in the long tradition of black heroic genius. His conceptions of manhood arise as a counter-discourse to categorical racism. See Victor Anderson, *Beyond Ontological Blackness: An Essay on African American Religious and Cultural Criticism* (New York: Continuum, 1995), 79.

60 Jefferson, *Notes on the State of Virginia*, 149.

61 Hinks, *David Walker's Appeal to the Coloured Citizens of the World*, 2.

62 By "race," I refer to taken for granted markers of identity constructed by nineteenth-century racialized notions.

63 Jefferson's *Declaration of Independence*. That the two documents, Walker's *Appeal* and Jefferson's *Declaration of Independence*, shared emancipatory intentions was not lost on Walker.

64 Hinks, *David Walker's Appeal to the Coloured Citizens of the World*, 4.

65 Ibid., 10.

66 Throughout the Old Testament, the writers esteem Egypt highly for its wisdom, military might, and wealth. See Bailey, "Beyond Identification."

67 Hinks, *David Walker's Appeal to the Coloured Citizens of the World*, 10.

68 Ibid.

69 Ibid.

70 Ibid.

71 Ibid., 10–11.

72 Ibid., 11.

73 Jefferson, *Notes on the State of Virginia*, 265.

74 Walker, *Walker's Appeal, in Four Articles*, 11.

75 Hinks, *David Walker's Appeal to the Coloured Citizens of the World*, 11.

76 Ibid., 11–12.

77 Emphasis mine.

78 Jefferson, *Notes on the State of Virginia*, 268–69.

79 Hinks, *David Walker's Appeal to the Coloured Citizens of the World*, 12.

80 Ibid., 12–13.

81 Exodus 2:6.

82 Ibid.

83 Ibid., 13.

84 Ibid., 14–15.

85 Ibid., 13.

86 Ibid.

87 W.E.B. Du Bois's dissertation takes up a masterful discussion of the complexity of enforcing the law. Du Bois, *The Suppression of the African Slave-Trade to the United States of America, 1638–1870* (New York: Longmans, Green, 1896).

88 John Hope Franklin, *From Slavery to Freedom: A History of Negro Americans*, 5th ed. (New York: Alfred A. Knopf, 1980), 130.

CHAPTER 2

1 The Hebrew word translated as "in the wilderness" is also the Hebrew title of the Book of Numbers, which continues the Exodus story.

2 The 1869 publication is the second, but earliest existing, edition. The 1,039-line epic poem was her most developed interpretive work on Exodus.

3 John Hope Franklin and Alfred A. Moss, Jr., *From Slavery to Freedom: A History of Negro Americans*, 6th ed. (New York: McGraw-Hill, 1988), 209.

4 Despite the intransigent President Andrew Johnson, the Republicans valiantly overrode fifteen of his twenty-nine vetoes. Robert J. Spitzer, *Veto: Touchstone of the American Presidency* (Albany: State University of New York Press, 1988), 72.

Thomas C. Holt, *Children of Fire: A History of African Americans* (New York: Hill and Wang, 2010). 170. See also Franklin and Moss, Jr., *From Slavery to Freedom*, 206–07.

5 This is W.E.B. Du Bois's estimate. Cited from Bruce J. Reynolds, "Black Farmers in America, 1865–2000: The Pursuit of Independent Farming and the Role of Cooperatives," ed. Rural Business Cooperative Service (Washington, DC: U.S. Department of Agriculture, 2003), 3.

6 Franklin and Moss, Jr., *From Slavery to Freedom*, 219–21.

7 Ibid., 221.

8 W.R.W. Stephens, *The Life and Letters of Edward A. Freeman* (New York: Macmillan and Co., 1895). 242.

9 Melba Joyce Boyd, *Politics and Poetics in the Life of Frances E. W. Harper 1825–1911*, African American Life Series (Detroit: Wayne State University Press, 1994), 42.

10 Frances Smith Foster, ed., *A Brighter Coming Day* (New York: Feminist Press at The City University of New York, 1990), 7.

11 Ibid., 99–100.

12 Ibid., 104.

13 William Still, *The Underground Railroad: A Record of Facts, Authentic Narrative, Letters, &C., Narrating the Hardships, Hair-Breadth Escapes and Death Struggles of The Slaves in Their Efforts of Freedom, as Related by Themselves and Others, or Witnessed by the Author; Together with Sketches of Some of the Largest Stockholders, and Most Liberal Aiders and Advisers, of the Road* (Philadephia: Porter and Coates, 1872), 792.

14 Foster, *A Brighter Coming Day*, 275.

15 For a fuller discussion of classical liberalism and its intersections with slavery in the American South, see Arthur Riss, *Race, Slavery and Liberalism in Nineteenth Century American Literature* (Cambridge: Cambridge University Press, 2006).

16 Boyd, *Politics and Poetics in the Life of Frances E. W. Harper 1825–1911*, 42. See also Still, *The Underground Railroad: A Record of Facts, Authentic Narrative, Letters, &C.*, 760.

17 Boyd, *Politics and Poetics in the Life of Frances E. W. Harper 1825–1911*, 43. See also Still, *The Underground Railroad: A Record of Facts, Authentic Narrative, Letters, &C.*, 779.

18 Foster, *A Brighter Coming Day*, 12–13. See also Barbara Welter, "The Cult of True Womanhood," *American Quarterly* 18, no. 2 (1966).

19 Foster, *A Brighter Coming Day*, 216.

20 Ibid., 217.

21 Still, *The Underground Railroad: A Record of Facts, Authentic Narrative, Letters, &C.*, 760–61.

22 Foster, *A Brighter Coming Day*, 16.

23 Still, *The Underground Railroad: A Record of Facts, Authentic Narrative, Letters, &C.*, 759.

24 Foster, *A Brighter Coming Day*, 285–86.

25 Ultimately, the cult of domesticity supported contemporaneous patriarchy. Its language celebrated women's presence and work in the home and, simultaneously, relegated them to same space.

26 Michael Stancliff, *Frances Ellen Watkins Harper: African American Reform Rhetoric and the Rise of a Modern Nation State* (New York: Routledge, 2011), 9.

27 Foster, *A Brighter Coming Day*, 288.

28 Ibid.

29 I refer to the common nineteenth-century understanding as articulated by W.E.B. Du Bois on February 23, 1893,

> I am glad I am living, I rejoice as a strong man to run a race, and I am strong—is it egotism is it assurance—or is it the silent call of the world spirit that makes me feel that I am royal and that beneath my sceptre a world of kings shall bow. The hot dark blood of that black forefather born king of men—is beating at my heart, and I know that I am either a genius or a fool. . . . this I do know: be the Truth what it may I will seek it on the pure assumption that it is worth seeking—and Heaven nor Hell, God nor Devil shall turn me from my purpose till I die. . . . The general proposition of working for the world's good becomes too soon sickly sentimentality. I therefore take the work that the Unknown lays in my hands and work for the rise of the Negro people, taking for granted that their best development means the best development of the world.

Here quoted from Frances L. Broderick, *W. E. B. Du Bois, Negro Leader in a Time of Crisis*, Volume 2 (Stanford: Stanford University Press, 1959), 28-29. Du Bois's reflections are replete with modernist understandings of race and its implications for racialized genius. He directs them toward what he understands as the common good of his race. Hazel V. Carby has recently offered an insightful interrogation of this position and its wider implications as it has traveled in black culture. See Carby, *Race Men* (Cambridge, MA: Harvard University Press, 1998).

30 Herbert Sussman, "The Study of Victorian Masculinities," *Victorian Literature and Culture* 20 (1992).

31 Foster, *A Brighter Coming Day*, 104.

32 Two excellent studies take up an analysis on this question of difference. Renita J. Weems, "The Hebrew Women are not Like the Egyptian Women: The Ideology of Race, Gender and Sexual Reproduction in Exodus1," *Semeia* 59 (1992): 25–34. Randall C. Bailey, "They're Nothing but Incestuous Bastards: The Polemical Use of Sex and Sexuality in Hebrew Canon Narratives," in *Reading from this Place: Social Location and Biblical Interpretation in the United States*, ed. Fernando F. Segovia and Mary Ann Tolbert (Minneapolis, MN: Fortress Press, 1995), 121–38.

33 Harper borrows the name Charmian from Plutarch's Parallel Lives LXXXV, 2-3 (Life of Antony). Charmian appears as one Cleopatra's handmaidens.

34 Francis Ellen Watkins Harper, *Moses: Story of the Nile* (Philadelphia: Merrihew and Son, 1869), 3.

35 Ibid., 4.

36 Ibid., 3.

37 Ibid., 11.

38 Ibid.

39 Ibid., 6.

40 The phrase "couch of pain" is a common euphemism for sickness in Victorian literature.

41 Harper, *Moses: Story of the Nile*, 6.

42 Ibid., 6–7.

43 Ibid.

44 Ibid., 9–10.

45 Ibid., 8–9.

46 Ibid., 9.

47 Ibid., 13.

48 Ibid., 14.

49 Ibid.

50 Ibid.

51 Ibid., 19.

52 Ibid., 14.

53 Ibid., 15.

54 Ibid.

55 Ibid.

56 Franklin and Moss, Jr., *From Slavery to Freedom*, 227.

57 Wayne E. Croft, "You Jes' Wait a Little: A Comparison of the Motif of Hope in African American Preaching During the Slave and Post-Civil War Periods," Dissertation (Drew University, 2009), 143.

58 Ibid., 156.

59 Lee D. Baker, *From Savage to Negro: Anthropology and the Construction of Race 1896–1954* (Los Angeles: University of California Press, 1998), 15.

60 John P. Jackson, Jr., and Nadine W. Weidman, *Race, Racism and Science: Social Impact and Implications* (Rutgers, NJ: Rutgers University Press, 2005), 50.

61 Baker, *From Savage to Negro*, 15.

62 William E. Hatcher, *John Jasper: The Unmatched Negro Philosopher and Preacher* (New York: Fleming H. Revell Company, 1908), 142–43.

63 Ibid., 143.

64 Ibid.

65 Ibid.

66 Ibid.

67 Ibid.

68 Ibid.

69 Ibid.

70 Ibid.

71 A document in Sixth Mount Zion's historical archives attests to Jasper's ability to deploy both Standard English and "the old slave dialect" at will. In fact, transcripts of the sermons vary with each delivery and with each transcriber. Edwin Archer Randolph, the first African American graduate of Yale Law School, who identifies himself as Jasper's friend, recorded the sermon in Standard English. Edwin Archer Randolph, *The Life of Rev. John Jasper, Pastor of Sixth Mt. Zion Baptist Church, Richmond, Va., from His Birth to the Present Time, with His Theory on the Rotation of the Sun*, Electronic Edition ed. (R.T. Hill and Co., 1884).

72 Houston A. Baker, Jr., *Modernism and the Harlem Renaissance* (Chicago: University of Chicago Press, 1987), 21. (Emphasis his.)

73 Ibid.

74 Ibid., 22. (Emphasis his.)

75 From Act I. Ossie Davis, Peter Udall, and Gary Geld, *Purlie Victorious* (New York, Samuel French Incorporated, 1971).

76 I have in mind the following definition: "The ironic reversal of a received racist image of the black as simian-like, the Signifying Monkey—he who dwells at the margins of discourse, ever punning, ever troping, ever embodying the ambiguities of language." Henry Louis Gates, "The Blackness of Blackness: A Critique of the Sign and the Signifying Monkey," in *Black Literature and Literary Theory*, ed. Henry Louis Gates (New York: Routledge, 1990), 286. Jasper presses his argument indirectly with humor and deflection.

77 Randolph, *The Life of Rev. John Jasper, Pastor of Sixth Mt. Zion Baptist Church*, 85.

78 Hatcher, *John Jasper: The Unmatched Negro Philosopher and Preacher*, 127.

79 Ibid., 134.

80 Ibid.

81 Ibid.

82 Ibid.

83 Ibid.

84 Ibid., 134–35.

85 Ibid., 135.

86 Ibid., 136–37.

87 Leon F. Litwack, *Been in the Storm So Long: The Aftermath of Slavery* (New York: Vintage Books, 1979), 167–70.

88 Ibid., 137.

89 Ibid.

90 Ibid., 137–38.

91 Ibid., 138.

92 Ibid., 141–42.

93 Ibid., 142.

94 Ibid.

95 Ibid., 142.

96 Ibid., 144.

97 In part, these scholars trafficked in a discourse that affirmed their interests in status quo racial hierarchies. The claim of objectivity only masks the very "interested" work of academic discourse.

98 Ibid.

99 Ibid., 146.

100 Ibid., 147.

101 Ibid., 147–48.

102 Ibid., 148–49.

CHAPTER 3

1 I am aware of the gender bias signified by the masculine pronoun. However, I employ it to emphasize the New Negro as a gendered being within the imagination of the era.

2 Manning Marable, *Race, Reform, and Rebellion: The Second Reconstruction and Beyond in Black America, 1945–2006*, 3rd ed. (Jackson: University Press of Mississippi, 2007), 9.

3 Ibid.

4 Franklin and Moss, Jr., *From Slavery to Freedom*, 310.

5 Ibid., 311.

6 Ibid., 312.

7 Marable, *Race, Reform, and Rebellion*, 32.

8 Franklin and Moss, Jr., *From Slavery to Freedom*, 312.

9 Ibid.

10 Ibid., 314.

11 Ibid., 315.

12 Nathan Irvin Huggins, *Harlem Renaissance* (New York: Oxford University Press, 1971), 55.

13 Ibid., 54.

14 Franklin and Moss, Jr., *From Slavery to Freedom*, 312.

15 W.E.B. Du Bois, "Returning Soldiers," *Crisis*, May 1919.

16 For the seminal work on the topic and the volume that established the term "New Negro," see Alain Locke, ed., *The New Negro: Voices of the Harlem Renaissance* (New York: Simon & Schuster, 1992).

17 Langston Hughes, "The Negro Artist and the Racial Mountain," *Nation* 1926.

18 Zora Neale Hurston, "Spirituals and Neo-Spirituals," in *Voices from the Harlem Renaissance*, ed. Nathan Huggins (New York: Oxford University Press, 1995), 344.

19 Huggins, *Harlem Renaissance*, 74.

20 See the excellent work done in chapters 3 and 4 of Tiffany Ruby Patterson, *Zora Neale Hurston and a History of Southern Life* (Philadelphia: Temple University Press, 2005).

21 Zora Neale Hurston, "How it Feels to Be Colored Me," in *The African-American Experience: Black History and Culture Through Speeches, Letters, Editorials, Poems, Songs and Stories*, ed. Kai Wright (New York: Workman Publishing, 2009), 449.

22 Victor Anderson, *Creative Exchange: A Constructive Theology of African American Religious Experience* (Minneapolis, MN: Fortress Press, 2008), 33. See also Edward Farley, *Deep Symbols: Their Post Modern Effacement and Reclamation* (Valley Forge, PA: Trinity Press International, 1996).

23 Hurston, "How it Feels to Be Colored Me," 449.

24 Zora Neale Hurston, *Dust Tracks on the Road: An Autobiography*, ed. Robert E. Hemenway (Urbana: University of Illinois, 1984), 15–16.

25 Hurston, "How it Feels to Be Colored Me," 448.

26 Hurston, *Dust Tracks on the Road: An Autobiography*, 266.

27 Ibid., 266–67.

28 Ibid., 55.

29 Ibid.

30 Patterson, *Zora Neale Hurston and a History of Southern Life*, 15.

31 Hurston, *Dust Tracks on the Road: An Autobiography*, 21.

32 Ibid.

33 Zora Neal Hurston, *Moses, Man of the Mountain* (New York: Library of America, 1995), 341. Throughout the novel, she uses sharp, rich dialogue, a hallmark of her fiction, to attend to differences in class and ethnicity. The Hebrew characters, except for Moses, speak as any rural folk might. She casts Egyptian speech, however, in Standard English.

34 In Exodus 4 Moses must introduce them to this deity who will deliver them.

35 Zora Neal Hurston, *Moses, Man of the Mountain* (New York: Harper Collins, 1991), 341.

36 Ibid., 343.

37 Hurston, *Moses, Man of the Mountain*, 341.

38 Ibid.

39 Ibid.

40 Ibid.

41 Ibid.

42 Ibid., 371.

43 Ibid., 445.

44 Ibid., 445–46.

45 Ibid., 573.

46 Ibid., 581–82.

47 Ibid., 583–84.

CHAPTER 4

1 Wil Haygood, *King of the Cats: The Life and Times of Adam Clayton Powell, Jr.* (New York: Amistad, 2006), 13.

2 Adam Clayton Powell, *Adam by Adam: The Autobiography of Adam Clayton Powell, Jr.* (New York: Kensington Publishing Corporation, 1971), 37.

3 Lewis V. Baldwin, *There is a Balm in Gilead: The Cultural Roots of Martin Luther King, Jr.* (Minneapolis, MN: Fortress Press, 1991), 39–41.

4 Charles V. Hamilton, *Adam Clayton Powell, Jr.: The Political Biography of an American Dilemma* (New York: Cooper Square Press, 2002), 9.

5 Baldwin, *There is a Balm in Gilead*, 235. [Emphasis King's.]

6 For example, see "Segregation Charged in New York," *Spartanburg Herald-Journal*, June 21, 1959.

7 www.nytimes.com/2010/01/06/nyregion/06harlem.html.

8 http://www.census.gov/population/www/documentation/twps0076/ALtab.pdf.

9 Reynolds, "Black Farmers in America, 1865–2000. http://www.rurdev.usda.gov/rbs/pub/rr194.pdf

10 Marable, *Race, Reform, and Rebellion*, 10.

11 Ibid.

12 Franklin and Moss, Jr., *From Slavery to Freedom*, 210.

13 This network of schools included Atlanta University (1865), Bennett College (1873), Claflin College (1869), Clark University (1869), Fisk College (1866), Gammon Theological Seminary (1869), Hampton Institute (1868), Howard University (1867), Meharry Medical College (1876), Morris Brown College (1881), Talledega College (1867), and Tuskegee Institute (1881) among others.

14 In 1890, the state of Mississippi, where blacks outnumbered whites, amended its constitution and effectively disenfranchised 123,000 blacks. South Carolina followed suit in 1896. In 1900 Alabama cut the number of registered black voters from 181,000 to 3,000. John Hope Franklin, *From Slavery to Freedom: A History of Negro Americans*, Fifth ed. (New York: Alfred A. Knopf, 1980), 236–37.

15 Ibid., 238.

16 Franklin and Moss, Jr., *From Slavery to Freedom: A History of Negro Americans*, 280.

17 Marable, *Race, Reform, and Rebellion*, 10.

18 For example, between 1900 and 1914, more than 1,100 African Americans were lynched in Knoxville, Tennessee and whites destroyed black property valued at $50,000. Countless similar occurrences throughout the nation carried the force of public spectacle and were meant to frighten entire communities into submission. Franklin, *From Slavery to Freedom: A History of Negro Americans*, 282; Marable, *Race, Reform, and Rebellion*, 11.

19 Powell, *Adam by Adam: The Autobiography of Adam Clayton Powell, Jr.*, 24.

20 Hamilton, *Adam Clayton Powell, Jr.*, 49.

21 Powell, *Adam by Adam: The Autobiography of Adam Clayton Powell, Jr.*, 32.

22 Haygood, *King of the Cats*, 14.

23 Powell, *Adam by Adam: The Autobiography of Adam Clayton Powell, Jr.*, 33.

24 Hamilton, *Adam Clayton Powell, Jr.*, 60.

25 Haygood, *King of the Cats*, 77. But see Hamilton, *Adam Clayton Powell, Jr.*, 97.

26 Hamilton, *Adam Clayton Powell, Jr.*, 482.

27 Ibid.

28 Peter J. Paris's study contains a thorough discussion of Powell's theological positions and the ways they informed his political orientation. Peter J. Paris, *Black Religious Leaders: Conflict in Unity* (Louisville, KY: Westminster John Knox Press, 1991), 145–81.

29 I refer to the monumental work by Gunnar Myrdal, *An American Dilemma: The Negro Problem and Modern Democracy* (New Brunswick, NJ: Transaction, 1996).

30 Powell dates this sermon's delivery to November 29, 1959. However, in the sermon, Powell references a speech given by Senator McCarthy attacking President Truman for a public and scathing critique of McCarthyism just a week earlier. McCarthy delivered the speech in question on November 24, 1953. Given the date of McCarthy's speech, Powell delivered his sermon on the Sunday before Thanksgiving in 1953 rather than 1959. See Adam Clayton Powell, *Keep the Faith, Baby!* (New York: Trident, 1967), 239. For the text of McCarthy's speech, see "Text of McCarthy Speech to Nation," *New York Times*, November 25, 1953.

31 Marable, *Race, Reform, and Rebellion*, 27.

32 Ibid., 28.

33 Ibid., 27.

34 "Big Lie" was the phrase President Truman used to refer to McCarthyism. Powell uses the same phrase to refer to McCarthyism as false religion.

35 Powell, *Keep the Faith, Baby!*, 239.

36 Ibid., 241–42.

37 The golden calf was not a replacement for God, but rather a representation of Yahweh in Moses' absence. However, as a symbol of the divine, the calf did more to distort God's presence than to clarify it. In the same way, Powell believed that McCarthyism distorted noble patriotic impulses toward freedom.

38 Powell, *Keep the Faith, Baby!*, 242.

39 Ibid., 243.

40 Ibid.

41 Ibid.

42 Ibid.

43 Ibid.

44 Ibid., 243–44.

45 Ibid., 244.

46 Clayborn Carson et al., eds., *The Papers of Martin Luther King, Jr.: Volume VI: Advocate of the Social Gospel, September 1948-March 1963*, vol. 6 (Berkeley: University of California Press, 2007), 48.

47 Robert M. Franklin, *Another Day's Journey: Black Churches Confronting the American Crisis* (Minneapolis, MN: Fortress Press, 1997), 45.

48 Baldwin, *There is a Balm in Gilead: The Cultural Roots of Martin Luther King, Jr.*, 16–17.

49 Martin Luther King, Jr., "Stride Toward Freedom," in *A Testament of Hope: The Essential Writings and Speeches of Martin Luther King, Jr.*, ed. James Melvin Washington (New York: HarperCollins, 1991), 420.

50 Ibid.

51 Ibid., 421.

52 Ibid., 420.

53 Ibid., 421.

54 Ibid.

55 Baldwin, *There is a Balm in Gilead: The Cultural Roots of Martin Luther King, Jr.*, 21–22.

56 See Alex Ayers, ed., *The Wisdom of Martin Luther King, Jr.* (New York: Penguin Books, 1993), 133–35. Quoted from Lewis V. Baldwin, "On the Relation of the Christian to the State: The Development of a Kingian Ethic," in *The Legacy of Martin Luther King, Jr.: The Boundaries of Law, Politics, and Religion*, ed. Lewis V. Baldwin, et al. (Notre Dame, IN: Unversity of Notre Dame Press, 2002), 82.

57 Baldwin, *There is a Balm in Gilead: The Cultural Roots of Martin Luther King, Jr.*, 183.

58 Ibid., 176–77.

59 In 1915, David Warren Griffith released "Birth of a Nation," the first feature-length motion picture in the United States. Replete with demeaning stereotypes of African Americans, the movie celebrated the rise of the Ku Klux Klan. For a history of the film and the controversy surrounding it, see the recent study by Stokes. Melvyn Stokes, *D. W. Griffith's* Birth of a Nation: *A History of "The Most Controversial Motion Picture of All Time"* (New York: Oxford University Press, 2007). Here, King's "Birth of a *New* Nation" celebrates a freedom that ideologically and politically supplants those values of the nation envisioned by Griffith.

60 Lewis V. Baldwin suggests that the Montgomery Bus Boycott and the theological and religious crises that King faced during that time and afterward "led him to a profoundly religious understanding of his leadership and mission." Baldwin, *There is a Balm in Gilead: The Cultural Roots of Martin Luther King, Jr.*, 187–89.

61 Martin Luther King, Jr., *Strength to Love* (Minneapolis, MN: Fortress Press, 1981), 77.

62 Ibid., 78.

63 Ibid., 77–78.

64 Ibid., 78.

65 Ibid., 78–79. At the same time, King's work is also intercontextual. He takes up the careful interpretive work of weaving the exodus and his contemporaneous social world together into a seamless whole so that each gives meaning to the other. Much as Absalom Jones related the story through descriptors of the contemporaneous conditions of African Americans held in slavery, King resorts to his vision of African Americans' experience in the United States. The ancient practice of corvée becomes "humiliating oppression, ungodly exploitation, and crushing domination."

66 Ibid., 79.

67 Martin Luther King Jr., "Birth of a New Nation," in *A Call to Conscience: The Landmark Speeches of Dr. Martin Luther King, Jr.*, ed. Clayborn Carson and Kris Shepard (New York: Warner Books, 2001), 17.

68 Ibid.

69 Ibid.

70 Ibid., 19.

71 Ibid., 20.

72 Ibid., 18.

73 Ibid., 28.

74 David Walker, *Walker's Appeal, in Four Articles; Together with a Preamble, to the Coloured Citizens of the World, but in Particular, and Very Expressly, to Those of the United States of America, Written in Boston, State of Massachusetts, September 28, 1829* (Boston: David Walker, 1830). See article I.

75 King, Jr., "Birth of a New Nation," 39.

76 Reinhold Niebuhr, *Moral Man and Immoral Society: A Study in Ethics and Politics* (New York; London: C. Scribner's, 1932).

77 King, Jr., *Strength to Love*, 78.

78 Ibid., 84.

79 Ibid.

80 Absalom Jones, "A Thanksgiving Sermon." With the refrain, "I am come down," Jones celebrates the congressional act of 1808 criminalizing the importation of Africans to be held as slaves. He understands the legislation to be a result of divine intervention.

81 King, Jr., *Strength to Love*, 81.

82 Ibid.

83 Ibid., 82.

84 Ibid.

85 King, Jr., "Stride Toward Freedom," 21.

86 Ibid., 21–22.

87 Ibid. I understand "sense of place" as a constellation of values, persons, and a geographical location that constitutes a core identity. See Baldwin, *There is a Balm in Gilead: The Cultural Roots of Martin Luther King, Jr.*, 30.

88 King Jr., "Stride Toward Freedom," 22.

89 Ibid., 23.

90 Ibid., 23–24.

91 Ibid., 28.

92 Ibid., 29.

93 Ibid., 30.

CHAPTER 5

1 Marable, *Race, Reform, and Rebellion*, 79.

2 Franklin and Moss, Jr., *From Slavery to Freedom*, 463.

3 Ibid., 454.

4 Huey P. Newton, *To Die for the People: The Writings of Huey P. Newton* (New York: Vintage Books, 1972), 3–5.

5 Angela D. Dillard, *Faith in the City: Preaching Radical Social Change in Detroit* (Ann Arbor: University of Michigan Press, 2010), 238.

6 For a critical appraisal of confluences and distinctions in Cleage's thought with that of Black Liberation Theology's primary figure, James Cone, see Amos Jones, Jr., "In Defense of the Apostle Paul: A Discussion with Albert Cleage and James Cone," D.Min. Thesis (Vanderbilt University, 1975). For the seminal articulation of Black Theology, see James H. Cone, *Black Theology and Black Power* (New York: Seabury Press, 1969).

7 Dillard, *Faith in the City*, 238.

8 Hiley H. Ward, *Prophet of the Black Nation* (Philadelphia: Pilgrim Press, 1969), 38–39.

9 Ibid., 38.

10 Dillard, *Faith in the City*, 241.

11 Ibid., 238.

12 Ibid., 242.

13 Ward, *Prophet of the Black Nation*, 43.

14 Ibid., 42.

15 Ibid., 43.

16 Dillard, *Faith in the City*, 242.

17 Ward, *Prophet of the Black Nation*, 53.

18 Ibid., 102.

19 Ibid.

20 Dillard, *Faith in the City*, 243.

21 Ward, *Prophet of the Black Nation*, 55. Dillard, *Faith in the City*, 245.

22 Albert B. Cleage, *Black Christian Nationalism: New Directions for the Black Church* (Detroit, MI: Morrow Quill Paperbacks, 1972), xxvii.

23 Ibid., xxv.

24 Ward, *Prophet of the Black Nation*, 103.

25 Ibid.

26 Ibid.

27 Cleage, *Black Christian Nationalism*, xxvi.

28 Ibid., xix.

29 Although two years later, King might have agreed with Cleage. By 1966, Cleage and King were closer in ideology that Cleage would probably admit.

30 Cleage's position follows Hurston in its nationalist orientation. For both, group consciousness and nationalist confidence were essential to black freedom. Hurston locates both in the Exodus story's wilderness experience. In Hurston's novel, Moses forces the Israelites to rely upon themselves for survival amidst the challenges of their wandering. Moses even orchestrates small skirmishes and later, larger battles to build the Israelites' confidence in their military

abilities against other more established nations. Cleage saw King's work in a similar vein.

31 Albert B. Cleage, *The Black Messiah*, 1st AWP ed. (Trenton, NJ: Africa World Press, 1989), 206.

32 Ibid., 207.

33 King's nonviolent philosophy assumed a concomitant humanity in the oppressor and the oppressed. Only then could he in good conscience subject black women and men to the violent horror of white suppression during the demonstrations. However, Cleage held no such belief.

34 Cleage, *The Black Messiah*, 209.

35 In a 1967 speech King declared,

> I have come here tonight to plead with you. Believe in yourself and believe that you are somebody. I said to a group last night: Nobody else can do this for us. No document can do this for us. No Lincolnian emancipation proclamation can do this for us. No Johnsonian civil rights bill can do this for us. If the Negro is to be free, he must move down into the inner resources of his own soul and sign with a pen and ink of self-assertive manhood his own emancipation proclamation. Don't let anybody take your manhood. Be proud of our heritage . . . we don't have anything to be ashamed of. Somebody told a lie one day. They couched it in language. They made everything Black ugly and evil. Look in your dictionaries and see the synonyms of the word Black. It's always something degrading and low and sinister. Look at the word White, it's always something pure, high and clean. Well I want to get the language right tonight. I want to get the language so right that everyone here will cry out: 'Yes, I'm Black, I'm proud of it. I'm Black and I'm beautiful!'"

King uses similar language in speeches during later portions of his life. For example, see Martin Luther King, Jr., "Where do We Go From Here," in *A Call to Conscience: The Landmark Speeches of Dr. Martin Luther King, Jr.*, ed. Clayborn Carson and Kris Shepard (New York: Warner Books, 2001), 171–99.

36 Cleage, *Black Christian Nationalism*, xxvii. Emphasis his.

37 In this, Cleage agrees with Malcolm X's analogy, "It's just like when you've got some coffee that's too black, which means it's too strong. What do you do? You integrate it with cream; you make it weak. But if you pour too much cream in it, you won't even know you ever had coffee. It used to be hot; it becomes cool. It used to be strong; it becomes weak. It used to wake you up, now it puts you to sleep."

38 Cleage, *Black Christian Nationalism*, 230. Emphasis his.

39 Ibid., 231. Cleage follows both Edward Blyden and Martin Delany who developed the concept earlier. See Edward W. Blyden, "The Call of Providence to the Descendants of Africa in America (1862)," in *I Am Because We Are: Readings in Black Philosophy*, ed. Fred Lee Hord and Jonathan Scott Lee (Amherst: University of Massachusetts Press, 1995), 121–33.

40 I refer to Raboteau's concept of the Black Church serving black outside of white strategies of surveillance. Albert J. Raboteau, *Slave Religion: The "Invisible Institution" in the Antebellum South* (New York: Oxford University Press, 2004).

41 Cleage makes good use of the Numbers 12 account where Moses marries a Cushite woman. He relies upon the work of Egyptologist Joseph ben-Jochanan and Rabbi Hilu Paris. Twenty years after Cleage delivered his sermon biblical scholars such as Charles Copher would, using traditional methods native to biblical studies, raise similar questions. Cleage, *Black Christian Nationalism*, 4.

42 Ibid., 3.

43 Ibid., 189.

44 Pneumatology, the study or doctrine of the Holy Spirit, is a tenet of any Christian theology. His understanding that the Holy Spirit acts within the life-world and specifically upon human sociality is an orthodox belief.

45 Cleage, *Black Christian Nationalism*, 251.

46 He believed that the entire universe was constituted by God's creative energy whose telos was both the affirmation and fulfillment of life.

47 Cleage, *Black Christian Nationalism*, 232.

48 Cleage, *The Black Messiah*, 183.

49 Cleage, *Black Christian Nationalism*, 7.

50 Cleage, *The Black Messiah*, 181.

51 Ibid., 183.

52 Albert B. Cleage, "But God Hardened Pharaoh's Heart," in *The Black Messiah* (Trenton, NJ: Africa World Press, 1989); Cleage, "What Can We Give Our Youth," in *The Black Messiah* (Trenton, NJ: Africa World Press, 1989); Cleage, "The Promised Land."; Cleage, "Coming In Out of the Wilderness."

53 Peniel E. Joseph, *Waiting 'Til the Midnight Hour: A Narrative History of Black Power in America* (New York: Henry Holt and Company, 2006), 185.

54 First, the claim makes God responsible for Egypt's suffering. Each time Pharaoh refuses to relent, ordinary Egyptians experience repercussions throughout the land ranging from skin disease to the deaths of their firstborn sons. They had not chosen Pharaoh to lead them, nor did the average Egyptian benefit from biblical Israel's bondage. Likewise the converse must be true: God sanctioned biblical Israel's suffering. Second, the claim questions the ability of the oppressor to repent and the possibility of redemption, two pillars of the CRM's philosophy. Thus, if God prevents the oppressor from changing, then reconciliation is unachievable.

55 The Hebrew word that English translators render "heart" refers to the seat of reason rather than the seat of emotion and better corresponds to the contemporary use of the word, "mind."

56 Cleage, "But God Hardened Pharaoh's Heart," 149.

57 Ibid., 143–44.

58 Ibid., 144.

59 Ibid.

60 Cleage, "What Can We Give Our Youth," 245.

61 Cleage, "But God Hardened Pharaoh's Heart," 154.
62 Ibid.
63 Cleage, "What Can We Give Our Youth," 242.
64 Ibid., 243.
65 Ibid.
66 Ibid.
67 Ibid., 243–44.
68 Ibid., 243.
69 Ibid., 253.
70 Cleage, "Coming In Out of the Wilderness," 270.
71 Ibid., 271.
72 Cleage, "What Can We Give Our Youth," 253.

CONCLUSION

1 William D. Hart, *Afro-eccentricity: Beyond the Standard Narrative of Black Religion*, 1st ed. (New York: Palgrave Macmillan, 2011), 2–3.
2 Such rules are determined by its theology (beliefs about God and the world), and its structures (organization, polities, conventions, values, and the like).

BIBLIOGRAPHY

Achebe, Chinua. *Things Fall Apart*. New York: Alfred A. Knopf, 1992.

Allen, Richard. "Life Experience and Gospel Labors." In *Afro-American Religious History: A Documentary History*, edited by Milton C. Sernett. 135–49. Durham, NC: Duke University Press, 1985.

———. *Life Experience and Gospel Labors*. Chapel Hill: University of North Carolina Press at Chapel Hill, 2000. F. Ford and M. Ripley, 1880.

Anderson, Cheryl B. *Women, Ideology, and Violence: Critical Theory and the Construction of Gender in the Book of the Covenant and the Deuteronomic Law*. New York: T&T Clark International, 2004.

———. "Reflections in an Interethnic/Racial Era on Interethnic/Racial Marriage in Ezra." In *They Were All Together in One Place: Toward Minority Biblical Criticism*, edited by Randall C. Bailey, Tat-siong Benny Liew, and Fernando F. Segovia. 47–64. Atlanta: Society of Biblical Literature, 2009.

Anderson, Victor. *Beyond Ontological Blackness: An Essay on African American Religious and Cultural Criticism*. New York: Continuum, 1995.

———. *Creative Exchange: A Constructive Theology of African American Religious Experience*. Minneapolis, MN: Fortress Press, 2008.

Auerbach, Eric. *Mimesis: The Representation of Reality in Western Literature*. Translated by Willard Ropes Trask. Princeton, NJ: Princeton University Press, 1968.

Ayers, Alex, ed. *The Wisdom of Martin Luther King, Jr*. New York: Penguin Books, 1993.

Aymer, Margaret. *First Pure, Then Peaceable: Frederick Douglass, Darkness and the Epistle of James*. New York: T&T Clark, 2008.

Bailey, Randall C. "Beyond Identification: The Use of Africans in Old Testatment Poetry and Narratives." In *Stony the Road We Trod: African American Biblical Interpretation*, edited by Cain Hope Felder. Minneapolis, MN: Fortress Press, 1991.

———. "They're Nothing but Incestuous Bastards: The Polemical Use of Sex and Sexuality in Hebrew Canon Narratives." In *Reading from This Place: Social Location and Biblical Interpretation in the United States*, edited by Fernando F. Segovia and Mary Ann Tolbert. Minneapolis, MN: Fortress Press, 1995.

———. "The Danger of Ignoring One's Own Cultural Bias." In *The Postcolonial Bible*, edited by R. S. Sugirtharajah. Sheffield: Sheffield Academic Press, 1998.

———. "Academic Biblical Interpretation among African Americans in the United States." In *African Americans and the Bible: Sacred Texts and Social Textures*, edited by Vincent Wimbush. 697–709. New York: Continuum, 2000.

———, ed. *Yet with a Steady Beat: Contemporary U.S. Afrocentric Biblical Interpretation*, Semeia Studies Atlanta Society of Biblical Literature, 2003.

———. "The Biblical Basis for a Political Theology of Liberation." In *Blow the Trumpet in Zion*, edited by Iva E. Carruthers, Frederick D. Haynes, and Jeremiah A. Wright, Jr. Minneapolis, MN: Fortress Press, 2005.

Baker, Jr., Houston A. *Modernism and the Harlem Renaissance*. Chicago: University of Chicago Press, 1987.

Baker, Lee D. *From Savage to Negro: Anthropology and the Construction of Race 1896–1954*. Los Angeles: University of California Press, 1998.

Baldwin, Lewis V. *There Is a Balm in Gilead: The Cultural Roots of Martin Luther King, Jr.* Minneapolis, MN: Fortress Press, 1991.

———. "On the Relation of the Christian to the State: The Development of a Kingian Ethic." In *The Legacy of Martin Luther King, Jr.: The Boundaries of Law, Politics, and Religion*, edited by Lewis V. Baldwin, Rufus Burrow, Barbara A. Holmes, and Susan Holmes Winfield. 77–123. Notre Dame, IN: Unversity of Notre Dame Press, 2002.

Banneker, Benamin. "Letter from Benjamin Banneker." In *Early Negro Writing 1760–1837*, edited by Dorothy Porter. 324–29. Baltimore: Black Classic Press, 1995.

Blackburn, Robin. *The Making of New World Slavery: From the Baroque to the Modern, 1492–1800*. New York: Verso, 1998.

Blount, Brian K. *Cultural Interpretation: Reorienting New Testament Criticism*. Minneapolis, MN: Fortress Press, 1995.

———. *Can I Get a Witness?: Reading Revelation through African American Culture*. 1st ed. Louisville, KY: Westminster John Knox Press, 2005.Blount, Brian K., Cain Hope Felder, Clarice Jannette Martin, and Emerson B. Powery. *True to Our Native Land: An African American New Testament Commentary*. Minneapolis, MN: Fortress Press, 2007.

Blyden, Edward W. "The Call of Providence to the Descendants of Africa in America (1862)." In *I Am Because We Are: Readings in Black Philosophy*, edited by Fred Lee Hord and Jonathan Scott Lee. 121–33. Amherst: University of Massachusetts Press, 1995.

Boyd, Melba Joyce. *Politics and Poetics in the Life of Frances E. W. Harper 1825–1911*. African American Life Series. Detroit, MI: Wayne State University Press, 1994.

Braxton, Joanne M. ed. *The Collected Poetry of Paul Laurence Dunbar*. Charlottesville: University of Virginia Press, 1993.

Broderick, Frances L. *W. E. B. Du Bois, Negro Leader in a Time of Crisis*, Volume 2. Stanford: Stanford University Press, 1959.

Brown, Michael Joseph. *Blackening of the Bible: The Aims of African American Biblical Interpretation*. Harrisburg, PA: Trinity Press International, 2004.

Byron, Gay L. *Symbolic Blackness and Ethnic Difference in Early Christian Literature*. New York: Routledge, 2002.

Callahan, Allen Dwight. *The Talking Book: African Americans and the Bible*. New Haven, CT: Yale University Press, 2006.

Carby, Hazel V. *Race Men*. Cambridge, MA: Harvard University Press, 1998.

Carson, Clayborn, Susan Carson, Susan Englander, Troy Jackson, and Gerald L. Smith, eds. *The Papers of Martin Luther King, Jr.: Volume VI: Advocate of the Social Gospel, September 1948–March 1963*. Vol. 6. Berkeley: University of California Press, 2007.

Cleage, Albert B. *Black Christian Nationalism: New Directions for the Black Church*. Detroit, MI: Morrow Quill Paperbacks, 1972.

———. *The Black Messiah*. 1st AWP ed. Trenton, NJ: Africa World Press, 1989.

———. "But God Hardened Pharaoh's Heart." In *The Black Messiah*. 143–55. Trenton, NJ: Africa World Press, 1989.

———. "Coming In Out of the Wilderness." In *The Black Messiah*. 266–78. Trenton, NJ: Africa World Press, 1989.

———. "The Promised Land." In *The Black Messiah*. 254–65. Trenton, NJ: Africa World Press, 1989.

———. "What Can We Give Our Youth." In *The Black Messiah*. 241–53. Trenton, NJ: Africa World Press, 1989.

Cone, James H. *Black Theology and Black Power*. New York: Seabury Press, 1969.

Copher, Charles B. *Black Biblical Studies: An Anthology of Charles B. Copher*. Chicago: Black Light Fellowship, 1993.

Croft, Wayne E. "You Jes' Wait a Little: A Comparison of the Motif of Hope in African American Preaching During the Slave and Post-Civil War Periods." Dissertation, Drew University, 2009.

Crowder, Stephanie Buckhanon. *Simon of Cyrene: A Case of Roman Conscription*. New York: Peter Lang, 2002.

Davies, K. G. *The Royal African Company. The Emergence of International Business 1200–1800*. Vol. 5. 7 vols. London: Routledge, 1999.

Dillard, Angela D. *Faith in the City: Preaching Radical Social Change in Detroit*. Ann Arbor: University of Michigan Press, 2010.

Du Bois, W.E.B. *The Suppression of the African Slave-Trade to the United States of America, 1638–1870*. New York: Longmans, Green, 1896.

———. "Returning Soldiers." *Crisis*, May 1919.

———. *The Philadelphia Negro*. New York: Schocken Books, 1967.

Farley, Edward. *Deep Symbols: Their Post Modern Effacement and Reclamation*. Valley Forge, PA: Trinity Press International, 1996.

Felder, Cain Hope. *Troubling Biblical Waters: Race, Class, and Family*. The Bishop Henry Mcneal Turner Studies in North American Black Religion V. 3. Maryknoll, NY: Orbis Books, 1989.

———. *Stony the Road We Trod: African American Biblical Interpretation*. Minneapolis, MN: Fortress Press, 1991.

Foster, Frances Smith, ed. *A Brighter Coming Day*. New York: Feminist Press at The City University of New York, 1990.

Foucault, Michel. *"Society Must Be Defended": Lectures at the Collège de France, 1975–1976*. Trans. David Macy. New York: Picador, 2003.

Franklin, John Hope. *From Slavery to Freedom: A History of Negro Americans*. 5th ed. New York: Alfred A. Knopf, 1980.

Franklin, John Hope, and Alfred A. Moss, Jr. *From Slavery to Freedom: A History of Negro Americans*. 6th ed. New York: McGraw-Hill, 1988.

Franklin, Robert M. *Another Day's Journey: Black Churches Confronting the American Crisis*. Minneapolis, MN: Fortress Press, 1997.

Gadamer, Hans-Geog. *Truth and Method*. Trans. Joel Weinsheimer and Donald G. Marshall, 2nd ed. New York: Continuum, 1998.

Gafney, Wilda. *Daughters of Miriam: Women Prophets in Ancient Israel*. Minneapolis, MN: Fortress Press, 2008.

Garnet, Henry Highland. *Walker's Appeal and Garnet's Address to the Slaves of the United States*. Charleston, SC: BiblioBazaar, 2008. J. H. Tobit, 1848.

Gates, Henry Louis. "The Trope of the Talking Book." In *The Signifying Monkey: A Theory of African-American Literary Criticism*. New York: Oxford, 1988.

_____. "The Blackness of Blackness: A Critique of the Sign and the Signifying Monkey." In *Black Literature and Literary Theory*, edited by Henry Louis Gates. 285–321. New York: Routledge, 1990.

Geertz, Clifford. *The Interpretation of Cultures*. New York: Basic Books, 1973.

Glaude, Jr., Eddie S. *Exodus! Religion, Race, and Nation in Early Nineteenth-Century Black America*. Chicago: University of Chicago Press, 2000.

Gronniosaw, James Albert Ukawsaw. "A Narrative of the Most Remarkable Particular in the Life of James Albert Ukawsaw Gronniosaw, an African Prince, as Related by Himself." In *Unchained Voices: An Anthology of Black Authors in the English-Speaking World of the 18th Century*, edited by Vincent Carretta. 32–58. Lexington: University of Kentucky Press, 1996.

Hall, Stuart, ed. *Representation: Cultural Representations and Signifying Practices*. Thousand Oaks, CA: Sage Publications, 1997.

Hamilton, Charles V. *Adam Clayton Powell, Jr.: The Political Biography of an American Dilemma*. New York: Cooper Square Press, 2002.

Harding, Vincent. *There Is a River: The Black Struggle for Freedom in America*. New York: Vintage Books, 1983.

Harper, Francis Ellen Watkins. *Moses: Story of the Nile*. Philadelphia: Merrihew and Son, 1869.

Hart, William D. *Afro-Eccentricity: Beyond the Standard Narrative of Black Religion*. 1st ed. New York: Palgrave Macmillan, 2011.

Hatcher, William E. *John Jasper: The Unmatched Negro Philosopher and Preacher*. New York: Fleming H. Revell Company, 1908.

Haygood, Wil. *King of the Cats: The Life and Times of Adam Clayton Powell, Jr*. New York: Amistad, 2006.

Hegel, Georg Wilhelm Friedrich. *The Philosophy of History*. Trans. C. J. Freidrich. New York: Dover, 1956.

Higginbotham, Jr., A. Leon. *In the Matter of Color: Race and the American Legal Process: The Colonial Period*. New York: Oxford University Press, 1980.

Hinks, Peter P., ed. *To Awaken My Afflicted Brethren: David Walker and the Problem of Antebellum Slave Resistance*. University Park: Pennsylvania State University Press, 2000.

———. *David Walker's Appeal to the Coloured Citizens of the World*. University Park: Pennsylvania State University Press, 2008.

Holt, Thomas C. *Children of Fire: A History of African Americans*. New York: Hill and Wang, 2010.

Horton, James Oliver, and Lois E. Horton. *Black Bostonians: Family Life and Community Struggle in the Antebellum North*. New York: Holmes and Meier, 1999.

Huggins, Nathan Irvin. *Harlem Renaissance*. New York: Oxford University Press, 1971.

Hughes, Langston. "The Negro Artist and the Racial Mountain." *Nation*, 1926.

Hume, David. *The Philosophical Works of David Hume*. vol. 3. Boston: Little, Brown, and Company, 1854.

Hurston, Zora Neale. *Moses, Man of the Mountain*. New York: Library of America, 1995. 1939.

———. *Moses, Man of the Mountain*. Edited by Henry Louis Gates. New York: Harper Collins, 1991.

Hurston, Zora Neale. *Dust Tracks on the Road: An Autobiography*. Edited by Robert E. Hemenway. Urbana: University of Illinois, 1984. 1942.

———. "Spirituals and Neo-Spirituals." In *Voices from the Harlem Renaissance*, edited by Nathan Huggins. 344–46. New York: Oxford University Press, 1995.

———. "How It Feels to Be Colored Me." In *The African-American Experience: Black History and Culture through Speeches, Letters, Editorials, Poems, Songs and Stories*, edited by Kai Wright. 448–50. New York: Workman, 2009.

Jackson, Jr., John P, and Nadine W. Weidman. *Race, Racism and Science: Social Impact and Implications*. New Brunswick, NJ: Rutgers University Press, 2005.

Jacobs, Mignon, R. *Gender, Power, and Persuasion: The Genesis Narratives and Contemporary Portraits*. Grand Rapids, MI: Baker Academic Press, 2007.

Janney, Samuel M. *The Life of William Penn with Selections from His Correspondence and Autobiography*. Philadelphia: Hogan, Perkins & Co., 1852.

Jefferson, Thomas. *Notes on the State of Virginia*. Philadelphia: Pritchard and Hall, 1788.

Jones, Absalom. "Petition of Absalom Jones and Seventy-Three Others." In *Early Negro Writing 1760–1837*, edited by Dorothy Porter. 330–32. Philadelphia: Black Classic Press, 1995.

———. "A Thanksgiving Sermon." In *Early Negro Writing 1760–1837*, edited by Dorothy Porter. 335–42. Philadelphia: Black Classic Press, 1995.

Jones, Amos, Jr. "In Defense of the Apostle Paul: A Discussion with Albert Cleage and James Cone." Dissertation, Vanderbilt University, 1975.

Joseph, Peniel E. *Waiting 'Til the Midnight Hour: A Narrative History of Black Power in America*. New York: Henry Holt, 2006.

Junior, Nyasha. "Womanist Biblical Interpretation." In *An Introduction to Feminist Biblical Interpretation in Honor of Katharine Doob Sakenfeld*, edited by Linda Day and Carolyn Pressler. 37–46. Louisville, KY: Westminster John Knox Press, 2006.

Kant, Immanuel. *Observations on the Feeling of the Beautiful and the Sublime*. Trans. John T. Goldthwait. Berkeley: University of California Press, 1991.

King, Jr., Martin Luther. *Strength to Love*. Minneapolis, MN: Fortress Press, 1981. 1963.

———. "Stride toward Freedom." In *A Testament of Hope: The Essential Writings and Speeches of Martin Luther King, Jr.*, edited by James Melvin Washington. 417–90. New York: HarperCollins, 1991.

———. "Birth of a New Nation." In *A Call to Conscience: The Landmark Speeches of Dr. Martin Luther King, Jr.*, edited by Clayborn Carson and Kris Shepard. 17–41. New York: Warner Books, 2001.

Litwack, Leon F. *Been in the Storm So Long: The Aftermath of Slavery*. New York: Vintage Books, 1979.

Locke, Alain, ed. *The New Negro: Voices of the Harlem Renaissance*. New York: Simon & Schuster, 1992.

Long, Charles H. *Significations: Signs, Symbols and Images in the Interpretation of Religion*. Minneapolis, MN: Fortress Press, 1986.

Marable, Manning. *Race, Reform, and Rebellion: The Second Reconstruction and Beyond in Black America, 1945–2006*. 3rd ed. Jackson: University Press of Mississippi, 2007.

Marbury, Herbert Robinson. "Ezra-Nehemiah." In *The Africana Bible: Reading Israel's Scriptures from Africa and the African Diaspora*, edited by Hugh R. Page, Randall C. Bailey, Valerie Bridgeman, Stacy Davis, Cheryl Kirk-Duggan, Madipoane Masenya, N. Samuel Murrell, and Rodney Steven Sadler. Minneapolis, MN: Fortress Press, 2010.

Mather, Cotton. *The Negro Christianized. An Essay to Excite and Assist That Good Work, the Instruction of Negro-Servants in Christianity*. Boston: B. Green, 1706.

Miller, Kelly. "Radicals and Conservatives." In *Radicals and Conservatives and Other Essays on the Negro in America*. New York: Schocken Books, 1968.

Myrdal, Gunnar. *An American Dilemma: The Negro Problem and Modern Democracy*. New Brunswick, NJ: Transaction, 1996.

Nash, Gary B. *Forging Freedom: The Formation of Philadelphia's Black Community, 1720–1840*. Cambridge, MA: Harvard University Press, 1988.

Newton, Huey P. *To Die for the People: The Writings of Huey P. Newton*. New York: Vintage Books, 1972.

Niebuhr, Reinhold. *Moral Man and Immoral Society: A Study in Ethics and Politics*. New York; London: C. Scribner's, 1932.

Noll, Mark A. "The Image of the United States as a Biblical Nation, 1776–1865." In *The Bible in America: Essays in Cultural History*, edited by Nathan O. Hatch and Mark A. Noll. 39–58. New York: Oxford University Press, 1982.

Page, Hugh R., Randall C. Bailey, Valerie Bridgeman, Stacy Davis, Cheryl Kirk-Duggan, Madipoane Masenya, N. Samuel Murrell, and Rodney Steven Sadler, eds. *The Africana Bible: Reading Israel's Scriptures from Africa and the African Diaspora*. Minneapolis, MN: Fortress Press, 2010.

Paris, Peter J. *Black Religious Leaders: Conflict in Unity*. Louisville, KY: Westminster John Knox Press, 1991.

Patterson, Tiffany Ruby. *Zora Neale Hurston and a History of Southern Life*. Philadelphia: Temple University Press, 2005.

Powell, Adam Clayton. *Keep the Faith, Baby!* New York: Trident, 1967.

———. *Adam by Adam: The Autobiography of Adam Clayton Powell, Jr.* New York: Kensington Publishing, 1971.

Raboteau, Albert J. *A Fire in the Bones.* Boston: Beacon Press, 1995.

———. *Slave Religion: The "Invisible Institution" in the Antebellum South.* New York: Oxford University Press, 2004.

Randolph, Edwin Archer. *The Life of Rev. John Jasper, Pastor of Sixth Mt. Zion Baptist Church, Richmond, Va., from His Birth to the Present Time, with His Theory on the Rotation of the Sun.* Electronic Edition ed.: R.T. Hill and Co., 1884.

Reagon, Bernice Johnson. *If You Don't Go, Don't Hinder Me: The African American Sacred Song Tradition.* Lincoln: Unversity of Nebraska Press, 2001.

Reynolds, Bruce J. "Black Farmers in America, 1865–2000: The Pursuit of Independent Farming and the Role of Cooperatives." Edited by Rural Business Cooperative Service. Washington, DC: U.S. Department of Agriculture, 2003.

Riss, Arthur. *Race, Slavery and Liberalism in Nineteenth Century American Literature.* Cambridge: Cambridge University Press, 2006.

Sadler, Rodney Steven. *Can a Cushite Change His Skin?: An Examination of Race, Ethnicity, and Othering in the Hebrew Bible.* Journal for the Study of the Old Testament. Supplement Series 425. New York: T&T Clark, 2005.

Said, Edward. *The World, the Text, and the Critic.* Cambridge, MA: Harvard University Press, 1983.

Sechrest, Love L. *A Former Jew: Paul and the Dialectics of Race.* Library of New Testament Studies. London; New York: T&T Clark, 2009.

Segovia, Fernando F. "And They Began to Speak in Other Tongues." In *Reading from This Place: Social Location and Biblical Interpretation in the United States*, edited by Fernando F. Segovia and Mary Ann Tolbert. 1–34. Minneapolis, MN: Fortress Press, 1995.

Smith, Abraham. "'I Saw the Book Talk': A Cultural Studies Approach to the Ethics of an African American Biblical Hermeneutics." *Semeia* 77 (1997): 115–38.

Spitzer, Robert J. *Veto: Touchstone of the American Presidency.* Albany: State University of New York Press, 1988.

Stancliff, Michael. *Frances Ellen Watkins Harper: African American Reform Rhetoric and the Rise of a Modern Nation State.* New York: Routledge, 2011.

Stephens, W.R.W. *The Life and Letters of Edward A. Freeman.* New York: Macmillan, 1895.

Still, William. *The Underground Railroad: A Record of Facts, Authentic Narrative, Letters, &C., Narrating the Hardships, Hair-Breadth Escapes and Death Struggles of the Slaves in Their Efforts of Freedom, as Related by Themselves and Others, or Witnessed by the Author; Together with Sketches of Some of the Largest Stockholders, and Most Liberal Aiders and Advisers, of the Road.* Philadephia: Porter and Coates, 1872.

Stokes, Melvyn. *D.W. Griffith's Birth of a Nation: A History of "the Most Controversial Motion Picture of All Time."* New York: Oxford University Press, 2007.

Sussman, Herbert. "The Study of Victorian Masculinities." *Victorian Literature and Culture* 20 (1992): 366–77.

Thomas, Rhondda Robinson. *Claiming Exodus: A Cultural History of Afro-Atlantic Identity, 1774–1903*. Waco, TX: Baylor University Press, 2013.

Walker, David. *Walker's Appeal, in Four Articles; Together with a Preamble, to the Coloured Citizens of the World, but in Particular, and Very Expressly, to Those of the United States of America, Written in Boston, State of Massachusetts, September 28, 1829*. Boston: David Walker, 1830.

Ward, Hiley H. *Prophet of the Black Nation*. Philadelphia: Pilgrim Press, 1969.

Weber, Max. *The Protestant Ethic and the Spirit of Capitalism with Other Writings on the Rise of the West*. Translated by Stephen Kalberg. 4th ed. New York: Oxford University Press, 2009.

Weems, Renita J. *Just a Sister Away: A Womanist Vision of Women's Relationships in the Bible*. San Diego: LuraMedia, 1988.

———. "Reading *Her Way* through the Struggle: African American Women and the Bible." In *Stony the Road We Trod: African American Biblical Interpretation*, edited by Cain Hope Felder. 57–77. Minneapolis: Fortress Press, 1991.

———. "The Hebrew Women Are Not Like the Egyptian Women: The Ideology of Race, Gender and Sexual Reproduction in Exodus1." *Semeia* 59 (1992): 25–34.

Welter, Barbara. "The Cult of True Womanhood." *American Quarterly* 18, no. 2 (1966): 151–74.

Williams, Raymond. *Sociology of Culture*. Chicago: University of Chicago Press, 1995.

Wimbush, Vincent L. "The Bible and African Americans: An Outline of an Interpretive History." In *Stony the Road We Trod: African American Biblical Interpretation*, edited by Cain Hope Felder. Minneapolis, MN: Fortress Press, 1991.

———. "A Meeting of Worlds: African Americans and the Bible." In *Teaching the Bible: The Discourses and Politics of Biblical Pedagogy*, edited by Fernando F. Segovia and Mary Ann Tolbert. 190–99. Maryknoll, NY: Orbis, 1998.

———. "Reading Darkness: Reading Scripture." In *African Americans and the Bible: Sacred Text and Social Textures*, edited by Vincent L. Wimbush. 1–49. New York: Continuum, 2003.

———. *The Bible and African Americans*. Minneapolis, MN: Fortress Press, 2003.

Wimbush, Vincent L. *The Bible and African Americans: A Brief History*. Facets. Minneapolis, MN: Fortress Press, 2003.

———. *Theorizing Scriptures: New Critical Orientations to a Cultural Phenomenon*. Signifying (on) Scriptures. New Brunswick, NJ: Rutgers University Press, 2008.

INDEX OF NAMES

INDEX OF SUBJECTS

ABOUT THE AUTHOR

Herbert Robinson Marbury is Associate Professor of Hebrew Bible and Ancient Near East at Vanderbilt University. He is the author of *Imperial Dominion and Priestly Genius.*

Made in the USA
Las Vegas, NV
04 January 2022

40348139R00157